Females,
Males,
Families

A Biosocial Approach

Females, Males, Families

A Biosocial Approach

Lila Leibowitz

Northeastern University

Duxbury Press

North Scituate, Massachusetts

Library of Congress Cataloging in Publication Data
Leibowitz, Lila.
    Females, males, families.
    Bibliography: p.
    Includes index.
    1. Family. 2. Sex differences. 3. Kin
selection (Evolution) 4. Familial behavior in
animals. I. Title.
HQ728.L495   301.42'1   77-18790
ISBN 0-87872-158-4

Duxbury Press
A Division of Wadsworth Publishing Company, Inc.

Females, Males, Families: A Biological Approach was edited and prepared
for composition by Service to Publishers, Inc. Interior design was
provided by Joanna Snyder and the cover was designed by Cindy Daniels.

L.C. Cat. Card No.: 77-18790
ISBN 0-87872-158-4
Printed in the United States of America

1 2 3 4 5 6 7 8 9 - 82 81 80 79 78

Contents

Preface

This book has several purposes. The primary one is to acquaint readers with some of the diverse ways in which human beings organize families. I have used a straightforward social-anthropological approach involving cross-cultural comparison of the customs and traditions of recent human societies to illustrate the variousness of human family arrangements. A secondary purpose is to explore and, to some degree, challenge the "new" biological view of human social behavior, which has recently gained considerable attention in both academic and lay circles.

We are in the midst of a revival of the notion that human societies are structured, and function, in terms of patterned behaviors that are fundamentally "fixed" in members of the human species. The view is exemplified by the belief that men and women are innately programmed to behave differently and that their different behavioral capacities became genetically prescribed during the course of evolution. While an examination of sex, sex roles, and families in other cultures provides some of the evidence that challenges this biological view, we must address an evolutionary argument in evolutionary terms. Consequently, I have adopted an evolutionary perspective and before reviewing the cross-cultural data in detail, discuss sex in nature, reproduction in the animal kingdom, the traits of males and females in a number of species, and the social and sex lives of some of our close relatives in the primate order. I have set the historical and cross-cultural data pertaining to human beings against an evolutionary trajectory—that of expanding behavioral plasticity—to develop a model of how the institution of family originated among humans. Because of the evolutionary perspective, the data I have used are drawn from ethology, primatology, physical anthropology, and archeology as well as from social anthropology, sociology, and history. I therefore cover material normally dealt with in courses on kinship, family, sex roles, the anthropology of women, women's studies, and human origins. Hopefully, the data and analyses will stimulate discussion in such courses and encourage close inspection of the issues raised by the "new" biological view of human social behavior.

The number of people contributing to this book by stimulating me and forcing me to clarify my often obscure ideas is very large. To Norman Kaplan, whose untimely death prevented him from seeing what he made possible, I owe a debt which, sadly, I cannot ever repay. Encouragement as well as useful hours of discussion were given me by Nate Raymond, Mary Russell, Mike Spence, Jerry Anderson, Dan McCall, Jack Levin, and Pat Golden. Among those who tried to make certain that I did not mangle the English language or my typewriter were Naomi Goldfield, Valerie Cahoone, Tony Emrich, and Phyllis Watson. The professional criticisms of Sue Ellen Jacobs, Carol Stack, Celia Moore, Karen Sachs, Ann Beuf, Barrie Thorne, Brigitte Jordan, and Robert Meier saved me from some, if not all, of my logical and informational errors. Jerry Lyons calmed me down and made me productive despite all odds, and John Moroney periodically comforted me. The members of my family, Richard, Karla, and Jean, contributed to this book by suffering through it with me and by demonstrating their adaptability by devising new ways to cope with the difficult and ever-changing situations I created as I buried myself in the manuscript. This book is theirs in many more ways than they can imagine.

Lila Leibowitz

Introduction:

Definitions, Social Theories and Sexual Politics

A book by an anthropologist that discusses the sex life of the Marquesan Islanders is hardly surprising. But a book by an anthropologist that is about "family"—and touches on bird behavior, sex differences in monkey and ape populations, and alternative life-styles in industrial societies—needs some comment. The range of subject matter is a result of the fact that the institution of family, a social phenomenon usually studied by sociologists, is viewed here from an anthropological—evolutionary and cross-cultural—perspective. Three major issues having to do with the evolution of family are dealt with. The book first examines the prehistory of the biobehavioral base on which families are built. It then addresses the diversity of contemporary human family arrangements and the common denominators that underlie them. Finally, it proposes a model of how the family, an institution involving many diverse social arrangements, arose on the base of the flexible behavioral capacities of the higher primates. Since these issues reflect a concern with processes occurring over a very long time span, it is not surprising that the book ranges widely.

To deal effectively with the identification of the nature of the biobehavioral background on which family arrangements emerged, a general overview of sex and sexual reproduction in the organic world at large is presented. Since data on the physical and behavioral sex differences among humanity's closest relatives, the primates, challenge many widely held beliefs about the social significance of physical sex differences, how such sex differences may have evolved among behaviorally malleable nonhuman and human primates is explained from a new perspective. In the course of exploring the second issue, that of the diversity of family arrangements among living peoples, a revised definition of "family" is offered and tested, and the factors affecting family arrangements in our own and other cultures are examined. The

1

model of the origin of families presented in Chapter 6 and outlined later in this introduction puts together concepts and data drawn from the discussion of these issues.

The order in which the issues are presented represents the way in which the initial investigation developed. Each of the problems dealt with came up unexpectedly as I proceeded to teach a course on the sociology of the family—which my training in social anthropology had not quite prepared me for. I was immediately made aware of a definitional problem, that of fitting some uncommon family arrangements into commonly accepted definitions of the family. Later it became evident that problems lay hidden in the social theory of family origins that I confidently quoted to my students, who promptly raised serious questions about it. Finally, it was the highly relevant world of sexual politics and women's liberation that led me into the apparently irrelevant subject matter of animal behavior and nonhuman social adaptations with which this book begins. The history of how these problems arose and were handled will, I hope, help to introduce the issues and models investigated in this book.

PROBLEM ONE:
AVAILABLE DEFINITIONS OF THE FAMILY

As soon as I was assigned the job of teaching about the sociology of the family, I read as much of the literature as I could in the limited time that was available. The sociologists whose works I hastily perused, like the anthropologists who trained me, generally seemed to subscribe to the idea that human family arrangements are the result of cultural processes, and presented detailed analyses of class and ethnic differences in American families from that perspective. But the sociology texts included very little material on family arrangements in other cultures and hardly any at all on the various kin terminological systems that anthropologists traditionally focus attention on. Students exposed only to a sociology text about the family would never fully appreciate how various and divergent are the households, kin groups, and domestic units in other societies. To illustrate the variability of human family arrangements, readings from several ethnographic studies were often assigned to augment the sociology text.

Anthropologists, on the other hand, rarely write about the family as such. But standard ethnographic reports, which are essentially detailed descriptions of how people live, include maps of resident areas and charts that show how people classify one another as regards blood and marriage bonds. Classical ethnographies include descriptions of how people make a living, who they work with, and how they distrib-

A family group in the Himalayas. Among the many diverse family arrangements human beings have devised are households in which several men share a wife or wives, or several women share husbands. Photo by John Bishop.

ute the products of their labors. After Freud, anthropologists began to include more data on sexual mores and habits and on the upbringing of children. A sound ethnographical study grew to have more and more data on aspects of what we call the family. The information, although scattered under such headings as "technology," "division of labor," "kinship," and "child care," became increasingly available. The diversity of non-Western family arrangements dictates to some extent such a fragmentation of data and has encouraged anthropologists to pursue sophisticated discussions of the nature and function of kinship systems (which can be made to appear as sort of elegant geometries of relationships) rather than discussions of the confusing ramifications of "family."

Despite this lack of emphasis, I found when I turned to the sociologists that they are not tuned to the problems of cross-cultural variations in family (and their definitions reflect this), so I turned again to anthropology. In G.P. Murdock's *Social Structure*,[1] a pioneering cross-cultural analysis of the vast body of ethnographic materials in the

Yale Human Relations Area Files, I found definitions and descriptions of the units of social structure with which anthropologists usually deal. Although the book does not pay much attention to an analysis of "family," it does define the term. Nineteenth-century anthropologists talked a lot about the family without defining what they meant, and those of the early twentieth century rarely used the term at all. Kroeber's monumental *Anthropology*,[2] for example, uses the word only twice. Murdock's definition was the first, and for awhile the *only* cross-cultural definition of the family available. Unfortunately, his definition is not a very good one.

According to Murdock, the family is a "social group characterized by common residence, economic cooperation and reproduction."[3] It involves a group of people who live together, work in conjunction with one another to meet their needs, and have children. However, the term "family" by itself is very ambiguous, he notes, because there are at least three distinct types of social groups for which the term is used. One type of group is the nuclear family, consisting of "a married man and woman with their offspring."[4] Another type of group is the polygamous family, of which there are two kinds: polygynous families, which include a man, his wives, and their offspring; and polyandrous families, which include a wife, her husbands, and their offspring. Typically the extended family, a third type of group, includes, along with a married man and woman, one or more of their married sons or daughters and their spouses, and the unmarried children

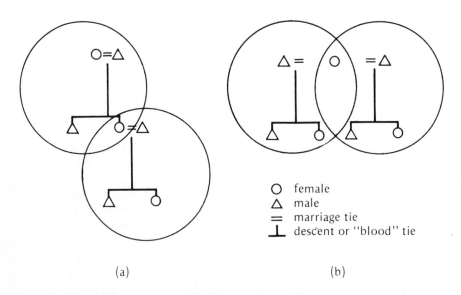

(a)   (b)

FIGURE 1   *Linked nuclear families (circled) in extended (a) and polygamous (b) family groups.*

of any of these pairs. Polygamous and extended families, Murdock points out, really consist of nuclear families affiliated with one another (Figure 1). Although these three types of family exhibit important points of difference, they are fundamentally similar in that they are all settings for economic cooperation and reproduction. Furthermore, he contends that since extended and polygamous families are built around affiliations between nuclear groups, the nuclear family is a universal human social grouping.[5] This contention, which has social evolutionary implications, will be discussed in detail later.

Murdock's definition of family as a social group characterized by common residence, economic cooperation, and reproduction seems straightforward enough. It is problematic, however, in that we can always find some society where one or more of these criteria do *not* apply to the social units that are recognizably "family." Some examples of such situations follow. We begin with an oft-quoted paragraph from Meyer Fortes' classic description of Ashanti life:

> As night falls young boys and girls can be seen hurrying in all directions carrying large pots of cooked food. One can often see food being carried out of a house and a few minutes later an almost equal amount of food being carried into it. The food is being taken by the children from the houses in which their mothers reside to those in which their fathers live. Thus one learns that husband and wife often belong to different domestic groups, the children perhaps sleeping in their mothers' houses and eating with their fathers.[6]

The Ashanti, a matrilineal group (one that assigns kinship through the mother), are not the only people whose residence arrangements are a departure from Murdock's model. Among the Catholic Celts in contemporary Ireland, a patrilineal people, husbands remain with their consanguineal or "blood" relatives after marriage, and wives stay on with their own parents.[7] On some kibbutzim in Israel, married pairs live in a room together, eat in a communal dining room, work in a communal corporation, and their children sleep, and eat, and are educated in communal nurseries and dormitories.[8] In England, men's clubs are incidental or auxiliary residences for upper-class British husbands, but in a number of societies men's clubhouses are the regular living places of married men.

These few examples show that "The family need not live together . . . to be a family," as one of the critics of Murdock's definition put it.[9] A few of the many anthropologists who criticized it offered other definitions or partial descriptions, which are, however, just as susceptible to criticism as Murdock's model. Take this one, for instance. The family "is a social group that may or may not be a local

5

or spatial group."[10] Yet the family may not be a social group at all, if by "group" we mean, as sociologists usually do, that its members interact with each other regularly or often. The following nineteenth-century situation represents a rare, but nonetheless real case. Among the Nayar, a warrior caste of the Malabar coast of India, a woman acquired a "tali" or ceremonial husband around the time she began to menstruate. He was her official husband, without whom her children would be considered illegitimate, but she saw him only once—at the marriage rites. Once married she was expected to entertain "sambund-han" husbands, men who were no more than night visitors to the household she and her children lived in.[11] Where is the family group in such a case?

The Ashanti, Kibbutz, and Nayar "families" lack both common residence and economic cooperation among family members. A tali husband, who may never sleep with his wife, is not part of her residence group and is not effectively involved in the family's reproductive aspects at all. Neither is a West African "female husband" or a Chukchi woman, who, like her West African counterpart, takes a wife. The children born to the wives of these husbands are those of the male lovers they are encouraged to take. The disparities between such arrangements and Murdock's definition show up its weaknesses. They indicate some of the difficulties Murdock's critics have run into in searching for a definition of the family that characterizes all the varying familial arrangements that human beings have managed to devise. Yet more difficulties are apparent when these and other "families" are looked at in detail. (See Chapter 4 for examples.)

Redefining the Family

Why, I began to ask myself, if the family is so difficult to define cross-culturally, do sociologists and anthropologists insist that the family is universal among human beings? There must be common denominators among the various social phenomena to which the term "family" is applied. It was clear that these are not "shared residence, economic cooperation, and reproductive activities," or even the quality of togetherness, of being a group. My classes therefore began to examine the question: What other factors unite these social entities under the heading "family"? In the course of our discussions, several features of family arrangements in all cultures became evident and seven common cross-cultural family characteristics emerged.[12]

1. Everything that is recognized as a family is a subunit of a larger social aggregate. Whether or not the members of the subunit interact with one another as a group, they are or can be identified as members of the subunit by the people around them.

2. The kind of subunits that we recognize as families are a "regularized" feature of the social aggregates in which they are embedded. In other words, for the society at large, family subunits are a permanent feature of the social landscape. The existence and recognition of these subunits is not linked to seasonal or environmental conditions in such a way that, for instance, it is only when food is scarce that the population breaks up into "subunits," yet when supplies are abundant, these units melt into an amorphous collectivity. Family subunits may be a permanent feature of the social aggregate, but each subunit is transitory. Sometimes it is expected that people who establish a new subunit do so for life. Sometimes societies discourage this (see the Irigwe, Chapter 4). Family subunits are constantly being disintegrated everywhere, by death or divorce, but some type of family unit is always around.

3. In all instances the subunits we recognize as families have something to do with defining the status of children. Everywhere children who are given membership, by birth or adoption, in such subunits are restricted as to whom they are permitted to have intercourse with and/or marry. Membership in these regularized subunits of larger social aggregates allocates to children a place in the larger social network, while minimally setting limits on whom they can mate with and marry.

4. The societal subunits designated by the term "family" are generated by temporally bound, publicly acknowledged agreements or contracts, and membership in them is based on the existence of a contract, usually a marriage contract. A contract, in the sense used here, is a tie involving obligations established informally or formally between parties which the community at large recognizes and can enforce. The consent of the individuals who become parties to such a contract is not necessary for the community to recognize the tie or insist on the fulfillment of the obligations. Because the family subunit is based on such a contractual tie between individuals, it differs significantly from several other kinds of subunits in human societies which also regulate mating and marriage (clans, lineages, etc.). These other subunits endure over many generations, and membership in them is determined by rules of descent, which govern relationships "forever."

By contrast, the family subunit lasts no longer than the contract (at best only as long as the parties to the contract are alive or regarded as effectively so), and only by virtue of the contract's binding its members to one another.

Before enumerating other family characteristics, the determination of family membership by contract rather than descent deserves a little further attention. Although it is obvious that husbands and wives (with or without their consent) are linked to each other as spouses through a contract, it is not so obvious that a child's family membership (its consent is not necessary) is just as much a matter of contract. Since we ask unwed mothers to "surrender" their infants for adoption, it seems we are used to thinking that a child automatically "belongs" to its mother's family, even when it is not a "complete" one. This is not a universal assumption, however. Among the Lakher of southeast Asia, the emphasis on a child's link to its father's group is so strong that children are viewed as related to their mothers only by virtue of her marriage to their father. If there is a divorce, the relationship between mother and child is dissolved. In theory, a son could marry his mother after she has divorced his father. In actuality, it is perfectly reasonable for him to marry his half-sister, a daughter his mother bears to a husband other than his father.[13] More directly to the point, in Christian England up until 1734 a child born out of wedlock did not belong to or with its mother. It was "the child of nobody" (filius nullius) or "the child of everybody" (filius populi), a child of the parish. It had no "family." (Bastards who remained bachelors or spinsters never got to be members of a family.) The 1734 Poor Laws assigned the unmarried mother an obligation which had previously been tied to the marriage contract, responsibility for her children up to the age of seven; and later the age was raised to sixteen.[14] The "matrifocal family" that sociologists have recently made much of is clearly more of a legal or social unit than a natural descent unit. In this, it is like all other forms of family.

We are so accustomed to thinking that membership in the social subunit that we call "family" is automatically a matter of descent that the term has been used (loosely) to describe animal pairs with their young. The term "matrifocal family" has recently even been extended to include the mother–young relational networks that are often maintained among mammals who live in large social groupings or aggregates and is sometimes used to refer to isolated mother–young groups. These uses of the term "family" seem inappropriate. The subunits identified as families among humans are not necessarily groups at all, and membership in them, even when they bear a striking resemblance to the groupings of other animals, is determined differently. To be a member of a human family unit, a contract, a socially acknowledged "deal" or a socially enforced relationship between various parties, is necessary. Which leads us to the next point.

5.   The social contracts that constitute marriage may forge ties between people who are of different sexes, *or* different as to group identity, *or*, as is usually the case, different in both respects. However, a difference in both respects is not necessary. While we often think of marriage as tying together as spouses people of the opposite sex, the

"woman-to-woman marriages" of West Africa tie together people of the same sex. Furthermore, although anthropologists are fond of pointing out that marriages usually tie members of different social units or groups together, that certainly does not hold true for the brother–sister marriages of Incan, Hawaiian, and Egyptian royalty, where the siblings belong to the same subunit or group. Since nowhere are marriages between same-sex siblings recorded, marriages seem to be based on some degree of social *or* sexual "oppositeness." But whether it lies in sex, or subunit or group identity, or both, varies.

6. Marriage contracts may involve nothing more than a public acknowledgment that two parties share a joint status as regards children. Nayar marriages have rather elaborate rituals attached to them, yet ultimately all that the tali husband does is publicly ensure the legitimacy of his wife's children. This is the one thing that marital arrangements everywhere accomplish, regardless of how simple or complicated the contracts and rituals are that accompany them.

7. The final common characteristic of the entities we call family is that the contracts generating them are everywhere "individualized," that is, the contracts always specify particular individuals as parties to the contract: they "name names." This does not necessarily mean that the individuals named as spouses are the only people linked by the marriage contract. It does mean, however, that specific individuals are always identified as participating in a contract, even when these individuals are only acting as agents of groups. This point warrants further clarification.

Marriage contracts often are built around establishing obligations between groups of people. But stable social groups do not marry each other en masse, with all the men of one such group taking as spouses all the women of another, and vice versa, in effect creating one big happy "family." Although it was once believed that a generalized exchange of mates between such groups occurs in some non-Western societies—in fact who is spouse to whom is made clear even when each of the individuals named in a contract is acting as the representative of a kin group or other social entity. One can see this clearly in royal marriages used to establish or solidify ties between nation-states. It is also evident in the humbler instances of the sororate and levirate. In the institution of the sororate, when a man's wife dies a woman who is classified as her sister is expected to take her place. In the levirate, a deceased husband is replaced by his "brother." The marital contract in these cases is clearly one between groups. The particular individuals named as spouses are readily replaceable. Yet even in these situations individuals are specified in the original and subsequent marital contracts. When a woman by marriage acquires sexual rights and obligations to a group of brothers (a kind of marriage agreement known as fraternal polyandry), or a man's marriage gives him sexual rights and obligations to a group of sisters (a situation called sororal polygyny), the group relationships established by the marriage contracts are obvious. That a marriage contract may incorporate many people is very clear from the arrangements found among the Pahari[15] of India, where an eldest brother marries a woman in the name of all his younger brothers. Subsequently, either he or a younger brother can marry another woman or women. These wives, too, have the right to sleep with all the brothers. Interestingly enough, the shared wives are not necessarily or usually sisters. Thus, despite the fact that every brother has sexual access to every wife and vice versa, and despite the fact that the marriage contracts generate intertwining group obligations, this is not a situation in which one group marries another. Wives are normally drawn from a number of kin groups, and each is married separately by a specific man who represents his group of brothers. The marital contracts are clearly individualized, with specific individuals named in each.

Genuine "group marriage" does not now appear to exist. At any rate, if, as has been proposed, a sort of general exchange of mates between stable, tightly knit groups was once a form of marriage, such group exchanges of mates could not have generated the social subunits we identify as family without further subcontracting or individualizing the spouse assignments. Recognizing that marital contracts are individualized consequently plays a part in coming to grips with the issue of how human family arrangements originated, especially since the notion of unindividualized group mate exchanges gives the erroneous impression that closed groups with a permanent membership are characteristic of simple human foraging societies, when, in fact, loosely articulated, highly fluid groupings are a common adaptation of collecting–hunting peoples.

Marriage contracts do not necessarily spell out obligations between the groups associated with each spouse. Often such obligations are informal and generated by the marriage itself, appearing after the fact, so to speak. In our own society, for example, legal adults can marry, have children, and live as a recognized family without the kin of either spouse ever knowing about it. Our contracts cover only spouses, not their kin, although bonds are frequently forged between the relatives of the marriage partners after the marriage. This is neither especially new in Anglo-Western tradition[16] nor uniquely Western. Among the Ojibwa of eastern Canada,[17] as among loosely knit collecting–hunting peoples elsewhere, while kin may be involved in making or fulfilling contracts, individuals are quite free to forge their own ties. The way in which contracts incorporate people other than one's named as spouses varies widely, but marriage contracts always specify a link between named individuals. They are always "individualized."

This final common characteristic is very clear in the case of the nuclear family form, where the individualization of the marriage contract and the fact that the group it creates is a subunit of a larger social entity are both clearly evident. The nuclear family grouping is particularly significant in discussions of how family may have emerged among humans for several reasons, not the least being that it is the most frequent arrangement among collecting–hunting peoples today. As we shall soon see, this individualized character of all marriage contracts is often overlooked, evidently because theorists who have built sociocultural models of the origins of human family arrangements regard individualization as either synonymous with isolation from kin ties (and therefore characteristic of recent societies) or as so obviously a part of marriage as to constitute a natural or quasi-natural aspect of the marriage contract.

The definition I offered my students takes into account all the common features that we have discussed: The family, a regularized subunit of a larger social entity, is established by a publicly acknowledged contract which links specific individuals of the opposite sex and/or from different membership units of the larger entity, and establishes with whom the children included in the subunit can and cannot make similar contracts. Although this definition includes things not usually incorporated in the definitions found in texts on the sociology of the family, it excludes a number of features commonly associated with definitions of "family." Nevertheless, it does cover the cases at hand.

PROBLEM TWO:
SOCIAL THEORIES AND FAMILY ORIGINS

Although our characterization of the family resolves the dilemmas of definition raised by placing sociological and anthropological concepts and data side by side, it raises another issue. Neither sociology nor anthropology texts usually deal with the next problem, even though they often talk about the family as a sociological phenomenon based on and subject to cultural forces. Clearly, the conditions that make the family possible, in our definition, depend on the prior existence of language. After all, how can you have a "contract" or a recognizable subunit that is not a group without words or symbols to designate relationships? Because a cultural basis for the family was indicated by the sociological literature and by the definition of the family that I had arrived at, it seemed appropriate to introduce into the next term's syllabus the issue of family origins and some readings on a theory that pointed to the social roots of family arrangements.

For such a theory I turned once again to the anthropological literature, since sociologists rarely worry about this sort of issue.

The most up-to-date discussion touching on family origins was that of Claude Levi-Strauss. Levi-Strauss, a highly respected anthropologist, holds that the institution of marriage is a communication structure and an aspect of economic exchange. In his first major work[18] he proposed a model of the origins of the institution of marriage. His model is an extension of a notion presented by the nineteenth-century anthropologist E.B. Tylor, who argued that incest taboos reflect the dictum "marry out or die out." The implications of this dictum are that incest taboos arose when people from different localities began to forge economic and political alliances through marriage which reduced intergroup hostilities and broadened each group's resource base. Levi-Strauss developed a hypothetical reconstruction of these events. His reconstruction can be outlined simply.

Initially, roving groups of people who relied heavily for their subsistence on the game they hunted were interested in getting objects and goods they themselves could not find or produce locally. When a group met another which was interested in what it had to offer, the two groups might exchange goods. If the exchange worked out to everybody's advantage, trade became a regular feature of their encounters. As the continuing exchanges proved worthwhile, the groups became interested in keeping trade going and having options on each other's goods. By trading women, giving each other their "sisters" as mates, an alliance was cemented and the exchange bonds between them were perpetuated. Trading "sisters" and exchanging women became regularized and required. Incest taboos and marriage were established this way. This model expands on Tylor's notion, and sees both marriage and incest rules as having been adopted because such rules expedited and ensured economic transactions.

Levi-Strauss' reconstruction is more concerned with the basis and origins of incest taboos and marriage than with the "family" per se, for the reconstruction is designed to set the stage for a discussion not of family, but of the forms and functions of non-Western types of kinship systems. The formulation is actually somewhat ambiguous as regards family origins, for the notion of "sister exchange" implies either "group marriage" or that Levi-Strauss meant that a family subunit of some sort existed before the institution of marriage made an appearance. Yet since sociologists treat marriage and family as being intertwined (a notion with which anthropologists who regard family as a uniquely human institution do not usually disagree), and since the term "sister" could—in a book about kinship—be interpreted as a shorthand expression for "women of my generation who were born to the same females who gave birth to the men of my generation in my local group," the reconstruction could be seen as implying that marriage and family arose together as a result of the regularization of certain kinds of economic transactions. This seemed a likely and useful interpretation because it fits so well with several other models of early human societies which American evolutionary theorists were presenting in the 1960s and which I hastened to report to my classes.

During the 1950s and early 1960s American anthropologists began getting involved in social evolutionary theory building, a form of inquiry and investigation that had been out of style for years. They built up models of early human society based on the belief that human beings are the only primates that hunt, and that hunting is the mainstay of all simple human subsistence economics. In addition, they also held that only men hunt. This image of hunting led them to conclude that the organization of hunting–gathering societies rests on arranging relationships so that the important activities of men are performed most efficiently. If groups of men who grew up together stay together to cooperatively exploit the home regions they know best, they will hunt better than if they separate or move to new localities. It follows, then, that relationships should be organized so that men bring their wives into their home group, and not vice versa. So the idea was put forth, and widely accepted, that male-centered hunting bands are characteristic of collecting–hunting societies. Such bands, it was thought, are both patrilocal (wives are brought into them to live with their husbands) and patrilineal (descent and group membership are reckoned through the male line). Because many monkeys and our closer ape relatives live in rather large groupings which, at the time, were believed to be both tightly knit and held together by males, it looked as if projecting this hunting band arrangement back to our ancestors made a lot of sense. These projections were offered up in my class as validating Levi-Strauss' model and, together with it, helping to explain the cultural basis and origins of human family arrangements.

Then a student pointed out that in one of the assigned sociological readings for the course a prestigious sociologist says: "The human family is an 'extension' of a subhuman precultural entity."[19] This sociologist holds not only that the nuclear family is a universal form, but that women naturally play "affective" or nurturing roles in the family and society, while men do the "instrumental" things, like making a living. A second student raised the point that another of the assigned readings[20] calls collecting–hunting societies made up of independent nuclear families "the simplest level of socio-cultural integration." Equating "simplest" with "first," this student pointed out that the Levi-Strauss model of sister exchanges does not lead to the creation of family subunits unless men claim one or more of the women they exchange as their own and the men's claims are socially acknowledged.

He went on and argued that men must have been claiming

individual women for themselves before marriage was invented, for not only are band societies more complex than simple independent nuclear families, but the band model holds that men were more important and powerful than women, which suggests that some men could have been more important and powerful than others, giving them the wherewithal to keep the most desirable women to themselves. I pointed out that the sexual division of labor peculiar to human beings cannot develop if males are so busy controlling the sexual activities of "their" females that they cannot go off to hunt. The student persisted. The family is a result of the human male's natural tendency to monopolize and jealously guard "his" females. Anyway, females naturally are not as promiscuously inclined as males. "Aren't they?" someone else asked. "Then why do they have to be guarded?" And so the discussion went.

At about the time that my students were showing me that there is something wrong with the patrilineal band model, and that Levi-Strauss' formulations do not explain the family sociologically at all, I ran into an anthropology text[21] that regards family as the offshoot of "one-male multiple female" mating and rearing groups such as those found among some baboons. (This patterned social adaptation is discussed in detail in Chapter 2.) This text made it very evident that not only many college students, but sophisticated behavioral scientists as well, regard the family among human beings to be grounded on biological differences in the social dispositions of males and females.

That many Americans are ready to accept this notion was brought home to me when a popular book that attributes the female physique as well as the family to "pair bonding" sold fantastically well.[22] Yet the very diversity of human family arrangements contradicts such a notion. The sketchy model of the sociological origins of the family that I had been using was obviously unsatisfactory enough to leave room for biological theories of family origins to be taken seriously, in my classroom and elsewhere. Again I had a problem. What was wrong with the model? By the late 1960s new data and new analyses of old data were indicating some of its failures.

The next time I taught the sociology of the family course, I took into account points of information that were previously unknown or overlooked in discussions of family origins. These points included the following. Human beings are not the only primates that hunt, and both human and nonhuman primates regularly kill small animals for food without weapons. While our closest primate relatives commonly interact with one another in groups, these groups are frequently fluid assemblages within loosely articulated populations, sometimes large and sometimes small. Interestingly, among the nonhuman primates, females often are the core of such groups, or, better said, the least widely ranging members of the assemblages.[23] Human collector–hunters, both male and female, range much more widely than other primates but do so in loosely articulated groups. Collected foods, whether brought in by men or women, and whether consisting of vegetable items or small animals, normally constitute the major portion of their diet. While medium-sized and large game animals are often hunted by men, in most foraging societies women are the main contributors to subsistence.[24] Further important points with regard to the origins of families are that the frequency of the nuclear family form is high among collector–hunters, that most collecting-hunting peoples reckon descent bilaterally (through both parents) rather than patrilineally (through males only), and that among most collector–hunters, husbands are as likely to join their wives as vice versa.[25] Of interest with respect to the model of family origins I was using is the fact that the collecting-hunting peoples tend to trade with whomever they can whenever they can, establishing wideflung trade networks. All these data (which are spelled out in greater detail in Chapters 2, 5, and 6) indicate that the model of early human society my students were finding so unsatisfactory was not only inadequate but was based on poor information. These data also indicate, although I did not recognize it for some time, that a fully sociological theory of family origins has to deal with the sexual division of labor and its roots.

Rethinking the Roots of the Family: The Behavior Base

The paragraphs that follow sketch out the model—and some of the reasoning and data on which it is built—that I began to put together to explain family origins in subsequent semesters of my course. The model is based on the view that a capacity for adapting to local conditions and forming fluid, flexible groupings is fundamental to the human condition. This capacity is found in many higher primates, where a prolonged dependency period allows infants to acquire information while their mothers take care of their survival needs. The unusually slow rate of development of human infants and the strong mother–child bonds that grow up in conjunction with this delayed maturation are also evidently a precondition of the capacity for and learning of language. But a mother–child bond is not, by itself, "family." While an enduring mother–child relationship is encouraged and maintained in most societies, it is not universally called for.

Furthermore, since similar bonds are found not only among higher primates but elsewhere among large mammals, the pattern is not uniquely associated with human family arrangements. Consequently, the prolonged mother–child relationship, undoubtedly central in early human family groups, is not viewed here as an original form of the family, but rather as a precondition for the social and linguistic capacities that allowed human beings to develop the tools and foraging techniques, the sexual division of labor, and the trade networks which gave rise to the conditions that led to the emergence of the uniquely human institution of the family.

Taking Game:
The "Hunting" Background

The conditions that led to the emergence of the institution of the family began to be established when human foragers began taking game regularly and hunting became habitual and then systematic.[26] For reasons that will soon become clear while the habit of taking game may have become established in groups of any size, hunting systematically in a planned and coordinated manner must have developed among those of our ancestors who found themselves members of large, though perhaps loose, assemblages. Presumably such assemblages were similar to those found among ground-foraging baboons, who live in regions where an abundance of small game and big predators encourages them to seek safety and security in large groups.[27]

One of the interesting things about hunting among contemporary collecting–hunting peoples is that it is conducted in several ways. One method of hunting (which in all its forms is usually a peripheral or secondary subsistence activity) is rather casual and involves more-or-less independent actions by individuals. A man or a woman may take game, with or without the cooperation of others, while out collecting whenever he or she encounters an animal small enough, weak enough, and slow enough to be grabbed or run down. The size of the group the hunter–forager belongs to is irrelevant. (This sort of "hunting" is also done by members of nonhuman primate populations.)

Another common method of hunting is called a "surround." More systematic, in that it requires planning, this method calls for organizing and coordinating the activities of a large number of people. As unobtrusively as possible, the hunters spread out along the perimeter of an area where small or medium-sized game animals can be found. Then the hunters make themselves conspicuous and noisily close in on the encircled animals, forcing them into a smaller and smaller space, where they are trapped. If they are not large or dangerous, killing and dismembering the animals requires simple tools and weapons, no more elaborate than those found by archeologists in early hominid sites. In "surrounds," defenseless and small animals can easily be beaten to death without much danger to the hunters.

Large groups of people also organize "drives" in which big and often dangerous animals are forced into a trap, such as a marsh or a ravine, or off a cliff. The hunters then either wait for the injured animals to die or approach for the kill when the animals are no longer able to defend themselves. One animal or a herd can be driven to its death. There are relatively recent archeological sites in which it appears that hunters wiped out whole herds, far more than they could consume, in this way.[28] None of the forms of hunting described here require particularly sophisticated tools, and in living collector–hunter populations both men and women participate in all of them.[29]

The one method of systematic hunting in which contemporary peoples usually observe a standardized division of labor along sexual lines is that in which hunters armed with projectile weapons track, pursue, and kill big, mobile animals. Women rarely take part in this sort of hunting, either in the chase or in the slaughter.[30] Projectile hunting tools are not found among the artifacts left behind by very early "hunters," those who lived from about 3 million years ago to those living 100,000 years ago. Projectile tools appear in deposits laid down long after hominid hunters had begun regularly leaving among their food scraps and garbage significant quantities of bones from small and medium-sized game as well as the occasional bones of large animals.[31] Apparently for a long time hunting consisted of individual efforts and also surrounds and drives—all forms of hunting in which both sexes participate. The appearance of projectile tools in the archeological record is late in the human record, about 100,000 years ago, and accompanies an increase in the animal debris found in human habitation sites. Evidently more and bigger animals were eaten and meat formed a larger proportion of the diet once these tools were in hand. This shows a change in the situation of early collector–hunters but tells us nothing about how they conducted their hunts with the new tools, and whether or not the associated work was divided along sex lines. But the customs of living collector–hunters indicate that projectile equipment, the tracking and pursuit of big game, and a sexual division of labor are somehow intertwined, and imply that the invention of projectile tools changed the social relationships of the food quest in a way that led to men taking responsibility for certain tasks and making women responsible for others. This indirect evidence of a significant change in the social circumstances of human foragers long after hunting had become an established means of augmenting a vegetable diet forces us to look in detail at another aspect of any model of family origins, the problem of accounting for the sexual division of labor, which is one of the cornerstones of family.

The Sexual Division of Labor

What is it about projectile hunting tools and their use that can lead to dividing labor along sex lines? There is evidently no physical reason for women not to hunt with these tools,[32] since in a few societies women do hunt with them quite successfully.[33] Furthermore, child care need not prevent a woman from taking part in the chase as long as there are other nursing mothers or mother surrogates around that a woman can leave her infant or children with. Sometimes, in fact, women foragers do go off for as long and travel as far as men hunters.[34] If neither physique nor child care prevent it, why is this kind of systematic hunting—the tracking, pursuit, and killing of animals with projectile weapons—nearly always "men's work"? To answer this question, we must look at two factors that play a part in shaping the social relations of peoples who hunt big game with such weaponry. The first has to do with the fact that projectile weapons are associated with a way of hunting that makes small, even tiny, groups highly efficient. The second has to do with the fact that small groups using these tools to their fullest advantage have special infant and child care problems.

The use of throwing or shooting instruments, such as bolas, spears and spear throwers, slings and slingshots (which are practically impossible to identify archeologically), and bows and arrows, permits hunters to kill or mortally injure from a distance, a distance that makes it safe enough to hunt large animals with tusks or antlers. Armed with one or another of these instruments a few people or a lone hunter who is stealthy and cautious can supply the meat for a number of others. Remaining inconspicuous is a key to hunting successfully with such instruments. Contrast this with the fact that a large group of people gathered together for a surround or drive ultimately depends on being conspicuous. Once animals that survive a surround or drive are alerted to the dangers posed by human beings, they flee whenever they detect a human presence. Thus hunting in large groups can result in making game hard to find, or, if whole herds or populations of game animals are wiped out, making it very scarce indeed. Small inconspicuous groups equipped with projectiles are far more effective game takers than large ones. The invention of projectile weaponry seems to have created a situation in which small groups became better at hunting than large groups. Not only that, but where game is normally rich, and defenseless ground-foraging primates are secure from predators only as long as they remain together in large groups, the new tools must have affected group size sharply, for the new tools provided a means of defending small groups which was not previously available.

It is very likely that small groupings were around before these tools and techniques were developed. Like modern baboon populations, early human beings must have been able to suit group size to local circumstances.[35] Where resources were scarce it is highly probable that long before they were armed with projectiles at least some humans found it possible to survive in small or even pair groupings. Some early humans probably moved about in groups too small to conduct surrounds or drives, and if they ate meat at all, it was the meat of the tiny or defenseless or immature animals that a person out collecting could pick up. Before projectile tools made an appearance, there was little reason to develop a division of labor along sexual lines in such groups because collecting and hunting are not really distinct activities. Unencumbered males may have been able to bring in more meat than females with heavy or noisy or active youngsters in tow, as happens in populations of nonhuman primates that hunt today, but both sexes would have collected game in much the same way. Thus while small groups, even "family-sized" ones, were probably present before projectile tools were invented, these early small groups were not a likely locus for task and role differentiation. The techniques and tools for pursuing big game changed things. It was after they appeared that small groups rather than large ones probably became the site of significant social innovation. Small groups, particularly, faced circumstances that made division of labor along sexual lines a necessity.

To examine the factors that suggest that the custom of allocating some tasks to men and others to women became established in this setting I ask my students to imagine a two-adult group situation. The kind of situation I outline for them is one which the data at hand indicate projectile armed forager–hunters might have had to deal with as they went about the business of trying to survive. After I point out that hypothesis building always consists of imagining relationships and processes in terms of data, we proceed to postulate and analyze the following set of extreme circumstances and conditions which affect the lives of many collector–hunters today.

Vegetable foods are or become scarce. Game, too, is scarce. The scarcity of food, whether seasonal, chronic, or episodic, forces the dispersal of a population of early humans who are accustomed to eating meat and who are equipped with projectile weapons that allow them to harvest it readily. Which people should go with whom? There are youngsters to be cared for. Food must continue to be foraged— vegetables and small animals collected, and when possible, big game stalked and pursued. Predators may even have to be fended off (although predators learn quickly to avoid humans who can hurt them). Clearly any young infant has to be accompanied by a woman who can nurse it. The likeliest woman to do so is its mother. Since there will be few or no other nursing women in her party, she will probably have to stay with or close to the baby most or all of the time. If she limits her activities, however, she can, at the same time, also watch over an older child (probably her own), a child who cannot move quickly or quietly, or travel far enough to accompany a hunter. While she is free to perform foraging and processing tasks that do not take her far afield, she is not in a position to go off for an unspecified length of time to chase game. Logically, then, someone who is free to do so ought to accompany her. Her companion, if male, cannot breast-feed the infant, so he will be forced to do whatever hunting is necessary or possible. And unless the older children are big enough to join him and remain still and inconspicuous while he stalks game, his baby-sitting services will be limited. If he has to keep his weapons ready to use quickly, he cannot even carry a baby when he and the woman are traveling.

Although there are some tasks that either person can perform, there are some which are—for the sake of mutual survival—performed by one and not the other. A division of labor along sex lines, very much like that found in a nuclear family, is called for in this very minimal dispersal group. If the two adults in the group enjoy free sexual access to one another, this small dispersal group resembles a nuclear family quite closely. Any male–female dispersal pair with sexual access to each other will probably come to resemble a nuclear family, since a woman who does not have an infant is very likely to have one in time. Our hypothetical example indicates why the tools for big game hunting make a sexual division of labor a practical necessity in a small male/female group.

That women do not go in for big game hunting even where

Bushman women on a collecting expedition. Women do not participate in dangerous big game hunting, but travel far afield to collect vegetable foods. Photo by Marjorie Shostak, Anthro-Photo.

groups are larger than our extreme case calls for can be attributed to several factors. First, while adaptive and efficient groups for hunting are often larger than this tiny one, they are rarely so large or so permanent that a woman who is nursing can count on another woman being around to care for her infant and allow her to go off. Second, where efficient hunting groups are sometimes very large but seasonal changes require them to disperse periodically to prepare for dispersal roles, it is worthwhile for males to develop and maintain their hunting skills, exchanging information and practicing with other men when they are assembled and not under the critical pressures they face when supplies are short and dispersal is required. Third, hunting big game animals is dangerous, even with projectile weapons, and hunters are sometimes killed or injured. Losing a man affects infant care, reproductive rates, and collecting activities (which supply the bulk of the subsistence foods) far less than losing a woman. So assigning men to do the hunting has distinct advantages in groups of any size. In sum, then, this model sees a sexual division of labor as having become established after projectile-wielding collector–hunters began to find small groups an effective social base for subsistence activities.

When a division of labor along sex lines is generalized and carried into all sorts of settings and groupings, a mutual dependency is created between men and women. This dependency between the sexes means that whenever dispersal is necessary, for whatever reason, a man and a woman ought to be included in the minimal dispersal group. This could lead us to jump to the conclusion that environmental factors that led to dispersing are the basis on which "family"—or at least the nuclear families of collector–hunters—grew. But is a minimal dispersal group made up of a female and a male truly a family?

Minimal dispersal groups lack several of the defining characteristics of the family.[36] They are, for one thing, not regularized in all environments. Minimal dispersal groups need not persist or maintain their identity when dispersal is no longer necessary. As long as there are no rules or contracts binding the members of a male–female dispersal pair together with reassembly into larger groups, dispersal groups and pairs can break up for their members are free to look where they will for care, or sex, or support. Second, where food is chronically in short supply and tiny groups never have the chance of getting together, as long as there are no rules forcing people to seek mates outside their dispersal group, the isolated, self-sufficient dispersal group is not a "family" either. It is not really a subunit of a larger social entity. So, although environmental factors can lead to family-like groupings, sex division of labor and all, something besides environmental necessity is called for to account for the emergence of the rules, contracts, and the assignment of membership that create true families. What is that something? What human activity contains the elements of the rules that generate family?

Trade, Trade Networks, and Families

Large as well as minimal groups of people benefit from exchanging or trading goods with others. Levi-Strauss[37] points out that the advantages of trade are secured and stabilized when people as well as goods are moved from one group to another. People who move between groups may be emissaries who volunteer for the job, or "earnests" or pledges against debt who are drafted for it, but in either case they establish a link that facilitates trading. While anybody, adult or child, male or female, can serve as a link or a channel through which goods are funneled, since the sexes need one another for mating, and "need" one another economically once a sexual division of labor forces them into a mutual dependency, insisting that men and women must seek mates outside a defined set of associates is one way of ensuring that people have to move between groups.[38] Incest rules, then, force people to seek mates outside the group they are born into, even if this natal group is normally isolated and self-sufficient. Incest rules are a way of assuring that groups always move people between them for marriage, and marriage contracts project durable links between spouses, links that are supposed to be kept intact whether or not dispersal is necessary or called for. Levi-Strauss reasons that the institutionalization of incest rules and marriage contracts effectively solidified advantageous trade and political alliances. Trade is thus what we have been missing in our attempt to explain what generates the rules on which the regularized family is based.

While Levi-Strauss clearly identifies trade as a key factor in the emergence of marriage and incest taboos, his formulations are

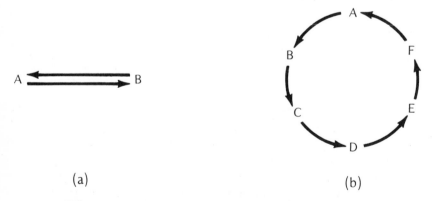

(a)   (b)

FIGURE 2   An exchange partnership (a) and a trade circle (b), showing how women are sometimes moved for marriages (arrows) between localized kin groups (A, B, C, etc.).

based on an image of tightly knit male-centered groups that go about moving women and goods through simple reciprocal trade partnerships or trade circles (Figure 2). As a result, his discussion does not address the fact that marriage contracts designate specific individuals as spouses and does not reveal that trade is implicated in the establishment of the rule that makes family a subunit of larger social aggregates.

We know that collector–hunters usually do not live in tightly knit groups but as members of fluid subgroupings of populations, that they trade with as many other people as they can, that local groups contract marriages in many directions simultaneously, and that either or both men and women may go off to be the link with peoples in other localities. Given these data it is not hard to identify what advantages led to specifying who married whom. The foundations of the rule creating family subunits comes into focus when we attempt to determine the effect that specifying the individual parties to a marriage contract has on trade among collector–hunters.

Populations of collector–hunters in which specific individuals are tied in marriage to specific people from groups other than their own are capable of establishing networks of trade relationships (Figure 3). A trade network moves goods from many sources to its member's

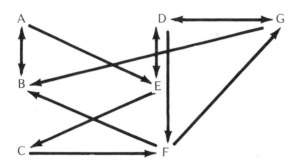

FIGURE 3   An exchange network generated by individuals, either men or women, moving at marriage (arrows) between localized kin groups (A, B, C, etc.).

units. What's scarce in one locality and plentiful elsewhere is moved through the many ties of individual marriages to reach distant and indirectly related peoples. A network of ties provides all its members with many suppliers, and assures them access to a variety of goods or resources. Making ties with a lot of suppliers from many places is easiest if trade and marriage contracts are arranged on a one-to-one basis—if a group moves one person here and one person there. The device of sending people off one by one, making marriages individual, also stabilizes intragroup relationships. For instance, if a specific man or woman dies, or if a couple does not get along well and splits up, their natal groups can offer another person to replace the dead or abandoned spouse. Ties are thus maintained. Yet if substitutions do not work, neither party need suffer much, for each has others to fall back on.

Insisting that marriage contracts specify individuals has other important effects on trading. One person can take spouses from several groups, thereby strengthening trade relationships in many directions. Furthermore, because children are assigned to specific "parents," a child's future marital ties are stipulated. Thus a trade network with complicated or elaborate ramifications is continued from one generation to another. Finally, of course, if dispersal is desirable or necessary, taking one spouse at a time is all that anybody can manage anyway, and specifying which individuals are supposed to go off together, whom they can rely on, and who children assigned to them can turn to keeps the network intact. Given these advantages, the central role in the emergence of the family played by individualizing marital contracts in the establishment and maintenance of trade becomes clear.

Before recounting how the one other issue dealt with in this book became a problem to be analyzed in class, I must add that I always warn students that models of evolutionary events and processes cannot easily be subject to laboratory or experimental "proof." Yet an evolutionary model can be examined in terms of whether it provides an adequate and elegant explanation of all the data it sets out to explain, whether it contains falsifiable concepts or false statements about observable processes and relationships, and whether it predicts accurately data that become known after the theory is formulated. Although not provable, evolutionary models can and should be tested.

PROBLEM THREE:
SEXUAL POLITICS AND PURE SCIENCE

The first issue to be explored in this book—the biobehavioral background against which the family emerged—is actually the last issue to which I devoted serious attention. Because the sociocultural basis of the family seemed to be well understood and widely accepted, I originally treated this issue perfunctorily in lectures and reading assignments. Events changed my approach rather rapidly and opened up for me an entirely new literature.

The mid and late 1960s saw the publication of a number of nontechnical books on the subject of human evolution which made "man's" instincts or behavioral potentials responsible for things such as contemporary wars,[39] the way boards of corporations are set up[40] —and the family! In a book which argues that the nuclear family is, if not universal, the only evolutionarily significant form of family (people who do not customarily live in nuclear groupings are regarded as off the main line of evolution and irrelevant), it is held that an ancient instinct for "pair bonding" among early humans gave rise to the family.[41] Because those early males who were strong enough and skillful enough to support a woman and her children supposedly preferred full-breasted, round-bottomed females, pair bonding is also seen to be responsible for the physical differences between men and women. Knowing that among the pair-bonded gibbons (small apes who are distant relatives of the human line) the sexes are not particularly differentiated, while among other primate species in which the sexes are differentiated pair bonding does not occur,[42] I wrote a critique of the model. In commenting on the book I pointed out the biases exhibited in its use of data.[43]

As I went over the course materials, I realized more and more that a male-oriented bias permeates not only the popular literature but the professional anthropological literature as well, and that it was necessary to *defend* the notion that our ancestors lived in loose, generally egalitarian groupings rather than in male-centered troops or bands. At this point the literature on animal behavior became of serious rather than casual interest to me. To discuss the origins of human family arrangements apparently could not be done without looking at what our primate relatives do, since even anthropologists who regard the family as a human invention harbor preconceptions about the social significance of sex differences which affect what they think early human social life was like. The literature discussing the "meaning" of sex differences in the animal kingdom was growing rapidly at this time as a major controversy was developing.

To counter the argument that women can, and often do, fulfill roles that are allocated to men in our society, a number of writers began to examine the physical differences between males and females in a variety of species. Citing sex differences in many species, they note that these are often the outward manifestation of fundamental behavioral differences between the sexes. The physical differentiation of men and women must, they argue, also have profound social behavioral concomitants. But does it? And do sex differences in the animal kingdom have the social consequences most frequently attributed to them? These questions have become very significant recently. Some women's liberationists, many anthropologists, and most Americans are predisposed to believing that just being male or female leads to certain kinds of social behavior patterns, even though they support equal rights for women. Anthropologists who regard themselves as proponents of Women's Liberation indicate that they

25

believe that the physical differences between men and women have "natural" social consequences which only our advanced state of culture makes meaningless.[44] Such views make it necessary to look closely at sex and sex differences in nature.

In exploring the literature on animal behavior to try to understand the biobehavioral background against which family emerged, it became clear that sex in the organic world is a phenomenon rarely appreciated for its diversity, that sex differences among non-human primates occur in social constellations which are both varied and variable, and that standard explanations of how and why sex differences evolved among primates do not reflect the realities of primate social life. Although examining how sexual differences evolved in primates was the last thing I devoted attention to in developing my course, the problem is an aspect of the first issue, the biobehavioral background of family, with which I deal in this book.

NOTES

1. George Peter Murdock, *Social Structure* (New York: Macmillan, 1949).

2. Alfred L. Kroeber, *Anthropology* [New York: Harcourt Brace, 1948 (originally published 1923)].

3. Murdock, *Social Structure*, p. 1.

4. Murdock, *Social Structure*, p. 2.

5. Murdock, *Social Structure*, p. 2.

6. Meyer Fortes, "An Ashanti Case Study," in *Social Structure*, ed. Meyer Fortes (New York: Russell and Russell, 1963), pp. 63-64.

7. Robin Fox, *Kinship and Marriage* (Harmondsworth, England: Penguin, 1967), p. 112.

8. Yonina Talmon-Garber, "The Case of Israel," in *The Family: Its Structure and Functions*, ed. Rose Coser (New York: St. Martin's Press, 1964), pp. 582-617.

9. Paul Bohannon, *Social Anthropology* (New York: Holt, Rinehart and Winston, 1963), p. 86.

10. Bohannon, *Social Anthropology*, p. 98.

11. E. Kathleen Gough, "The Nayars and the Definition of Marriage," in *Cultural and Social Anthropology, Selected Readings*, ed. Peter B. Hammond (New York: Macmillan, 1964), pp. 167-180.

12. Lila Leibowitz, "Founding Families," *Journal of Theoretical Biology*, *21*, 1968, pp. 153-169.

13. Edmund R. Leach, "Aspects of Bridewealth and Marriage Stability among the Kachin and Lakher," in *Rethinking Anthropology, Collected Essays*, ed. Edmund R. Leach (London: Athlone Press, 1963), pp. 114-123.

14. Herma Hill Kay, "The Family and Kinship System of Illegitimate Children in California Law," in *The Ethnography of Law*, ed. Laura Nader, American Anthropologist Special Publication, 67, no. 6 (Menasha, Wis.: American Anthropological Association, 1965), pp. 57-81.

15. Gerald D. Berreman, "Pahari Polyandry: A Comparison," *American Anthropologist*, *64*, no. 1, 1962, 11, pp. 60-75.

16. Peter Laslett, *The World We Have Lost* (New York: Scribner's, 1971). See especially Chapter 4.

17. Ruth Landes, *The Ojibwa Woman* (New York: W.W. Norton, 1971).

18. Claude Levi-Strauss, *The Elementary Structures of Kinship* [Boston: Beacon Press, 1969 (originally published 1949)].

19. Talcott Parsons, "The Incest Taboo in Relation to Social Structure," in *The Family: Its Structure and Functions*, ed. Rose Coser (New York: St. Martin's Press, 1964), pp. 48-69.

20. Julian Steward, *Theory of Culture Change: the Methodology of Multilinear Evolution* (Urbana, Ill.: University of Illinois Press, 1955).

21. Bernard Campbell, *Human Evolution* (Chicago: Aldine, 1966).

22. Desmond Morris, *The Naked Ape* (New York: McGraw-Hill, 1968).

23. Jane Van Lawick Goodall, *In the Shadow of Man* (New York: Dell, 1971).

24. Richard B. Lee, "What Hunters Do for a Living; or How to Make out on Scarce Resources," in *Man the Hunter*, eds. Richard B. Lee and Irven DeVore (Chicago: Aldine, 1968), pp. 30-43.

25. M.F. Nimkoff, "The Social System and the Family," in *Comparative Family Systems*, ed. M.F. Nimkoff (Boston: Houghton Mifflin, 1965), pp. 37-60.

26. The argument presented here is a modification of one that appears in Elman R. Service, *Primitive Social Organization* [New York: Random House, 1971 (originally published 1962)], and in Marshall D. Sahlins and Elman R. Service, *Evolution and Culture* (Ann Arbor, Mich.: University of Michigan Press, 1961).

27. Irven DeVore and K.R.L. Hall, "Baboon Ecology," in *Primate Behavior*, ed. Irven DeVore (New York: Holt, Rinehart and Winston, 1965), pp. 20–52.

28. C. Vance Haynes, Jr., "Elephant Hunting in North America," in *New World Archaeology*, selected and with an introduction by Ezra B.W. Zubrow, Margaret C. Fritz, and John M. Fritz (San Francisco: W.H. Freeman, 1974), pp. 204–212. Also in the same volume, Joe Ben Wheat, "A Paleo-Indian Bison Kill," pp. 213–221.

29. See, for example, Colin Turnbull's description of hunting in *The Forest People* (New York: Simon and Schuster, 1962). For further examples of collaborative hunting by men and women, see Nathaniel Raymond and Lila Leibowitz "The Division of Labor and Authority in Collecting–Hunting Societies," paper presented at the 1975 American Anthropological Association meeting, 1975, San Francisco.

30. Ernestine Friedl, *Women and Men: An Anthropologist's View* (New York: Holt, Rinehart and Winston, 1975). The author emphasizes this form of hunting in her analysis.

31. An easy-to-read summary of archeological investigation of early human sites appears in John E. Pfeiffer, *The Emergence of Man* (New York: Harper & Row, 1969).

32. Women may even be physiologically better suited than men for prolonged chases. In discussing the exploits of Ms. Christa Vahlensieck, who broke the world marathon record set by a male, Dr. Ernest Van Aaken of Waldniel, Germany, noted: "Women are born with greater natural stamina. Men will throw further, jump higher and run faster for short stretches. Forty percent of a man's body weight is muscle. In women, muscle amounts to only 23 percent. Instead of this, they have more hypodermal fatty tissue and that is the source of energy for hours-long exertion." He is quoted by Lloyd Shearer, *Parade Magazine*, March 23, 1975, p. 16.

33. Landes, *The Ojibwa Woman*.

34. Patricia Draper, "!Kung Women: Contrast in Sexual Egalitarianism in Foraging and Sedentary Contexts," in *Toward an Anthropology of Women*, ed. Rayne R. Reiter (New York: Monthly Review Press, 1975), pp. 77–109.

35. Chapter 2 presents a review of baboon ecological adaptations.

36. A discussion of minimal dispersal groups appears in Leibowitz, "Founding Families," 1968.

37. Levi-Strauss, *The Elementary Structure of Kinship*.

38. Claude Levi-Strauss, "The Family," in *Man, Culture and Society*, ed. Harry Shapiro (London: Oxford University Press, 1971), pp. 337–349.

39. Konrad Lorenz, *On Aggression* (New York: Harcourt, Brace and World, 1966).

40. Antony Jay, *Corporation Man* (New York: Random House, 1971).

41. Morris, *The Naked Ape*.

42. Chapter 2 examines this material in detail.

43. Lila Leibowitz, "Breasts, Buttocks and Body Hair," *Psychology Today*, *3*, no. 9, 1970, pp. 16–22.

44. Marvin Harris, in the first edition of his introductory anthropology text [which was titled *Culture, Man and Nature* (1971)] held this position but later modified it slightly. He also retitled his text *Culture, People and Nature* (New York: Thomas Y. Crowell, 1975).

1

Sex in Nature

Living organisms reproduce in two ways, asexually and sexually. Asexual reproduction occurs primarily among small or "simple" organisms when an individual germ cell divides and sets in motion the production of new organisms which are almost perfect replicas of the parent. Sexual reproduction is more complicated. Not only is more than one cell required for the process, it is the mode of reproduction characteristic of organisms that come in a great many sizes and shapes, are very diverse as to their bodily organization and complexity, and utilize a great many strategies to bring together the cells necessary for reproduction.

This chapter is a survey presenting a sampling of the diversity of ways in which sexual reproduction is accomplished by organisms of different forms and levels of complexity. It will make clear that sexual reproduction occurs in many ways that do not conform to some of our favorite notions about what sex involves, what male and female organisms are like, and how—in the animal kingdom—males and females are presumed to interact sexually and/or socially. This survey shows that maleness is not always associated with characteristics that we conceive of as being masculine, or femaleness with traits we think of as being feminine.

More important for a book about the social roots of the institution of the family, which has been conceptualized as the product of the biological attributes of human males and females, this survey indicates that the course of biological evolution has led to the emergence, in several species of mammals, of a biologically based condition which makes sexual and social behavior subject to individual or group experiences. It points out the difference between the species-wide stereotyped responses to sex-related stimuli (developed from genetic programs either in isolation or elicited or imprinted as the result of experience) and the flexibility of the social and sexual responses of some of the larger mammals, and indicates that the biologically based capacity to vary behaviors related to reproduction is neither uniquely human nor characteristic of only humanity's closest relatives in the primate order (whose diverse social and sexual adaptations are dealt with in later chapters).

30

THE ORIGINS OF SEXUAL REPRODUCTION

Sexual reproduction is an ancient process. It has been tentatively identified in rocks from Bitter Springs, Australia, where a small cataclysm 900 million years ago ended the lives of several single-celled animals and preserved in perpetuity the evidence of their sexual activities.[1] These fossils bear silent witness to the fact that for a long time living things on earth have been reproducing by the coming together of two individuals of the same general genetic structure, thus setting in motion the development of new individuals.

The fossilized cells from Bitter Springs died during meiosis. This cell process involves a halving of the number of certain chromosomes which control cell function. This division normally is followed by recombination and rejoining. Two by two, pairs of these halved cells reassemble, creating new "whole" individuals.

There are indications that even this type of simple sexual reproduction has antecedents. The fossilized Bitter Springs cells are by no means "simple" in themselves, since they contain distinct structures that resemble a nucleus, and cell walls. Similar single-celled organisms may have other specialized structures as well. Some biologists regard unicellular organisms as noncellular because they are more complex than the cells which make up multicellular organisms . Whatever they are called, they pose a problem. It is not clear how such "cells" evolved from complex protein molecules, but the processes implied suggest sex-like interdependencies.[2] Furthermore, a kind of presexual reproductive process has been observed in the laboratory among organisms of this type. Single-celled creatures that normally reproduce by division often live in colonies or clones, which consist of genetically identical individuals. These individuals represent the multiple replications of a single original cell. Sometimes a clone of such massed individuals joins with another just like it before replicating further.

How and if cloning is related to the "halving-before-joining" process, which is recognized as sexual reproduction, is as yet unknown. Genuine sexual reproduction may have arisen in an individual cell through a mutation that affected its replication procedures. It is even possible that sexual reproduction may have arisen several times and in several ways. In any case, true sexual reproduction has been around for a long time.

Why should sexual reproduction have taken hold and developed at all? What forces favored minute metabolizing structures that required two rather than one individual for the complex process of reproduction? In terms of bare efficiency, it would seem that where one alone suffices, two is more than enough or even too much. Life is preserved without twoness. There are billions of well-adapted asexual unicellular organisms around today. Asexual reproduction continues

31

as the means by which they perpetuate themselves. Yet sexually reproducing organisms appeared long ago, survived, proliferated, and evolved elaborate variations.

Current speculations on the reasons for the success and increasing complexity of sexual processes are straightforward. Where Darwin pointed out that variation is the basis of evolution, that evolution works by selectively favoring some variants of an organism over others, twentieth-century theorists point out that the existence of variation is itself advantageous to the perpetuation of living things. The more different kinds of living things there are, the more likely it is that *some* will survive; especially in changing environments. When a single-celled organism splits, its "daughters" are almost identical to it. When two cells combine, the offspring may be like one parent in some ways and like the other parent in other ways, but not exactly like either parent. Sexual reproduction involves combinations and recombinations of parental traits. It allows for a great many variants and a lot of changes from one generation to another—many more variants and a greater rate of change than can occur when a single individual replicates itself. The major advantages of twoness in reproductive activities lies in the production of variation.[3]

Reproductive twoness had irreversible evolutionary effects. It gave rise to new kinds of organisms and set the stage for new ways of existing. It introduced variation between creatures of the same general genetic makeup. But these early differences between individuals had nothing to do with their sex per se. There was no division of labor in reproductive tasks. Sexual reproduction and sex differences do not go hand in hand. In living creatures of the simple cellular kind which reproduce sexually it is not possible to define one of the cells as male and the other as female; they are generally similar in appearance and content. On this very simple level, there are no "sexes," just sexual reproduction.

The Basic Sex Differences

Although the basic requirement of two players on the reproductive team has remained the same, organisms that reproduce sexually have developed a number of different "strategies" for sexual reproduction. In evolutionary lines where sexually reproducing organisms stayed unicellular and relatively simple, the two contributors to the reproductive process usually are essentially alike. Any change in the cell alters the whole organism and affects its ability to survive. Among multicellular organisms, some cells can change without altering the life chances of the whole organism significantly, and genuine structural "sex differences" occur more readily. Minimally, sex differences appear in those cells that play a direct part in sexual reproduction. There are some cells which are almost exclusively miniscule containers of genetic materials. Others, larger ones, contain nutrients as well as genetic materials. The former, sperm, are classified as male, and the latter, ova or eggs, are classified as females. Despite the fact that we tend to think of sex differences as being a characteristic of individuals (i.e., of males and females who look and act differently), in a great many multicellular organisms, such differences are present, as we shall see, within individuals but not between individuals; that is, an individual produces *both* ova and sperm.

As we go up the scale of organic complexity, differences involve more than just specialized cells. Whole organs—structures made up of many cells—become specialized for ingesting, or digesting, or sensing, or breathing, or reproducing. The reproductive equipment of relatively complex plants and animals includes organs whose particular function is the generation of eggs or of sperm. With differences in reproductive organs, the structural attributes of maleness and femaleness are unquestionably present. Surely now we are dealing with "males" and "females," with sex differences.

SEXUAL REPRODUCTION WITHOUT SEXUAL "BEHAVIOR": PLANTS

Interestingly, the presence of specialized sexual parts does not necessarily lead nonbiologists to regard in sexual terms the organisms that possess them. Lay people do not tend to think of plants in terms of sex, that is, as having "male" qualities or "female" qualities. Nor do we regard flowering plants in such terms, even though some of us might regard the process of pollination, which is necessary for most seed-producing plants to actually produce seeds, as having some "sexual" aspects. The truth is that even though we generally use eros-free phrasing when telling children about "the birds and the bees," pollination is a sexual act; it involves the joining of sperm and ova.

One factor that clouds our awareness of this and similar types of sexual reproduction as "sex" is that we are not used to thinking in terms of a single organism incorporating both male and female parts. But when we learn that there are both male trees and female trees in some species (holly and lilacs being examples)—that some species of plants do indeed share with us clearcut distinctions between male individuals and female individuals—we still tend not to regard them as "sexual" organisms. This suggests that another factor preventing us from perceiving of plants as sexed and participating in sexual reproduction is their inactivity. Birds, bees, and wind *do* the work of

A bee foraging. In their movements from flower to flower while feeding, bees help plants to reproduce sexually. Photo by John Bishop.

mating for plants; mates do not seek or choose their sexual partners. Indeed, neither do the agents of insemination act as "seekers" in sexual terms. Plants just stand and grow, winds blow, bees seek honey, and birds merely brush by. Insemination is incidental to these events. Sex in our culture is seldom just incidental. The idea that maleness and femaleness are qualities of whole organisms is permeated by the precept that males and females participate actively in mating and in sexual reproduction. Maleness and femaleness are also associated with differences in behavior, maleness commonly with an "active" principle, femaleness commonly with "passivity" and sustenance.[4] Plants do not behave as our culture expects sexual organisms to behave. Therefore, we are apt to think of sex as an *animal* instinct.

SEX IN INVERTEBRATE ANIMALS

Even in the animal kingdom, sex and sex differences occur in ways that do not conform to our expectations. In some species individuals produce both male and female reproductive cells, just as some plants do. Among some invertebrate species in which this double-sex condition—hermaphroditism—is the norm, hermaphrodites are neither rare nor aberrant, nor are they infertile. Like self-inseminating flowers, they are sexually self-sufficient. Scallops are a case in point. The nudibranches—slug-like creatures who look like what their name suggests—are another. They reproduce sexually, yet need no mates.

But invertebrate animals are not always hermaphroditic. Permanent sex distinctions between male and female individuals are common, and sexual dimorphism—the occurrence of two distinct forms, one for each sex—is frequent. Among insects, particularly, there are extreme differentiations in form as well as in sexual function. Indeed, there are far more "sexes" than two in some species if we take form and function as being diagnostic of sex.

The social insects—bees, wasps, termites, ants—show striking variations on the theme of sex differences and sex reproductive techniques, and some species exhibit *polymorphism* (poly, many; morph, forms) for different sex roles.[5] The role of bees in pollination was discussed earlier without any reference to the complexity and variety of bees and bee-to-bee social arrangements. The famed honeybee hive organization, which is built around a few egg-laying queen mothers, many infertile female workers, and a small number of male drones, is but one in a wide spectrum of bee adaptations. Other types of bees have other ways of coping with the problems of surviving and reproducing. In addition to the well-known social hive-living bees, there are bees who live more or less solitary lives, do not build hives, produce no sterile female workers, and lack dramatic differences in the numbers of males and females. Among solitary species, most males and females reproduce, and the differences between sexes are less marked than those found among the honeybees.

The many social or hive-living species differ widely in the complexity of their social organizations. Some have hives that are merely cooperative nests. Others have complex, sophisticated structures that harbor just a few fertile female queens, a great many infertile female workers, and several fertile male nonworking drones. The queens of some species are inseminated only once in their reproductive careers, so that a whole hive can be the offspring of a single mating. Queens of other species may mate more frequently and store and use the sperm of several males. Sometimes ostensibly sterile worker females mate and lay eggs. (Even the unmated worker female may lay viable eggs.) Nevertheless, egg laying usually falls only to queens, who look different from workers and drones. The care of eggs and their feeding, and the care of the developing young, fall to workers, as do foraging and food-processing activities. In complex hives, many tasks may occupy different kinds of workers, for bee species differ in degree of dimorphism or polymorphism. In the survival sweepstakes, bees have followed various courses and have elaborated sex differences and reproductive arrangements in special and unique ways.

Ant arrangements and patterns, like those of the bees,

include a variety of strategies for reproduction and nurturing. The winged fertile queen and her few potential male consorts are usually surrounded by myriads of mateless and infertile female workers. In some species there are several forms of worker females, each with physical features especially suited to a highly specialized task. There are nursery workers who spend their lives within the nest caring for the immature and developing young. There are honey-jar ants whose enlarged abdomens serve as food repositories. They carry food from the outer portions of the nest to the inner sanctums. There are soldier ants, "spartan" neuter females, with the kind of strength, agility, and high activity levels that permit them to fit well their roles of nest guardians and foragers. There are even ants who act not just as door keepers but as doors.[6] Each looks a little bit different from the others. Role differences by sex and subsex are clearly evidenced by anatomy. Among ants, anatomy and destiny are one.

The sex life of aphids is also built around a kind of polymorphism in which differences in body structure and appearance clearly reflect variants in sexual functioning. Although plant lice, or aphids, are associated with ants and ant colonies (ants sometimes keep "herds" of aphids because they produce a sweetish liquid prized by the herders), aphid "polymorphism" is quite different from that of ants.

An ant nest includes at all times ants of several forms (queens, workers, males, etc.). Workers and males, although they look different from the queens, usually share the same genetic makeup. Aphids might be called generationally or sequentially polymorphic because parents and offspring differ in their forms and functioning. What happens is this: Aphids utilize several modes of reproduction. During warm seasons, when food is plentiful, wingless females produce many eggs which hatch without fertilization. If the plant on which the aphids are living dies, the wingless females lay eggs that produce winged females. These fly to new plants, where they lay eggs that produce more wingless females. So far, all the generations of descendants are identical in genotype to the originals. At the end of the warm season, in the fall, when food is no longer plentiful, the eggs that are laid hatch into both males and winged females. In the course of seeking out winter accommodations, sexual matings occur between males and females of different genotypes. Changes in diet, temperature, and light in the environment thus initiate changes in sexual forms and functioning; this is a kind of polymorphism that occurs over time. Destiny, it seems, determines their anatomy.

The number of species and individuals in the class Arthropoda (which includes insects and spiders) that exhibit social arrangements and reproductive patterns that we might consider to be "odd" or "unusual" is enormous, greater by far than the number of mammals and birds that have ever lived or may ever live on the earth. The "not-so-social" insects also exhibit a great many reproductive adaptations. There are some species in which the females expend great amounts of energy on offspring they will never see, spinning cocoons or incapacitating prey on which their eggs are laid and the larvae develop. In other species females simply scatter their eggs, letting them fall where they may, prey to whatever fate overtakes them. In general, arthropod females are larger than males and live longer. Female spiders that cannibalize their lovers after copulating with them exhibit an unusual but nevertheless "natural" reproductive behavior pattern.

SEX IN THE LOWER VERTEBRATES

Human beings are quite different in total body organization from the creatures we have been discussing, which often look so different from us that nonbiologists may not want to recognize them as true "animals." As reproductively successful and numerous as invertebrates are, their sexual behavior often seems strange to us. After all, we are vertebrates, related to all other animals which have a centralized neural cord, a head end and a tail end, a left side and a right side that are mirror images of each other, and a back and a belly. So, sex and sex differences among a few vertebrates whose "animal" attributes we see easily and acknowledge readily might be more recognizably "sexual" than those of other animals.

Displayed in the cases in "Fish Bowl Hall" (as my children used to call it) at the Museum of Natural History in New York are models and pictures of protandrous fish, species in which the individual is first male, then becomes female. A nearby exhibit shows other protogynous species, which reverse the order, first female, then male. Marine biologists have worked with several such sex-changing species of fish.[7] These scientists have learned how to stimulate female conversions to male forms. When all the obvious males are removed from a breeding population, sex changes are set off among some of the remaining "females." Although at any given time, most individuals in a sex-changing species can be classified as either male or female, each individual at birth is potentially male *and* female.

Sex-changing fish represent just one among several ways in which sex differentiation has been developed among fish. Among most species of fish whether an individual is male or female is determined at the time of conception. In some, the sexes look alike; in others, sex differences are marked. In some species females broadcast eggs freely, then leave them to be inseminated and developed, or to be eaten.[8] In others, females guard the fertilized eggs from predators, and in still others, males guard the eggs. Sometimes, females brood their eggs in special body sacs from which the young ultimately emerge alive and swimming. Among sea horses, males are sac holders and perform the function of brooder. Some sharks give birth to live young. Others are egg layers. Some male fish fight for territories. Others join schools. Indeed, fish are quite variable as to the natural forms which their sexual adaptations take. Interestingly, sometimes their destiny dictates their anatomy.

Amphibian and reptilian vertebrates apparently evolved from ancient fish populations, and their recent representatives developed strategies for a sexual division of labor which are only slightly less various than those of fish. The ancestors of all birds and mammals are certain ancient amphibians and reptiles.

SEXUAL DIVERSITY IN BIRDS

Birds, like mammals, are relatively late arrivals on the evolutionary scene, and like mammals, they are warm-blooded. One would expect the birds to have sexual patterns that are more familiar and natural to us than those of other classes of vertebrates, and in one respect sex in birds is persistently very much like that of mammals; there are no species in either class given to changing sex in midlife, and the sexes are normally differentiated with regards to their reproductive organs. But mistakes do happen.[9] Medieval tales of cockatrices, monsters with a deadly glance that hatch from eggs laid by roosters, are based on the occurrence of hens that develop the sexual insignia of roosters but retain the hen's egg-making equipment. Since such "hens" cannot normally attract mates, their eggs do not have much opportunity to produce live offspring. (Unhatchable eggs are, of course, the best eggs from which to have monsters arise.) We know very little about how often hermaphroditic mistakes occur in most populations of birds, but we can be almost certain of one thing: in creatures of such exquisite reproductive refinement as birds and mammals, hermaphrodites and sexually anomalous individuals are functionally sterile. Thus, a male–female dichotomy is part and parcel of the avian adaptation.

Given this fundamental sexual dichotomy, the sex differences and sex life of bird species are still considerably more varied than one might expect. Sex differences and their social correlates are not necessarily as simple as those conveyed in our normal tale of "the birds and the bees." What male and female birds of different species look like and what they do as regards reproductive accommodations covers a broad range of variant adaptations.

One idealized picture of sex behavior among birds often has the male robin (or bluebird or redwing) singing his heart out in lyric joy, wooing a fair young female. Bird songs are love songs, it would seem. But, actually, songs serve many purposes. The most lyric of male redwing songs are reserved for periods in which no females are around, when males are competing for territories.[10] And African bell shrikes "sing" just to keep in touch.[11]

Another idyllic concept of bird life has the mother bird sitting on her eggs while she is fed by the father bird. Then both join forces to fill the gaping beaks of their ravenous and noisy nestlings. Illustrations that accompany the telling of such tales often show birds that are blue or have red breasts. The elegantly attired hoopoes, a species in which the sexes look alike, do go in for this sort of thing, but since their rather casual nests are befouled by malodorous secretions from the female and her young, the pretty hoopoes make less than ideal illustrations of this pattern.[12]

Although it is not too common, another picture of bird life and domesticity is that characterized by the rooster, lording it over a flock of cackling and somewhat stupid hens. Perhaps this image is also idyllic from some people's point of view.

Despite these varying ideas that we have of birds, ornithologists (naturalists who study bird life) are well aware that evolution has favored birds with considerably more inventive ways of handling reproduction than our story tellers would have. The female of the common cuckoo, whose activities have given rise to the term "cuckold" (a term applied to husbands whose wives wander), lives a profligate life.[13] She leaves her eggs in the nests of birds who are the victims of their limited perceptual capacities. They are deceived, often enough, into accepting the cuckoo's eggs and brooding and rearing cuckoo foster children, to the detriment of the nestlings who are their own offspring. Female cuckoos, like the male cuckoos they resemble, in the meantime disport themselves free of domestic duties. Canada geese, which also come in look-alike pairs, are quite unlike cuckoos, bound to one another for life. Both males and females involve themselves heavily in brooding *and* in the caretaking of the young. The bright-red male cardinal is as loyal to his dull mate and almost as solicitous a father as a Canada gander. In the reeds close to where Canada geese nest, eye-catching male red-winged blackbirds compete anew each year for territories in which one or more dull-brown females (this year's mates) will nest.[14] Among cattle egrets, males and females look and act so much alike that only inborn highly stereotyped patterned rituals during mating permit human observers, and perhaps cospecies members, to distinguish males from females.[15] There are many other species in which we find that the sexes look different and also go in for different stereotyped rituals. Gaudy self-advertising plumage bedecks males in many species in which the more modestly attired females are camouflaged and seem to try to escape notice. Peacocks are spectacular, peahens drab. Male cardinals are scarlet, females brownish; the male painted bunting has a red breast, purple head, and green back, the female is just green. Although bright male plumage is commonly associated with annual courtship and changing mates, cardinals, for example, are permanent spouses. There is no single patterning of avian anatomy that signals behavioral destiny.

Not well known are the many species in which females are the larger and showier sex. Such is often the case among birds with "polyandrous" adaptations (females having multiple male mates), such as the plains-living African phalaropes and the shore-living Central American jacanas.[16] Where polyandry prevails among birds, the females move from one nest-building male to another, leaving each with clutches of eggs to care for and rear, and are, as a rule, larger and more aggressive than their male mates. But, as with most rules, exceptions can be found. Among the flightless polyandrous great rheas of the pampas of Uraguay and Argentina, females are almost indistinguishable from the males.[17] Males and females flock together at the beginning of the breeding season. The males at that time undergo a darkening of their plumage and become very aggressive toward one another. When a male has successfully driven off other males, he turns to actively pursuing the females, who continue to forage together in flocks. The females largely ignore his overtures until they are ready to permit mounting. Once the male services all the females of a flock (and all are mated over a two- to three-day period), the male's next activity is to scrape out a nest. If no eggs are deposited in the nest, he scrapes out another the next day, and another the day after that, until the females are ready to lay. Then the most recent nest becomes the repository of the several eggs laid by each female over a period of a week or so. As the male settles down to the business of incubation, his aggressiveness toward other rheas increases. Even erstwhile mates anxious to contribute to his egg collection are attacked. Finally, the incubating male is deserted, left alone to cope with from twenty to fifty eggs, while the females go off en masse with another male, and then another, and then another. There is contact with ten to twelve males during the season, which lasts 120 days or so. Female rheas are simultaneously less aggressive and less motherly than males. In any event, rhea reproductive arrangements, which represent an evolutionarily successful pattern of sexual behavior, involve only a seasonal sexual differentiation.

Birds, fish, insects, and simpler organisms have evolved a great many ways of organizing sexual reproduction. Among them the sex differences, as well as the social processes that accompany reproduction, take many forms. Evolution has not given to these sexually reproducing organisms a single pattern of sex differences or sex roles. No particular pattern or social arrangement is more natural than any other. Quite the contrary, selection has favored the development of many different arrangements. At the very least, this richness and diversity should suggest that sexual reproduction exists within a framework of variability. Let us keep this in mind when we come to consider whether a population that has alternative ways of organizing mating and nurturing and has the ability to be variable in its adaptation has an adaptive advantage that other populations may lack.

The variations in reproductive processes that we have cited are variations among species. In most instances, all the members of a species conform more or less to a sex-appropriate pattern. Individuals do not significantly depart from genetically determined forms in either their appearance or their sexual behaviors. Even in protandrous or protogynous species, body changes occur automatically. Individuals see, smell, feel, or otherwise perceive only a limited set of cues, and each individual is hatched or born more or less "knowing" what to respond to, and how to respond to stimuli associated with reproductive activities. This raises an interesting problem. Although it is commonly believed that all variants of sexual and nurturing behavior involve relationships between individuals, this may not be quite accurate. In the types of stereotyped reproductive processes that we have looked at, in some species the individuals may not even perceive each other as individuals.

For example, a male turkey's "courtship" display makes a good deal of sense to us, as aiding and abetting reproduction. But is it truly "courtship"? His strutting, feather spreading, and posturings are equally exuberant whether he is confronted with a live and responsive female or whether nothing more than the stuffed head of a female turkey is presented to him. Evidently, he is unable to discriminate between the two situations. Thus, although under normal circumstances his behavior accomplishes the same end as courtship, as we usually think of it, it is built on a somewhat different base than our own. Most of what the male turkey "sees" apparently does not influence his behavior at all. A very limited set of cues trigger an automatic set of mating-related behavioral responses, even when those responses are inappropriate. Similarly, a hen turkey's vigorous protection and care of her poults (chicks) is seemingly "maternal behavior," but if the hen is deafened and unable to hear their chirps, she will kill them. The individual turkey's reproductive behaviors appear to be complex and goal directed yet involve only a few stimulus–response sequences. Since being able to fly imposes restrictions on head size and weight, the amount of room for information-processing equipment is severely limited in turkeys, but it is not so limited that environmental circumstances play no part at all in their reproductive activities. The males and females of three populations of the same turkey species, although exhibiting the same individual patterns of courtship and display, organize social groupings and subgroups differently.

In the Welder Wildlife Refuge in Texas, an open grassland subject to erratic weather conditions and inhabited by many predators, flocks of one sort or another are maintained year round and an astounding degree of social stratification occurs in the adult male flocks. So rigid is this stratification that most of the males never have an opportunity to mate. During mating season the males of "subflock" sibling groups usually "court" and strut in unison before the hens. This takes place annually on "leks" or display grounds. But while all the adult males participate in displays, very few (6 of 170 during the year of observation) account for all the matings during this peak part of the breeding season. After the females leave the display grounds to nest, the male sibling groups circulate among them performing their rituals, but rarely leading to further matings. Eastern wild turkeys, living in woodlands, generally favor smaller social units and pursue a mating-season pattern in which each male who can, stays with several hens in a harem group until they are bred. In a part of Oklahoma less drought-ridden than the Welder area, the species follows an intermediate pattern, males displaying on leks but not usually mating until afterward, and then going off to form harem groups.[18]

Since most birds mature rather quickly (in about 1 percent of their life span), the means by which birds achieve some of their complex behavioral formats often involve inborn perceptual focusing mechanisms which, when triggered, set off actions that require a minimum of experience or "learning" to elicit them. Experience, however, plays a part in the development and perfecting of many species-wide stereotyped responses.[19] With practice, chicks improve the accuracy of their food-getting pecks. Perceptual sharpening and the precision of stereotypic actions often depend on the immature individual being exposed to certain conditions which normally occur when species members are young. If the animal is not exposed to these experiences, a particular behavior may not develop at all or it may develop along peculiar, and usually maladaptive, lines. Although some birds, such as jays, crows, and parrots, are bigger-brained and more able problem solvers than turkeys, they are still subject to the limitations imposed by limited brain capacities. With regard to sex-associated behavior, however, they are still "bird-brained." Stereotyped sex differences in behavior related to reproduction show up even in these bigger-brained birds, whether the sexes look alike or not. Anatomical similarity does not mean that the sexes behave alike at all.

SEX IN SMALL MAMMALS

Mammals, like birds, are warm-blooded higher vertebrates. Unlike birds, mammals give birth to live young who must be suckled.

Mammalian infants, like the hatched young of birds, make their entrance dependent, hungry, and immature. They have to be taken care of. Small mammals and mammals who live where the seasons harshly alternate scarcity with plenty mature quickly, as do nearly all birds. But unlike birds, even the smallest mammals supply sustenance of their offspring only through the mother, whose mammary glands produce milk, a specialized baby food purified, predigested, and refined for infant consumption more thoroughly than regurgitation could accomplish.

Clearly visible differences between the sexes are what zoologists commonly refer to when they talk about sexual dimorphism. If the males and females of a species are easily distinguished from one another, the species is considered phenotypically sexually dimorphic. (When males and females look alike but differ in their reproductive organs and the chromosomes that control their development, the species is recognized as genotypically dimorphic but is not usually referred to or classed as dimorphic.) Color distinguishes the red male cardinal from his brownish mate. Combs or crests or fancy tail assemblages distinguish the cocks from the hens of many species, or size and build differences distinguish them. Yet male and female pigeons, jays, sparrows, egrets, and gulls, although differing as to reproductive organs, are visually identical. Some species show no dimorphism at all, although females and males still have different reproductive functions. Many mammals exhibit a great deal of sexual dimorphism. Either males or females have one or more obvious physical characteristics (e.g., horns, bony crests, antlers, furry patches, seasonal or permanent swellings) that are absent or not well developed in members of the opposite sex. Physically obvious structures may provide an easily recognized sign of gender among lions, or walruses, or red deer, but among horses, foxes, and rats, the main visible clue to an animal's gender is its genitals. If structural differences are minimal, the species is simply not considered dimorphic.[20]

Mammalian sexual differentiation, even in its most minimal form, involves some very complicated anatomical and physiological features. Male bodies have external or extrusive genitalia to introduce sperm into the female's body. Females have elaborate internal structures to house fetuses as well as fetus-feeding tissues. Although both males and females have nipples on their ventral surfaces, teats for feeding infants normally become engorged with milk in the females only.

These minimal bodily differences, in a very real sense, constitute biologically based anatomical determinations of certain kinds of social interactions. Any mammalian species that has survived has done so by assuring that at least some of its males inseminate some females, an act of physical proximity that clearly involves social interaction. The interaction may be brief, however, as among black bears and the solitary cats, where lone females drive males from their territories and dens and raise their young unaided. While mating does not necessarily call for prolonged interaction, nursing does, and males cannot take over nursing. Both mating and nursing, tied as they are to different physical structures, require that the sexes in mammals minimally fulfill certain specific tasks. Although it is physically possible for male birds to take over brooding and feeding the newborn, and for bird babies to be hatched and nurtured without a biological parent in attendance, mammalian anatomical adaptations afford few such opportunities in the reproductive sphere. Anatomically, mammals have fewer alternative ways of securing survival and reproduction than do birds. Reproductive-task specialization is normally assured by a very fundamental physical sex differentiation.

It would seem on the surface, then, that highly specialized anatomy should result in highly structured behavior. We should expect to find that even when sexual dimorphism is absent in a mammalian species, sex differentiates the social behaviors associated with mating and with care of the young more rigidly for mammals than for birds. At the very least, mating and nursing behaviors ought to be more or less automatic. Where sexual dimorphism is marked, we ought to find sharper highly structured behavioral differences in general behavior. Indeed, some stereotyping of sex-related behavior occurs among many small, fast-maturing mammals (and dimorphism accompanies differences in activity profiles of the sexes in some larger mammals). However, mammalian evolution has taken interesting turns, and mammals, both dimorphic and nondimorphic ones, behave in some rather unexpected ways.

Although male and female laboratory rats differ visibly hardly at all, as anyone faced with determining a rat's sex soon discovers, male and female rats act differently, nevertheless. If brought up in a normal laboratory colony, the behavioral distinctions between the sexes are marked and fairly standardized, or stereotyped, in regard to mating and nurturing. Males react to nonvisual stimuli in certain ways, and females react to them in others. While females pay little or no attention to odors which signal that another female is in heat, males ignore a deodorized sexually receptive female but make sexual overtures to an undeodorized one. A nursing female responds maternally to an infant with her own odor, but males scarcely notice infants at all. Laboratory rats reared in an overcrowded colony do not exhibit the same patterns of behavior.[21] When overcrowded rats fail to mate, display poor or absent infant care, participate in frequent homosexual episodes, show increases in aggressive encounters, and suffer from pathological apathy and spontaneous abortions, one is reminded of similar happenings in human environments, such as city slums. The similarities between the disrupted social adaptations of overcrowded rats and the sorts of behaviors found among some of the people trapped in slum ghettos have suggested to several researchers that humans and rats respond to overcrowding in a similar manner and possibly for similar reasons.[22] Considering that as cities grew human populations increased whereas rat populations reproduce poorly or not at all under extraordinary crowding, the analogy between rats and humans appears to be unwarranted. This is especially so since rats operate in a perceptual and behavioral framework very different from ours—for instance, attacking group members that have been deodorized and strangers that don't smell "right," but accepting both if they have be rubbed in the nest's litter. The analogy between rats and human beings becomes even more awkward when we realize that rodents other than rats do not respond to overcrowding the way rats do.

Bahamian hutus, members of a rare and obscure rodent species that lives only on the semidesert of East Plana Cay, tolerate abnormally close contact in cages without the aggression common among many other rodents placed in similar circumstances. In fact, the squeaks of crowded caged hutus attract other hutus. Lemmings, on the other hand, have an extremely high level of social intolerance, which serves as a stimulus for the spectacular migrations for which they are famous. Lemmings under unusually crowded conditions become embroiled in conflicts that are so sharp that maternal behavior breaks down and their young perish form neglect and canibalsim. Yet even in these circumstances, mating, conception, and birth continue unabated among lemmings, whereas similar circumstances encourage apathy, homosexuality, and aborted pregnancies in rats.[23]

It is as yet unclear what mechanisms permit some behaviors to persist and others to break down in one species of rodent and not in another, but it is certainly clear that among these small mammals, both experience and preprogrammed reactions to the sorts of stimuli with which the animals normally come in contact during their maturation shape their reproductive behavior. Like birds, these small mammals cannot survive to adulthood without experiencing care and feeding. Like birds, these small mammals grow quickly and have neither the time nor the neurological space to acquire through experience much of the information to assure their survival and reproduction as a species. Despite their look-alike sexes and the need for experience to strengthen or ensure appropriate reproductive patterns (female rats never exposed to feces and nest litter do not make nests for their infants, but those who are exposed to them do so without further "instruction"), these small creatures are at least partly dependent on "preprogramming" for the behaviors that permit them to perpetuate themselves and their species. Unusual crowding evidently introduces confusing stimulational experiences. Confusing experiences during maturation evidently disrupt the development of standardized or stereotyped behavior patterns in members of either or both sexes among all these rodents, since their populations suffer a decline in growth rates (a decline which in the case of lemmings is, in the long run, adaptive). By contrast, among human beings, those who are overcrowded continue to beget children. Crowding among humans evidently does not disrupt their reproductive abilities at all. We can obviously adapt to odd or unusual situations, taking on behavior which may or may not prove to be destructive in the long run, but rats and other rodents are not quite so malleable.

With only the behavior of these few rodents in front of us, it already appears that it is not safe to take too much for granted about the sex life of mammals "in general." We can already see that it is not wise to assume that all mammals adapt or learn sex-role behaviors more readily than creatures of other orders. Some small ones seem to be subject to the same limitations as those affecting birds, who are members of another order. Neither is it safe to assume that the social capacities of one species of mammal are like those of another, even a closely related species. Nor is it safe to assume that if the sexes look alike, they respond to stimuli in the same way. This already hints at the possibility that visually obvious sex differences among mammals may not be indicative of differences in inborn social behavior patterns, responses, or capacities. This challenges a number of myths about sex roles and how they relate to physical sex differences—myths which in fact need to be challenged.

SOME MISCONCEPTIONS ABOUT LARGE MAMMALS

How do the dramatically dimorphic deer act in the wild? Do popular concepts conform to the views of professional naturalists? The story of Bambi is an idealization and distortion of the social adaptations and sex-role behaviors of deer. It is instructive to view the story and some of the assumptions about sex differences out of which they grew and then look at the data which field naturalists consider.

Deer include "any of the several ruminants of the family Cervdae, most of the males of which have solid deciduous horns or antlers."[24] Antlered and horned animals such as elk, deer, and moose, it is commonly assumed, use their horns primarily to serve a particular purpose. Horns and antlers are seen as weapons against predators and in intraspecific conflict. The possession of horns, it is often believed, is indicative of the presence of a propensity toward, and the advantageousness of, aggressive as well as protective behaviors. If males have horns or antlers and females do not, or have smaller versions than their male counterparts, it is usually assumed that the males have evolved their headgear primarily because of reproductive advantages that accrue to the males who are most aggressive and can protect their females. Presumably in such species males are both protective of females and somewhat aggressive in their dominance over them. Why some naturalists doubt this notion will soon be made clear.

Part of the Bambi story is built around an incomplete knowledge of the habits of the temperate-zone woodland deer whose heads and horns decorate many a hunter's home. There are many species of deer, and several are common game animals taken for meat as well as for trophies. The more astounding the spread of their horns, the more prized the trophy. Often enough, wall displays include locked pairs of horns, sometimes with skulls attached, that huntsmen did not fell. Such pairs give us a glimpse of males sharing a final double agony, the outcome of a violent encounter instituted by aggressive action on the part of one or both stags.[25]

Because of naturalists' field observations it is possible to assess what is, in fact, taking place. At the onset of the mating season male deer seeking out newly assembled groups of sexually receptive females confront one another. They parade their wares and some engage in horn-to-horn combat. Although combat is rarely fatal, death,

Two stags in combat. The victorious male may find no females to mate with. Photo by Tom McHugh, Photo Researchers, Inc.

as those tangled antlers demonstrate, does occur on occasion. Undoubtedly, the image of these embattled males suggests to many the kind of male with the kind of role attributed to Bambi's father. The striking death tableau predisposes us to a certain kind of picture of the events presumably leading to or springing from these fatal conflicts.

It is easy to visualize the most reproductively significant male deer as the elegant great-horned winner of a conflict standing on the crown of a hill with the sun setting behind him, lording it over the clustered females he has won, and fathering and protecting their offspring. It is easy to visualize such a male as leader and protector, aloof but available to the herd when danger threatens.

This is the Bambi myth. It is a pretty story, but the battles that occur between antlered male deer do not often result in this winner-take-all social arrangement. Entangled aspirants are effectively removed from all active breeding, and exhausted competitors may find themselves also out of the animal breeding reservoir. On the other hand, those males marginal to the major encounters, the less aggressive onlookers, often occupy themselves in the most fruitful direct approaches to prospective mates, attracting and herding off as many females as will follow or allow themselves to be pressed. The combatants, too preoccupied to participate, are out of this action. For them the battle may continue to rage long after the does and their escorts disappear from the scene. The battle-scarred victor can have no mates at all and no herd to lead. Whether the males who succeed in capturing mates even "lead" their herds is somewhat questionable, since those males who succeed in acquiring mates have only brief—but productive—encounters with their mates and soon leave. When and if a single animal regularly sets the direction of the seasonal moving group, she is a doe.[26] Pregnant females find that protection from predators lies in togetherness, so they remain close to one another, although when spring comes and trees leaf, forage is easy to come by, and fawns are born; safety no longer lies in numbers. Camouflage and speed afford protection. The female herds break up, the does separate, and mothers stay away from their young as much as possible, especially right after they've been born. The tiny spotted infants are left alone and unattended much of the day, almost vanishing in the sun-dappled shadows under low-growing branches. If the fawn seems to be in danger of discovery by a threatening predator, the almost invisible mother quite suddenly makes an appearance. Clattering and thrashing noisily she runs off, leading the pursuer astray. A successful mother is among other things, built for swift flight, unimpeded by antlers. Antlers provide her neither protection nor mating advantages.[27]

The notion that large antlered males evolved because antlers primarily serve protective or combat functions is hard to maintain when we consider the ancient forms of giant deer. The Irish elk (which was neither Irish nor an elk) holds the all-time record for antler development, up to a 12-foot span, probably shed and regrown annually.[28] Whether an Irish elk stag could use its antlers efficiently for protection or combat is doubtful. Although stags are often depicted as impaling wolves with these horns or tossing them aloft in combat, the rapid twisting and turning of 90 pounds worth of Irish elk antlers would have created enormous problems. The points of the tines on these antlers face backward. Such turnaround tines on antlers this big are a problem in combat or in protective weaponry, for a stag would have had to turn his head upside down and put it between his legs to impale anything. Among the Irish elk, antlers might well have served as highly visible advertisements for males seeking out females in the grassy, sparsely wooded country to which the species was adapted. Indeed, only as attractants do these incredible antlers appear to make much sense. If, then, the most successful suitors among deer are mainly the showiest, we have to rewrite the Bambi story, but would the story continue to appeal to an American audience? Mild-mannered stags running off with harems of females are hard to see as heroic. Velvet-eyed does who desert their young as much as possible are hard to envision as motherly. All-female herds with female leaders also seem to violate our concepts of sexual and natural order. Yet several deer species share these behavioral traits.

Female-led herds are neither necessarily seasonal nor characteristic of herbivores with dimorphic decorations. Tusks adorn female as well as male elephants. Female elephant herds remain together year round and year after year.[29] Elephant babies are constantly supervised and nurse freely at any of the females who are producing milk. The herd leader, who is the mother or grandmother of some of the younger elephants, often "assists" at the birth of elephant babies, standing by, perhaps to guard against predators, and often helping the wobbling newborn baby to its feet. Skilled at finding food and fighting predators, she is never challenged for her job. Adult male elephants belong mostly to bachelor herds and join the nursery herd briefly for mating. The slow-moving nursery herd benefits from their absence. With the adult males roving and eating elsewhere, the slow-moving nursery group has more to eat and drink, especially during drought.

Carnivorous males surely must carry into their domestic arrangements a bit of the "agressiveness" that their hunting abilities presumably call forth. Perhaps herbivorous males are meeker than was imagined, but meat-eating hunters surely have to be tough to survive. Among felines, even house cats are predators, and domestic tomcats have aggressive reputations. Yet one cannot generalize easily about the social lives of member species of the cat family. Feline behavioral adaptations vary. Bobcats are best described as bad-tempered, uncompromising solitaries.[30] Lions and lionesses prefer living in groups, or prides. Domesticated cats seem to exhibit great individual differences in temperament with respect to their social or solitary preferences. (We have two who differ: Sam, a male, who manages to tolerate the dogs, cats, tiny kittens, and rabbits that occasionally visit with us; and Missy, a female, who barely tolerated her own badly nourished kittens, and—after fifteen years—barely tolerates Sam.) Of all the cats, lions and lionesses exhibit the most marked sexual dimorphism, the lions wearing manes that lionesses lack. Obvious even from a distance, the manes make lions seem even larger than they are.

One would anticipate that lions are more "aggressive" than lionesses. Regal to look upon and intimidating to hear, lions have been viewed as lords of their own manor and credited with the hunting prowess, "political" power, and sexual prerogatives admired in Middle Eastern and Medieval European monarchies. The more kingly the lion, presumably the greater his abilities, his kingdom, and his sexual conquests. This image of the lion, promulgated since pre-Christian times, has given way before field data. But it has been replaced with a somewhat simplified view that male lions serve few functions and are lazy exploiters of tolerant lionesses, perhaps because it has been rather difficult to acknowledge that they sometimes serve social functions usually identified as falling to females of the species.

Before summarizing the kind of social organization that field studies reveal, the story of Frasier, a captive lion whose experiences anticipated some of the surprises field studies uncovered, deserves recounting.[31] At a wild animal farm-cum-sanctuary-cum-zoo in Florida, a pride of females that had been successfully established was presented with a series of young, vigorous male candidates, with the hope of producing some baby lions. All the candidates were shrugged off. As one rejected lion succeeded another, the problems at first looked serious, and then evidently began to look funny. Almost as a joke, an amiable elderly lion named Frasier was introduced one day to the uncooperating pride, apparently with the belief that he was expendable, more likely a sacrificial lamb than a lion destined to succeed. Alive and well the next day, he stayed on and on and on, living to father a highly profitable progeny. His obituary records that when he was approaching death and too weak to walk unsupported, the lionesses who were his pridemates helped him walk by leaning against him.

When we look at circumstances in the wild, Frasier's experiences appear to be atypical. He enjoyed uninterrupted group membership until death, following a prolonged period of weakness at a late age. He was the only adult male in the pride for the whole of his life there, and, as a result, he probably fathered more cubs (thirty-five) than a wild lion normally has a chance to. For in the wild, male lions rarely live out their lives as members of a singe pride. Of twelve prides studied, by George Schaller[32] only three had the same males after a period of just three years.

Lions and other inhabitants of the tropics (e.g., elephants, monkeys, and apes) are not subject to significant seasonal changes in temperature. Prides do not follow a seasonal cycle of assemblage, breeding, and dispersal, and they rarely change their locales. Nonpride members are not so immobile; nomadic individuals of either sex, or small groups of males, range widely at any time of year over areas that include the territories that permanent prides establish for themselves.

The core of a pride consists of a group of females to which one to four males are attached. Although most of the females probably grew up together, the fact that Elsa, the lioness of "Born Free" fame, ultimately established herself in a pride in which she had no relatives indicates that there is some openness in the recruitment of females. Where there are females, there are usually young. Prides rarely lack two generations.

Nomadic lionesses give birth as often as do pride lionesses but rear fewer cubs successfully. Nomadic lions, male and female, whose contacts with each other tend to be amicable as they cross and recross the plains, do not do too well as hunters and have trouble keeping hyenas, vultures, and other scavengers off their kill, a problem that groups do not face. These difficulties are partially alleviated when three or four males band together, but without the social cement of cooperation in the continuing care of cubs, all-male groups are not particularly long-lived, especially since, as it turns out, males are rather poor hunters.

How come males are poor hunters? Although both lions and lionesses are well endowed with claws and teeth to grasp and kill prey, they lack speed. Silent stalking brings the hunter or huntress close to the hunted. That magnificent mane, that erstwhile symbol of the male lion's prowess and power, unfortunately contributes to making him a conspicuous and inefficient stalker. George Schaller found that in seventy-one hunts by groups of mixed sex, males took the initiative only twice. Out of a total of 1210 lions observed stalking and running, only 3 percent were males. In a typical communal hunt, males stay well behind their female hunting companions. Out of sight of the prey, they are also in a position to protect trailing cubs from danger. Although poor hunters, they are excellent baby-sitters.

Males are important to the well-being of cubs in other ways. Our cat Sam would escort Missy's kittens to the feeding dish, sit back and watch them stuff themselves. His solicitousness astounded us. Male lions often allow cubs to feed on the uncomsumed remains of a kill while preventing female lionesses, who can cuff away even starving cubs, from eating. Missy's kittens were not Sam's. The cubs a lion cares for may not be his. Males evidently like cubs. Since males also kill the unprotected cubs of other prides, which cubs they care for and which they kill depends, apparently, on situational factors.

Although they are pride members only for awhile and poor hunters to boot, males contribute to the pride's permanent food supply in a roundabout way. They actively patrol and scent-mark a pride's range. They keep other lions away either by intimidation or by fighting, inflicting mortal wounds on occasion. (Human beings are by no means the only animals who kill their own kind.) Males thus maintain a space for the more-or-less exclusive use of pride members and keep a pride's provisions up.

Males who are big, obvious, active, and easily recognized keep competing lions and lionesses away. They are an asset to the group. Manes and masterfulness are functionally useful. Prides that choose imposing males have clear survival advantages. Yet these traits are virtues only in certain circumstances. Mild-mannered Frasier, who was far from imposing, found acceptance among females whose food supply was assured. In fact, he was welcomed when more vigorous males were rejected. It would seem that lionesses have the ability to assess their needs and to select their lions accordingly, and that both lions and lionesses display a capacity for learning and altering behavior.

SUMMARY

Sexual reproduction is a process that assures variation among organisms. It is a process that has become more complex and diverse during the millenia since it became instrumental in the diversification of organisms. Organisms that reproduce sexually take many forms and the process that secures their survival and success occurs in a great many ways.

In the animal kingdom, sexual reproduction is accomplished by means of diverse strategies. Sometimes species individuals are not differentiated into two sexes, but more often they are. Where two sexes are intrinsic to the species, members of each sex may play a fixed and special role in perpetuating the species, but how males and females contribute to species survival differs radically among species. Whether the sexes are visibly and permanently differentiated or not, the activities or actions that lead to successful reproduction among smaller and lower animals are largely controlled by genetically established perceptual capacities and responses to stimuli which are specific to the sex of the individual. Species-wide stereotyped behavior, whether purely an expression of an organism's developmental profile, or elicited or refined in the individual by experience, is critical for successfully producing new members of the species. The same generalization cannot be made about the sex behaviors of larger mammals.

Among larger mammals, while some species are sexually dimorphic and exhibit consistent sex differences in behaviors (patterned along lines that do not always conform to what we expect of the sexes), other dimorphic species demonstrate both variability and flexibility in their social and sexual adaptations. The experiences of Frasier and the fact that lions *and* lionesses may be "loners" or live in prides, indicate that among the larger mammals even far removed from the human line, physical attributes alone do not determine the social or sexual destiny of the individual.

Thus, this survey indicates that behavioral malleability and the capacity to learn run rather deep in the mammalian heritage, contributing significantly to the survival chances of species that produce relatively few offspring which take a long time to mature, even when the species is characterized by sexual dimorphism. The depth of such a genetically based heritage of malleability suggests, by itself, that the roots of the family are not grounded in genetically determined human behavioral predilections. The behavior of our close primate relatives leads to this conclusion even more forcefully, as we shall see in the next chapter.

NOTES

1. Louise A. Purrett, "When Life Began on Earth," *Science News, 101,* June 3, 1972, pp. 366-367.

2. Lynn I. Margulis, "Symbiosis and Evolution," *Scientific American, 225,* no. 2, August 1971, pp. 49-57. For reports of a contrary view, see "Parts of the Cell, How Did They Evolve?" *Science News, 105,* June 8, 1974, p. 365.

3. James F. Crow and Motoo Kimura, *An Introduction to Population Genetics* (New York: Harper & Row, 1970). These authors also point out that the development of sexual reproduction confers no immediate advantage on the individual in which this occurs, and in fact may be far more deleterious than advantageous to that individual. The benefit is only to the descendants, perhaps quite remote, and to the population as a whole.

4. The ancient Chinese regarded these principles—yang and yin—as complementary, too, and as fundamental to the operation of the

universe. Similarly, a contemporary Western theoretician [Claude Levi-Strauss, *The Savage Mind* (Chicago: University of Chicago Press, 1970)] associates human males with "culture" and females with "nature," and views culture (male) as the active intervention into natural (female) processes which are but passive States of Being. In the religious myths of India, however, it is a female, the Goddess Kali (who is often shown dancing on her husband Siva), who is regarded as the active aspect of the Absolute, while her consort is regarded as its passive, eternal aspect (James M. Freeman, "Trial by Fire," *Natural History*, *83*, no. 1, 1974, pp. 54-63). For a discussion of factors affecting the way in which male and female "states" or "principles" are interpreted, see Karen Sacks, "State Bias and Women's Status," *American Anthropologist*, *78*, no. 3, 1976, pp. 565-569.

5. Edward O. Wilson, *The Insect Societies* (Cambridge, Mass.: Harvard University Press, 1971). This extensive work provides masses of information on the social insects.

6. William S. Creighton, "Living Doors," *Natural History*, *86*, no. 10, 1967, pp. 71-73.

7. D. S. Robertson, "Social Control of Sex Reversal in a Coral Reef Fish," *Science*, *177*, September 15, 1972, pp. 1007-1009. See also C. Lavett Smith, "Hermaphroditism in Bahama Groupers," *Natural History*, *72*, no. 6, 1964, pp. 42-47, and Michael S. Cimino, "Meiosis in Triploid All-Female Fish (*Poeciliopsis poeciliidae*)," *Science*, *175*, March 31, 1972, pp. 1484-1485.

8. Vicki McMillan, "Mating of the Fathead," *Natural History*, *81*, no. 5, 1972, pp. 72-78.

9. F. Abdel-Hameed and R. N. Shaffner, "Intersexes and Sex Determination in Chickens," *Science*, *172*, May 28, 1971, pp. 962-964.

10. Joreen Piotrowski, "Of Gaggles, Prides and Packs," *The Curious Naturalist*, *9*, no. 10, 1970, p. 209.

11. W. H. Thorpe, "Duet Singing Birds," *Scientific American*, *229*, no. 2, 1971, pp. 70-79.

12. Charles Vaurie, "So Fair and Foul a Bird," *Natural History*, *82*, no. 6, 1973, pp. 60-65.

13. Karoly Koffan, "The Ways of a Parasitic Bird," *Natural History*, *72*, no. 6, 1963, pp. 48-53.

14. The information on North American birds (Canada geese, redwings, cardinals, etc.) comes from Edward Howe Forbush, *A Natural History of American Birds of Eastern and Central North America*, 1955, revised

and abridged with the addition of more than one hundred species by John Bichard (New York: Bramhall House). The book is written in an archaic style and is delightfully anecdotal bedtime reading.

15. William J. Weber, "A New World for the Cattle Egret," *Natural History, 81*, no. 2, 1972, pp. 26-33.

16. Otto Hohn, "The Phalarope," *Scientific American, 220*, no. 6, 1969, pp. 105-111.

17. Donald F. Bruning, "The Greater Rhea Chick and Egg Delivery Route," *Natural History, 82*, no. 3, 1973, pp. 68-75.

18. C. Robert Watts and Allen W. Stokes, "The Social Order of Turkeys," *Scientific American, 224*, no. 6, 1971, pp. 112-118.

19. Jack P. Hailman, "How an Instinct Is Learned," *Scientific American, 221*, no. 6, 1969, pp. 98-106.

20. Katherine Ralls, "Mammals in Which Females Are the Larger Sex," paper presented in the 1974 Radcliffe Institute Colloquium Series, Cambridge, Mass.

21. John B. Calhoun, "Population Density and Social Pathology," *Scientific American, 206*, no. 2, 1962, pp. 139-148.

22. Omer R. Galle, Walter R. Gove, and J. Miller McPherson, "Population Density and Pathology; What Are the Relations for Man?" *Science, 176*, April 7, 1972, pp. 23-30. Also Robert J. Trotter, "Cities, Crowding and Crime, *Science News, 106*, November 2, 1974, pp. 282-283.

23. Garrett C. Clough, "A Most Peaceable Rodent," *Natural History, 82*, no. 6, 1973, pp. 67-74.

24. *The Random House Dictionary of the English Language*, Unabridged (New York: Random House, 1967), p. 377.

25. In the 1940s the Bronx Zoo had (and may still have) a small museum building near its main entrance on Pelham Parkway. In it was an extraordinary exhibition of stag heads and entwined horns. I owe the explanation of what these heads represented in social and breeding terms to an anonymous museum guard. Helen Lambert, a colleague at Northeastern University and a member of the Biology Department, confirmed his statements. For a description of a clash between two Grant's gazelles, see Richard D. Estes, "Showdown in Ngorongoro Crater," *Natural History, 72*, no. 8, 1973, pp. 71-79.

26. Peter H. Klopfer, "Aggression and Its Evolution," *Psychiatry and Social Science Review*, *3*, no. 3, 1969, pp. 2-7.

27. I have rarely felt more ignorant than when my daughters and I frantically called the attention of a keeper at the Audobon Society Drumlin Farm facility to what we mistakenly thought was a deserted, sick fawn. Its mouth was covered with white foam. Its mother was at the farthest point from it in a field enclosure. We were told fawns bubble and burp like human babies and the doe knew what she was doing. The incident taught us to restrain our urge to rescue animal youngsters that may not need to be rescued.

28. Stephen Jay Gould, "The Misnamed, Mistreated and Misunderstood Irish Elk," *Natural History*, *82*, no. 3, 1973, pp. 10-19.

29. Robert Gray, "Meet the Family," *Ranger Rick, National Wildlife Federation Magazine*, *7*, no. 7, 1973, pp. 4-7 (special issue on elephants).

30. Theodore N. Barley, "The Elusive Bobcat," *Natural History*, *81*, no. 8, 1972, pp. 42-49.

31. *The Boston Globe*, July 14, 1972, p. 1. "Sensuous Lion Ends Amorous Days" is the headline on the obituary. The article includes an interview with a spokesman, John Foxen, for the Lion Country Safari at which Frazier lived.

32. George B. Schaller, "Predators of the Serengeti, Part I," *Natural History*, *71*, no. 2, 1972, pp. 38-49. See also Richard D. Estes, "Predators and Scavengers," *Natural History*, *76*, no. 3, 1967, pp. 38-47.

2

The Evolution of
Sex Differences in Primates

THEORIES REGARDING THE SOCIAL SIGNIFICANCE OF SEX DIFFERENCES

Theorists who regard family as shaped by or deriving from a genetically based sex difference in physique and behavior adopt either of two approaches. Some argue that the family, or something like the family, existed preculturally.[1] A species-wide social pattern involving a bond between a male and one or more females evolved, they say, in an environment that favored pair or one-male groups. This sort of social situation and the behaviors associated with it, they go on, became behaviorally programmed into the emerging hominid species as males and females who were genetically predisposed to establishing durable bonds with one another proved to be reproductively more successful than other males and females. The social adaptations of some non-human primates, particularly the nondimorphic gibbons and some of the sexually dimorphic baboons, are considered especially significant for this model of precultural family.

Other biologically oriented theorists reject the notion that a male bonded to one or more females is part of our past. Pointing to the behaviors of other nonhuman primates (primarily dimorphic semi-terrestrial or terrestrial species), they note the prevalence of large aggregates as an adaptive social form among them, and postulate that early humans must have lived in similar large groups, without family. Although these theorists view family as emerging within a cultural setting, they nevertheless hold that the kinds of roles men and women play in families (as well as in larger societal institutions) reflect bio-logically determined behavioral predispositions which are different for the sexes.[2] Such behavioral predispositions are treated as an extension or expression of the sex differences in body form that evolved within the framework of large groups. In the ancient multimale and female groups, it is held, the bigger and more aggressive males won for themselves socially dominant roles. Their dominance allowed them to father more offspring than the smaller, milder-mannered males could. When family ultimately emerged as an institution, the roles men and women adopted within its setting conformed to already established physical and behavioral sex differences.

Both of these behavior-determined models—one emphasizing a species-wide sex-related stereotyped social pattern, and the other merely stressing sex differences in behavioral potentials—attach great significance to the fact that men and women are somewhat physically differentiated from one another, and regard this physical dimorphism as tied to sex differences in behaviors or behavioral proclivities. Not too surprisingly, the presumed sex-differentiated abilities and proclivities pretty much conform to Western ideas about what is the appropriate social role of each sex.

In Chapter 1 we noted that sexual dimorphism and stereotyped sex-differentiated behaviors occur in a great many ways which do not conform to our culturally biased view of sex. It was also noted that some higher mammals do not exhibit stereotyping in their social and reproductive activities, and that their behavioral flexibility indicates a genetically based capacity for learning. This flexibility with respect to social and reproductive behaviors shows up, interestingly enough, in the behavior of both males and females of a species which is sexually dimorphic and well removed from the human line.

This chapter deals with the physical and social aspects of sex in species of the mammalian order to which human beings belong. Primates, as we shall soon see, are very varied in their adaptations. A few vaguely confirm the simple postulates about our past that have been drawn from them. Others do not. Many exhibit variability; they adapt to various sorts of situations in the wild or in captivity, by adopting different sorts of social behaviors and relationships. Many, but not all, primate species are sexually dimorphic. While dimorphism is commonly seen as linked to some sort of differentiation of sex roles and of behavioral capacities, the evidence indicates that it is an error to assume such simple links between physical and behavioral sex differences for many primate species. After inspecting situations which once again run counter to some very widely held notions, this chapter explores how sexual dimorphism could have evolved in conjunction with genetically based capacities for flexibility in sexual and social adjustments. The analysis suggests that social flexibility and behavioral adaptability are far more ancient and widespread in the primate order than is usually recognized. This underscores the view that family among humans is both relatively recent and a function of social and cultural adaptations. How data on one or another primate population are used to support biologically oriented theories about human family arrangements is pointed out in passing in the descriptions below, which focus, however, on sex differences—their variations and variability, and ultimately the reasons for these.

THE PRIMATES:
GENERAL PHYSICAL CHARACTERISTICS

Of the many primate species that exist, few have been systematically observed in the wild. Field studies of animal behavior are relatively new, and although nonhuman primates have gotten a good share of attention, a lot of data remain to be collected. New information on even the best-known species is coming to light all the time, so data are dated almost before they are published. The monkeys and apes discussed below have been chosen simply because there is a reasonably good-sized body of literature on them and students of human behavior use it regularly.

Primates are an order of mammals. The 170 or so species that are classified side by side with humans in the primate order are anatomically rather "unspecialized" in that they have anatomical features characteristic of the earliest mammals.

The original mammals had five fingers and five toes. Whereas bats can fly with their hands, deer run on them, and moles dig with them, primate hands are used for grabbing and holding things. Primates have retained five distinct fingers but have substituted nails for claws and acquired increased opposability of their thumbs, allowing them to pick up food and fleas daintily twixt thumb and fingers instead of relying on teeth or claws for scratching, biting, and tearing. These "generalized" hands, which have some rather elegant special aptitudes, accompany eyes that have overlapping fields of vision, which give great depth to the visual field. Hands and eyes together reflect a reduced reliance on the nose. Consequently, a much reduced snout characterizes most primates. Only the few small rat-faced shrews and insectivores that cause zoologists to debate whether or not they should be classified as primates[3] have kept the original form of mammalian snout.

The 44 teeth of the first mammals have been reduced in number. The small-snouted monkeys, apes, and hominids evolved several different specialized tooth patterns, because teeth evidently change their shape and number rapidly when dietary habits change, but how rapidly is also a question. Primates eat many things: nuts, seeds, leaves, grains, and meat. Primate tooth forms are frequently an indication of primate food adaptations, but are not, as we shall see, always viewed in that light.

Primates exhibit some unique physical traits associated with reproduction.[4] Nearly all are tied to an estrus cycle (among humans the "menstrual" cycle, a monthly female uterine blood letting), which is linked to the production of ova but sometimes occurs without ovulation. Among primates only one egg at a time is normally released during ovulation. Females usually produce one infant at each pregnancy. After birth, infants are carried around for at least as long as they were carried around before birth. Although some button-eyed little lemurs and bush babies, who look like they were designed by a toymaker, build nests and leave three or so tiny newborns in them at once, most primates invest far more time producing and caring for fewer infants than other mammals of comparable size. Most primates have only two nipples high on the chest wall at which the newborn nurses. Although present in males, the teats the nipples give access to are, for all practical purposes, full, fatty, and functional only in nursing females. Among human females, fat deposits on breasts appear at about the onset of menses, and remain thereafter, more or less, ever present. Among nonhuman primate females the breasts temporarily enlarge during pregnancy and nursing and recede afterward.

Sexual Dimorphism in the Primate Order; Sex Traits in Nonhuman Species

Within the primate order there are as many, if not more, different designs on the fundamental mammalian male–female dichotomy as in other mammalian orders. There is little dimorphism among the tiny golden marmosets—jewel-like creatures that seem to be escapees from the convoluted intricacies of an illuminated manuscript. There is little dimorphism among lion marmosets, who look like miniature Chinese bronzes come to life. There are great differences between a 400-pound crested silver-backed male gorilla and a 200-pound female or between the huge male and smaller female orangutan. Dimorphism among howler monkeys is neither as negligible as that among marmosets, nor is it on as grand a scale as that of gorillas.

The physical traits that distinguish male from female vary from species to species. Probably the most startling sex-differentiated markings among primates are those of the blue-faced, blue-bottomed mandrills. The blue backside and ribbed blue and scarlet muzzle of the male mandrill are unmatched eye-catchers. Against the background of the bare zoo cage, the face of the male mandrill looks like the flamboyant invention of a modern artist. Against the background of the green and flowering opulence of the rain forest of West Africa these markings are, undoubtedly, less conspicuous. Unfortunately, we know very little about the social habits of these brightly marked baboons because they live in an impenetrable habitat, are extremely shy, and avoid humans (they are heavily hunted), so we can only guess at the social significance of these markings. As we have seen, it is perhaps wisest to refrain from speculation.

The faces and bottoms of baboons are dull by comparison with those of mandrills. Among baboons the infants, male and female alike, are born with a bright pink rump, which becomes black and shiny in the first year. In both sexes the rump normally remains black from then on. It usually flashes in the sunlight, semaphoring the location of each individual all the time. The markings on adult baboon females, who are always smaller than adult males, are, in some populations, rather peculiar (gelada females look as if they are wearing necklaces), but everywhere females develop a sexual skin, not on the rump but in the perineal area around the anus and between the anus and the vagina. This perineal tissue swells, recedes, and changes color in conjunction with the changing hormonal balances of the female's menstrual cycle. In addition to these visual signs of a female's readiness for mating, a female's black rump changes to bright red during pregnancy, announcing a nonmating state to the group at large far more vividly than perineal swellings advertise her estrus states. If pink and red bottom swellings evolved primarily because they serve as sexual attractants, why a female is most vivid when she is least interested in sexual encounters is puzzling. According to one another,[5] no one has as yet explained why the fact of pregnancy is better advertised than is sexual readiness. Only a change in reproductive status, announced by the color markers, is evidently signaled.

Rhesus macaques are monkeys that have things arranged in yet another way. Hairy-rumped at birth, both males and females are bare around the root of the tail by adulthood. When a female rhesus reaches puberty, the skin around her tail, on the inside of her legs, and along the outside of the upper thigh swells. This happens just before her first menstruation. The swelling then decreases in size rapidly. During her first few estrus episodes, which are nonovulatory and infertile, these patches of skin redden and the hair on them falls out. The hair never grows back. In all macaque species the hairless sexual skin, where present, changes color under the influence of testosterone, a male hormone, and also changes color under the influence of social factors. An animal under attack, for instance, pales noticeably. But macaque dimorphism involves more than sex differences in inflating and deflating perineums. Males are much larger than females, more heavily marked, and, in addition, have more pronounced canine teeth. It is not at all difficult to tell the males from the females in a macaque troop, with or without swellings.

Perineal puffing is not particularly common among the tailless great apes. No visible physiological signs mark the stages in the female gorilla's hormonal cycle. Thus it is practically impossible to ascertain visually whether a female gorilla is in estrus. Mountain gorillas consume such vast quantities of bulky vegetable foods that big bellies are the rule, and it is even impossible to tell whether a female is pregnant. One field observer found that he could discover whether or not a female was pregnant only by waiting to see if a newborn put in an appearance.[6] Although it is hard to discern a female's sexual state, it is not hard to see which animals belong to which sex, for adult male gorillas are much bigger than females. Only some adult males grow prominent bony crests along the ridgeline and back of their skulls, but all turn silvery-backed during adulthood, while females stay dark-furred. Males also have larger canine teeth than females. Telling one sex from the other is easily accomplished without perineal indicators.

Equally distinctive dimorphism is present in orangutan populations. Silky-haired auburn orangutan males end about twice the size (160 pounds) of females (80 pounds). They have intimidating large canine teeth and enormous goiterous-looking throat sacs that resonate beautifully, giving their voices a booming quality absent from female vocalizations. Males also take a longer time than females reaching their full size, and show advanced age less dramatically than females, whose lush coats become bedraggled in their later years. David Horr thinks the arduousness of child-bearing wears out orangutan females rapidly, submitting females to stresses from which orangutan males are forever free.[7] Since adult male orangs, as we shall see, are startlingly solitary in their pursuits, a singular absence of social stresses, especially in child rearing, may contribute to their prolonged well-being.

Sex differences among chimpanzees are by no means as visually obtrusive as those of orangutans. However, chimpanzee females, like macaque monkeys, have eye-catching perineal sexual skins. Not only does this hairless sexual skin swell and subside rhythmically, indicating a female's estrus state, its mere presence distinguishes adult females from males. Thus, in one feature at least, chimpanzees are "more" dimorphic than gorillas or orangs. In other respects they are less sharply differentiated, for although chimpanzee males are usually (but not always) bigger, heavier, and later to mature than females, size differences between the sexes are not great (150 pounds average for males, 130 pounds for females).[8] Although chimps are less dimorphic than gorillas and orangs, they are more dimorphic than gibbons, since neither swellings nor size distinguish male from female gibbons. Male and female gibbons are so much alike that without seeing the genitals of these small (about 13 pounds) long-armed arboreal apes, a human observer cannot readily determine a gibbon's sex.

Human Sexual Dimorphism:
Traits and Variations

According to some scientists humans are tailless and hairless naked apes. There are, however, experts in the fossil history of the primates who think it more appropriate to regard apes as specialized hominids, offshoots from a basically hominid line that scattered fossil evidence indicates may have appeared nearly 25 million years ago.[9] Whether humans are specialized apes, or vice versa, men and women are neither as extremely differentiated as are the males and females of some species of apes nor as little differentiated as others. Keeping in mind, then, that even our closest primate relatives are pretty various about the way the sexes are physically distinguished, let's look at some of the sex differences that seem significant in human populations and begin with a nondifference, the sexual skins that on chimpanzee females, among others, serve to signal their estrus state and which human females lack.

Human females often experience uncomfortable and even painful premenstrual swellings but lack a perineal sexual skin. The engorged tissues may be hands or feet, bellies or breasts, or all at the same time. Precisely because swelling affects almost any kind of tissue it goes unnoticed except by the sufferer and by the manufacturers of pills for premenstrual discomfort. Like gibbons and gorillas, then, human females lack conspicuous menstrual-cycle markers, even though swollen tissues may play a part in or reflect sexual receptivity. (Fondling swollen breasts can induce pain instead of passion, and encourage rejection rather than responsiveness.) Since male tumescence or erection, although conspicuous, is not considered a trait that reflects dimorphism, humans are not notably dimorphic with regard to sexual swellings.

Some of the commonly recognized sex-differentiated features in humans, such as beards, breasts, and buttocks, do not distinguish the sexes in other primates. For instance, gorillas, regardless of sex, normally have hairless faces, and only among humans are breast and buttock shape usually sex-differentiated. One recent analysis argues that in human females fatty deposits on breasts and buttocks developed as substitutes for perineal sexual signals.[10] However, only human primates are effectively hairless and given to upright posture, and fat and fur act as energy conservers and insulation. Fat deposits seem to be somewhat functional for hairless human females as energy reserves and mammary insulators, and the amount of fat seems to determine the age at which menstruation begins.[11] As regards the pelvic bones underlying buttock development, an upright pregnant woman must distribute the weight of the infant she carries on as broad a base as possible. A similar pelvic baby basket is not particularly important for other primate mothers-to-be, whose arms normally bear some of her weight as she leans forward or suspends herself from overhead supports. That many human females tend toward rounder breasts and buttocks than most males may have little to do with swellings as sex signals and a great deal to do with how fat functions in pregnancy and prolonged nursing, and how muscles articulate with broad pelvic baskets. The assumption that humans have substituted one set of signals for another when they became upright (because perineal swellings are not compatible with upright posture) is also questionable. Our ancestors may not have had such swellings; although chimpanzees do, neither gibbons nor gorillas develop them. In any event, these commonly recognized sex-differentiating characteristics are not crucial for distinguishing males from females.

Most cultures usually, on the basis of the appearance of the genitals, divide humanity into two sexes at birth, long before secondary sex differences appear. Our culture does, yet in our culture not too long ago, sex differences were summed up in terms of secondary traits, for the Victorians barely acknowledged that males have penises and females vaginas. They instead emphasized that women differ from men in having rounded breasts and buttocks and in being beardless, while men are taller, heavier, and hairier than women. Men, the Victorians noted, are also deeper chested, deeper voiced, narrower hipped, and longer legged than women. In the Victorian tradition children's sexuality was denied or ignored at the same time that boys and girls were sharply differentiated in anticipation of their adult roles. The Victorians not only deemphasized the genital aspects of sex directly related to reproduction, they also minimized how much adults vary in those traits they saw as sexually significant. How significant and how variable are the features they chose?

Now, we all recognize that some women are taller than some men, that some women have light mustaches or flat chests while some men have fatty breasts, hairless chests, or high voices. We all know that clothes and customs obscure some sex differences and heighten others. We know that in Victorian Europe fashion decreed that men wear beards and women bustles. Today men and women can look alike in unisex clothes and hairstyles. But despite style similarities men can assert their hairy manliness in the revived vogue for mustaches and beards. Despite the fact that style changes have made us aware that some overlap and variability of sex traits is "natural," it seems equally true that some secondary sex differences never vary. Consequently, there seems to be little appreciation or attention given to how much and in what ways the sexes in various human populations differ. Because sex and sexuality are so important to us, however, some data have been collected about the variability of sex-associated traits in human and even nonhuman populations. This information is rarely discussed by evolutionary theorists of the Victorian tradition, who in general seem slow to acknowledge that sex differences are not the same in degree or kind in all human populations.

For instance, although beardlessness is associated by

Westerners with womanliness, the facial hair on males of American Indian, Eskimo, and Asian Mongolian descent is so distributed that light plucking, no more than middle-aged Caucasian women may feel compelled to indulge in, suffices to keep these male faces uncluttered. Body hair is sparse on both males and females in these populations. Adult males are balder-bodied and barer-chested (less male?) than many women of European extraction.

Although loath to admit it, and likely to remove it, white Euro-American women often have a good deal of fine hair on their arms, legs, and even between their breasts. Far worse than fine fuzz to many an adolescent girl are the coarse hairs that may sprout on the aureolas of her nipples at pubescence. Because of the hair on her chest, she is often convinced that she is a freak of some sort. Unwanted hair that appears at adolescence or later in life on women supports many an electrolysist, a hair-removal expert.

Although it is usual for girlish bodies to grow womanly with the acquisition of fatty tissue on the breasts at puberty, small-breasted or "boyishly" flat-chested adult females show up on ancient Egyptian frescoes, and in contemporary groups in the Middle East and Southeast Asia, while there are enough flat-chested American women to support an industry devoted to correcting this "defect." In fact, deep-breasted women are viewed as odd in many Asian cultures rather than as normal or attractive. Traditionally in Japan, where babies are nursed in public and men and women bathe together in generous bathtubs, decolleté necklines which reveal cleavage are not considered sexually stimulating. Exposing the nape of the neck, however, is. Not only do populations differ in how markedly females and males are distinguished by breast developments, they vary in how bustiness is regarded, and whether breasts or some other part of the body are seen as "sexy."

Most of the Middle Eastern and Asian populations in which male–female differences are not particularly marked are relatively slight in build. Sex differences in height and hip form are minimal: small enough to make it difficult to determine from skeletal remains alone what sex an individual belonged to. At Lepenski Vir, a prehistoric neolithic site located on the Danube in Europe, there now lives a population which shows the kind of dimorphism common to most European populations. Among the ancient inhabitants, however, we find "the women's bones scarcely look different from the men's; all must have shared the hard work on equal terms."[12] It seems that whether generally sturdy or slight of build, some populations show or showed little sex differences in height and only a bit in hip form.

The rounded buttock which is considered distinctly womanly in the Victorian world view is, to some degree, a shape imposed by localized fat deposits as well as by underlying pelvic structures. Heavy fat deposits on the buttocks in their most extreme form are given the name steatopygia. Steatopygia is frequently mentioned in introductory anthropology texts. It is often noted as a prominent characteristic of the women of the Kalahari desert. Prominant fat deposits show up on the men of the Kalahari as well, however. In European Paleolithic cave paintings prominent buttocks appear to grace both men (figures drawn with projecting penises) and women (figures drawn with pendulous breasts). Paleolithic artistic conventions have been found to reflect some pretty accurate observation. It is likely, then, that well-developed padding was common in the populations pictured, although remnant bones alone do not reveal it. It is worth noting that the people of the Kalahari are involved in Paleolithic ways of making a living; that is, they live off the animals they hunt and the food they collect. It might be that fatty buttocks are (or were) an advantage to both sexes under these circumstances. Yet there are collecting–hunting societies made up of humans without steatopygia. Today people who live as collector–hunters come in a variety of sizes, shapes, and colors and show a wide range of variation in butt form.

Fashion and food habits evidently play some part in the variability of sex-associated traits, emphasizing or diminishing physical features that epitomize cultural notions of what sex differences are important. In the past century or so European women have, if they could afford it, dressed, eaten, and exercised to achieve in quick succession Gibson-girl, flapper, pin-up, and Pepsi-generation figures, alternating between striving to expand and reduce their dimensions as best they could. They often achieved their goals, with measurable (and sometimes miserable) success. Western men have shaved or grown beards, exercised, padded their shoulders, or acquired prosperous-looking paunches. Thus sex differences not only are more or less marked in populations in different parts of the world, degrees of differences may vary over time. In European populations alone, in a few short generations real physical as well as stylistic changes took place.

Some sex-associated physical traits which are more basic than height, weight, hip, and breast form also appear in varied form often enough to raise some questions as to exactly how rigidly dimorphic the human species is. Genitals and genes are the foundation on which sex differences are built. Cross-sex anomalies, genitals that have both male and female features, are far from infrequent. Despite the fact that birth certificates record sex as either male or female, it has been estimated that between 2 and 3 out of every 100 newborn babies exhibit such anomalies.[13] That means that in the United States alone there may be more than 4 million people who are physically neither or both male and female and are classified either as males or females. Whether or not the condition corrects itself or is surgically corrected, they are expected to function as one or the other sexually as well as socially. Since gender-role socialization overrides such ambiguities successfully, their physical predicament usually remains private although their sexual functioning may be sorely impeded. In our culture intermediary types of sex organs can be kept hidden, but nevertheless constitute physical variants of a basic sex trait that is viewed as fundamentally dichotiomized.

Sex-chromosome variations are more subtle, since they often occur in people whose sex organs are clearly either male or female and can be recognized only through the use of sophisticated laboratory techniques.[14] Until quite recently it was believed that humans with obvious female traits have two X chromosomes and males have an X and a y chromosome. Current research is turning up individuals with patterns of chromosomes that were unanticipated. There are triple X "super" females and double y "super" males in addition to anatomically female individuals carrying y's, and males carrying extras of both chromosomes.[15] These are patterns of chromosome distribution that don't quite fall into simple dichotomous categories. Individuals with these unanticipated X and y chromosomes are, for the time being at least, viewed as genetically abnormal. Since most of the work on sex-gene typing has depended on sampling people who for one reason or another are in institutions, sex-gene anomalies are suspected of being linked to tendencies toward deviant behavior. Yet there are few data yet available on how often and what kinds of X–y patterns occur in the general population, or what aspects of physical or social behavior X and y chromosomes affect.

Some societies recognize more than two sexes, although data on how many societies do so is scant, largely for lack of investigation. Among the Navajo there is the category *nadle*. People born as genital hermaphrodites are placed in this category at birth. They are "real *nadle*." Genitally normal individuals can choose (as an alternative to masculine or feminine status) to "pretend they are *nadle*," thus freeing themselves from the restraints imposed by the Navajo division of labor. A person undertaking the status *nadle* can marry, which a true *nadle* is not permitted to do, and can take as a spouse either a man or a woman. Those who "pretend they are *nadle*" acquire the social and legal status of women, which is greater than that of men; can dispose of the private property of relatives without their permission, a right denied Navajo men and women; and act as mediators. Similarly, among the Mohave, *hwame* is the name applied to phenotypic females adopting masculine-defined roles, and *alyha* is the name applied to males adopting feminine-defined roles. Evidently, human sexual characteristics can be classified into more than two categories, and it is very likely that more societies than are now known to do so follow this practice.[16]

Yet, for all the variations on sex differences that we find in human populations, it is safe to say that humans as a whole are more likely to have dichotomizing sex differences than are gibbons, and have fewer and less obvious sex-differentiating traits than mandrills, gorillas, or orangutans. That is, in several primate species closely related to us sex differences of some sort are usual.

SOCIAL ROLES AND SEX DIFFERENCES: OLD THEORIES AND NEW DATA

How have the physical differences between the sexes in human and nonhuman primate populations been accounted for? If we look back at the tale of Bambi or the myths about life among the lions, we can see that the social aspect of sex has been treated as both a cause and an effect of physical sexual traits for a long time. Although we have revised our understanding of what part big antlers and shaggy manes play in the social and sexual adaptations of stags and lions, the notion that physical sex differences evolved because of sex-role differences is still widely used. This notion logically lends itself to the idea that as physical sex differences evolve, role differences are perpetuated, and vice versa. Thus, it is held that anatomy reflects not only history, but destiny as well. Most attempts to account for the sexual characteristics of various primate species, human and nonhuman alike, subscribe to this reasoning. It therefore behooves us to look at what sex roles and social patterns have been found in various primate species and how they relate to their physical characteristics. Later we shall examine an alternative approach which can explain the evolution of sex differences in primate species where role behaviors are flexible, or the members of each sex do not act as their appearance suggests they should.

In the late 1930s and early 1940s some studies of life among the rhesus macaques[17] and gibbons[18] were conducted by C. R. Carpenter. These studies provided substantial support for some of Freud's most famous postulates about human sexual proclivities. They helped further the then-current views about anatomy and its social consequences.

Rhesus Monkeys

For the sake of convenience, a number of rhesus were brought for close and careful observation to a small island off the east coast of Puerto Rico. Aside from setting up feeding stations which were regularly stocked, the animals were left alone to adapt without interference. In this "open zoo" the displaced monkeys formed themselves into several troops. In one of these, an aggressive male earned for himself the name Diablo. His activities and their effects lent some credence to Freud's suggestion that the Oedipus complex is rooted in humanity's buried past.

In Freud's reconstruction of history our ancestors lived in tight groups, each led by a domineering and jealous father. This old man of the tribe drove out all his sexual competitors and kept all the women to himself, exuberantly fathering as many offspring as time permitted. Finally, one such old man was slaughtered by his jealous and angry sons. The triumphant young men then distributed the females among themselves, and ended up feeling guilty about all of it. While a 9- to 10-pound rhesus male hardly seems a likely candidate for the position of old man of the tribe, Diablo's actions gave the impression that he was acting in just that way. Diablo did not drive out all his male competitors, but he intimidated most of them. The troop to which he belonged ranged widely and had a high frequency of copulatory episodes, for which he was directly or indirectly responsible.

A caged rhesus macaque male next to a rhesus female and her infant. Although the physical differences between males and females are similar in all rhesus populations, the social roles and relationships of males and females vary in different environments. Photo by John Bishop.

Although copulations among rhesus and most other primates is initiated when a female solicits a male (male testes recede and spermatogenesis ceases when females are not active in soliciting), a male may demur and often does. Diablo rarely refused. His aggressive and amatory activities had profound effects on how well the troop he was in ate, for after he was removed, his troop lost much of its range. In addition, the number of episodes of intercourse decreased, though females continued to solicit when in estrus, and became pregnant. Diablo's island idyll suggests that aggressive rhesus males have reproductive capacities and food-getting abilities that inevitably favor them, their group, and their offspring in evolutionary competitions.

Because of studies done in the 1960s and 1970s, we are beginning to learn about how rhesus macaques live in their native India. Many of these bright little monkeys long ago insinuated themselves into cities and temples. Others stayed on in the forests or forage in the tilled fields of the countryside. In all these settings they gather into groups or troops. It turns out that social groupings in different habitats differ significantly from one another. The setting in which they find themselves affects everything: how big a troop is, how close together groups are, how troops interact with each other, how members and subgroups of a troop relate to one another, and proportions of old to young and male to female members.

Groups living in temple areas are similar to those originally moved to Cayo Santiago, in that they receive a regular food supply through human agencies, and typically are free from molestation. In the year 1960, four troops (of 11, 17, 34, and 40 members) and two unattached males made their home around a place called Achal Tank, a temple area in the city of Aligarh.[19] Three of these troops stayed in or near the temple all the time, where regular offerings kept them well fed. The fourth troop left the temple for days at a time, venturing as far as 2 miles into the city. In the temple area, as in Cayo Santiago, however, home ranges overlapped. Only in the central temple area was there any evidence of exclusive control. There, one troop intimidated and displaced all the others regularly. Elsewhere, this did not hold true. No troop held a hegemony.

Despite the movement of some individuals (adult females and juvenile males) back and forth between groups, which might suggest easy intergroup relationships, intergroup contacts were often extremely hostile. Battles were usually brief but dramatic fifteen-minute free-for-alls in which males, females, and juveniles participated. Each Achal Tank troop harbored several subgroups, consisting of one or two older males, several juveniles, and females and infants. In one case five young adult males hung around together persistently, and it was this subgroup which initiated most of the intergroup contacts that flared into uproars. Within each troop males rarely came into direct conflict with one another. Yet in the well-provisioned temple setting, where males often permit females, juveniles, and infants to eat with them, they frequently attack the females and infants of their troop. In the wild, rhesus males pay little attention to infants (they rarely play with young animals as do the other macaques: e.g., male bonnet macaques, Japanese macaques, or as do chimpanzees and gorillas).[20] Their attacks on infants and females are common, however, only at shared feeding sites. The temple females, who, like their forest sisters, are either pregnant or nursing from the time they reach four years of age, associate peacefully with one another, grooming each other and playing with and grooming their ever-increasing number of offspring. (There's about a year between babies.) In many respects, temple and open-zoo troops resemble one another.

Trappers charge more money for town monkeys than they do for forest monkeys. They insist that forest monkeys, who are harder to catch (which might be taken for a sign of their intelligence) are stupid. Yet forest animals perform as well as town animals on standard learning and discrimination tests. Interestingly enough, however, town monkeys prove to be more curious and more interested in complex activities on psychological tests than their forest conspecifics.[21]

Even stronger contrasts between temple and forest animals show up in the social interactional framework of behavior. Forest-living rhesus troops are larger, more widely dispersed, and fight far less frequently than town dwellers. A single large forest male nearly always monopolizes the feeding site. Only during the breeding season might he occasionally permit his current consort to feed with him. Yet in or out of breeding season town males share their "table" with troop members, although sometimes ungraciously. In laboratory-generated competitions for food, town monkeys always succeed against forest monkeys. It is especially interesting that female town monkeys take food *before* males from the forest. Caged forest monkeys, male as well as female, accept strangers with relatively little conflict. Town monkeys, on the other hand, respond so viciously to strangers introduced to their cages that newcomers have been mauled, bitten, and sometimes killed. Forest and town rhesus macaques obviously learn to live differently in their different settings. Members of the same species, they modify and adapt their social behavior significantly, surviving and reproducing with aplomb in both settings.

This does not mean that all members of the species are equally or infinitely malleable, or that they all have the same perceptual capacities, or that they all can or will respond identically to the same stimuli. But it does argue that individual adaptibility is part of the species behavioral repertoire, and that the roles and behaviors assumed by an individual are significantly shaped by its life experiences. How much rhesus macaques are subject to the effects of socialization we will see in a later chapter.

The physical sex differences in rhesus monkeys are tied by many theorists to the kinds of male–female roles found in Diablo's troop. Diablo's easy sexual responsiveness, "leadership," and general aggressiveness are the model of the successful big male who dominates the males and females of his group, and fathers most of its young. Since rhesus social relations are interestingly diverse, and those forest-living monkeys uninfluenced by human presence are rather unlike Diablo's troop in habits, it would seem that an evolutionary model linking genetically determined physique to role behaviors has limited applicability even to rhesus. How does such a model apply to other primate species?

Gibbons

For gibbons this model does not apply at all. The sexes look alike. This lack of dimorphism is characteristic of nearly all primate species that are, like gibbons, almost totally arboreal. Many of these nondimorphic arboreal species live in large social groups. Among gibbons, however, the similarity between the sexes is tied to a social pattern that is built around a stable male–female mating pair in which males and females are equidominant. Carpenter, the first student of gibbon behavior, held that "there is no reason to believe that human families have ever been formed characteristically in any other way."[22] Morris argues that gibbon-like pair bonding is a fundamental human trait (associated with the more advanced types of humans), but believes that gibbons must have suffered a decline and fall from the "true" primate heritage of male dominance and female dependency.

Gibbons' social adaptations[23] are rather unlike those of rhesus. These small apes forage in the treetops, where each pair-centered group vociferously maintains a permanent range. Groups consist of from two to six individuals: a female, her mate, and immature young. In zoos, gibbon pairs copulate rather frequently, often as a result of male overtures. They copulate even during menstruation and pregnancy. In the wild, a thousand hours of watching 21 pairs turned up only two episodes of intercourse, initiated in both instances by the female. Despite a high level of copulatory activity, reproductive rates in zoos are no different than they are in the wild. Every two or three years a pair produces a new infant. The infant remains with them as it grows until it reaches sexual maturity, sometime between its eighth and tenth year. Normally a pair has several youngsters of different ages in tow. Male and female offspring alike begin to separate from the parental pair at approximately the same stage of maturation.

As gibbons grow up, they become more and more independent of their parents, gradually exploring the forest spaces around them, and as they grow older and sturdier, they do so more and more freely. When a youngster is approaching sexual maturity, the adult parent of its own sex becomes increasingly hostile toward it. Aggressive actions replace tenderness and tolerance. Eventually, maturing animals are driven from their natal groups.

By the time an animal is cast out, it is physically about ready to make a liason with a member of the opposite sex who has also been or is being expelled from its group. Sometimes that animal is a sibling. Gibbon brothers and sisters show no particular aversion to taking each other as mates. Indeed, circumstances may encourage them to make such alliances. Since mothers drive off maturing daughters and fathers drive off their maturing sons, adolescent brothers and sisters find themselves being abandoned in tandem and they are likely to become a mating pair.

Gibbons also show no particular aversion to parent–child mating. When an adult male is removed from a group, his role and sexual prerogatives are taken over by a mature son. Removing an adult female results in her place being taken by a daughter. When male and/or female gibbons show increasing intolerance for the maturing offspring of their own sex, they are beginning to treat them as they do all other adult gibbons rather than as their children.

Freud's contention that ancient and primitive sexual jealousies underlie the antagonisms he discovered between Viennese fathers and sons and mothers and daughters is beautifully illustrated by the gibbons. Gibbon behaviors appear to support early notions that incestuous inclinations run deep into our primate past. Gibbons do not really fit the Freudian model of the human family. Copulation is rare. The sexes look alike. Both members of the parental pair share equally in leadership, defense, and direction-setting activities. Both parents play with, inspect, manipulate, and groom infants with equal alacrity. Both go in for the same kinds of aggressive displays, vocalizations, teeth gnashing, head shaking, and lip smacking. Chronic sexuality does not characterize the relationship of a pair whose role behaviors are essentially identical. While mothers find themselves at odds with maturing daughters and fathers with their growing sons, the aggression directed toward maturing offspring takes the same form as the aggression directed toward strangers. Recent interpretations regard the gibbon pair as joint partners in maintaining an adequate food supply rather than as jealous spouses.

The physical and social egalitarianism of gibbons is unusual among the higher primates who are, for the most part, terrestrial and semiterrestrial. Foraging and traveling in the trees—secure and safe, it is held, accounts for gibbon males who are on occasion subdominant to females, sometimes smaller than they, and not very sexually oriented.

Many arboreal monkeys are similarly non-dimorphic. Is a lack of dimorphism, and equality in leadership, food access, and dominance part of the "high arboreal" primate niche?

Orangutans

Orangutans live in much the same area as gibbons.[24] In fact, members of the two species have been spotted within 100 feet of each other. They, too, spend much of their time in the high trees, but where a 13-pound gibbon can get around by arm-swinging through the branches, the heavier orangutans move much more cautiously, rarely trusting their full weight to one tree limb. Orangutans generally take their time. They are capable of extraordinary arboreal acrobatics but do not indulge in them often. Orangutans are also capable of amazing speed on the ground of the gallery forest when they are pursued, and spend much more time moving from place to place on the ground than had been realized.

Until quite recently, reports on orangutan behavior in the wild were scanty. A few bits and pieces indicated that orangs, unlike gibbons, make themselves sleeping platforms or nests, and that like gibbons, their social groups contain from two to six individuals. It was evident early, however, that the constitution and stability of orang groups was totally at odds with gibbon patterns. Hard and fast facts were few. Apocrypha, on the other hand, abounded. It was not at all clear that reports of orangutans at large meetings and "dances" were reliable. On the other hand, how could one be sure?

Systematic surveys show that orang groups today are never mass rallies, but it is also true there are no massive groups of orangutans left, only about 5000 or so in the wild. (It is estimated that about half of the world's population of orangutans is in zoos.[25]) Recent observations of the species in Celebes[26] uncovered groups that are made up of one or more adult females, with one or more subadult young; male–female pairs, with or without young; and quite often lone animals, unattached to groups and wandering freely. Noting that a male on three successive nights moved from nesting near a female infant and juvenile to a tree 400 feet from them the next night, and farther away the third night, one is led to conclude that groups are ephemeral. Because of patient observers like David Horr, we now know that there is a pattern underlying the instabilities, and that orangutans are not nearly as much fun to watch as apes and monkeys are reputed to be.

Orangs are, in fact, boring to observe. They spend an inordinate amount of time resting high in the trees or avoiding observers from an unreachable perch. It took a lot of neck-craning to get enough material together to discern what is essentially a rather simple—and unexpected—pattern of social relationships. Lone adult males travel over a wide area. Adult females with young keep to rather small ranges. The path a male follows usually touches or crosses several female range areas and overlaps the travel routes of other males. Long-term observations show that the female-centered groups are each individual mother–child units. The unit grows as a female's progeny increases. It shrinks as her grown-up children move away. While mature sons wander off to range widely, mature daughters set themselves up near their mothers, and join with them occasionally, bringing along their offspring. The female-centered small groups occasionally link up with one another or temporarily admit a male. It is as yet hard to tell whether the males who sometimes join the mother-centered groups are prodigal sons, brothers, or strangers. It is therefore impossible to tell yet whether brothers, sons, or strangers have special or characteristic kinds of social relations with the female-centered groups they join. One thing is clear, however. The males who temporarily associate with these female-centered groups are not often highly sexually motivated, for only sometimes are they sexually active.

Sexual intercourse between orangutans is nearly as infrequent as it is among gibbons, reports indicate. It is also usually a cooperative endeavor, encouraged or initiated by the female. However, in at least one instance an enterprising male managed a rape. Although human rapists are viewed as behaving like "wild animals" rape in the wild is so rare that this was the first eyewitness account of rape in an uncaged, undomesticated mammal species that I know of. Field-workers, who agree that the interactions between male and female orangutans are mostly placid, have observed a subadult male they named Mute exhibit a preference for unwilling sexual partners, although his constant female companion, to whom they gave the name Noisy, was never subjected to his sexual advances. (She turned elsewhere when she came into estrus.)[27] Mute and Noisy are an Odd Couple, for orang males are usually isolates, and vocalize frequently, letting other animals know exactly where they are. This vocalizing enables males to avoid each other, which they do as much as possible, and enables females to avoid the vocalizing males or not, as their inclinations dictate. Mute is a somewhat extraordinary orangutan male as to both the quality and evidently the quantity of his sexual relationships.

The smallish orang females are essentially self-sufficient, rearing their young without benefit of a male breadwinner, companion, or protector for years at a time. Since troops and male-centered groups do not exist, these large primate males do not compete with each other for positions in a dominance hierarchy, or for leadership or territorial mastery. The classic social-role distinctions associated with big males and small females also do not exist. Nor is the gibbon pair pattern evident, although the pair group has been suggested as likely for arboreal apes. It is possible that this remnant population of an endangered species has assumed a dispersed, cautious mode of living under the pressures of human encroachment and that there once was some truth to the tales of orangutan assemblies. If such is the case, and we may never have the opportunity to learn if it is, it would indicate an impressive degree of social adaptability. With or without such data, however, one thing is clear. The evidence at hand on contemporary orang social arrangements does not lend itself to the usual interpretations of the basis for or significance of sex differences among social primates.[28] Detailed analysis of sex-role behavior and mating practices among gorillas and chimpanzees indicates much the same thing.

The African Apes

If we take at face value similarities of blood types, gorillas and chimpanzees are much closer to human beings than either gibbons or orangutans. Their social habits also suggest closer affinity to the human heritage, for gorillas and chimps maintain larger social groupings than either gibbons or orangutans, and their groupings usually include males and females and young. If they are humanity's closest living relatives, their adaptations are of special interest to us here.

Despite differences in forms and degrees of dimorphism, both gorilla and chimp males are generally larger than species females and also have larger canine teeth. These males have consequently suffered from a poor press. Since Edgar Allen Poe wrote *The Murders in the Rue Morgue* and King Kong inconsiderately abducted Fay Wray, gorilla and chimpanzee males have been reputed to be subject to overpowering sexual cravings, especially toward Caucasian women. Darwin did much to establish the image of the aggressive and sexy ape by publishing an inaccurate and rather libelous version of gorilla social organization which Freud fitted nicely to his Old Man of the Tribe hypothesis. Until George Schaller spent a year or so among the gorillas, gorillas were considered dangerous rather than endangered. Chimpanzees had already somewhat redeemed themselves by being entertaining. Since chimpanzees are more numerous and smaller than gorillas, they are easier (and cheaper) to catch, transport, and train. Much sought after by theatrical entrepeneurs, they had opportunities to modify their image which gorillas never enjoyed. Nevertheless, trained performers are not the same as wild animals.

In light of these reputations, the first observers to go unarmed into the wild to investigate chimpanzees and gorillas on their home grounds were very, very brave indeed.[29] Jane Goodall had no difficulty discovering that male chimpanzees do not prefer blondes. In fact, rather than being pursued avidly she was at first, of necessity, a patient pursuer, for instead of attacking her, the chimps retreated before her. It took more than a year to win acceptance of her presence and many more years to establish true confidence. George Schaller instantly learned that gorillas, also, would rather flee than fight, and very quickly found that gorillas are sedate and their interactions are marked by tranquility. Both investigators must have been reassured by this early evidence of shyness and serenity, but uncertainties must have remained, and they deserve enormous credit for their accomplishments.

Gorillas: Schaller's first view of gorilla life was undoubtedly very tantalizing. Given the pugnacious picture of gorilla males that was then popular, who could have expected to run into evidence of their benign paternalism? Yet this is exactly what Schaller ran into. Coming suddenly upon a group of browsing animals, Schaller and a companion settled themselves to watch a day in the life of a gorilla group. A large silver-backed male spotted them, moved closer, and then sat down to browse with one eye on the unknown intruders. Soon a female gorilla holding an infant still damp from birth joined the silver back. The two animals sat thus, side by side, for several hours, the male occasionally reaching out to fondle the tiny infant, all the while keeping a quiet eye on the observers in the bushes nearby. The tableau remained undisturbed until, at last, as the day drew toward evening, the human observers got up to go back to their camp.[30] This peaceful vignette provided a preview of the social patterns and behaviors that were to be uncovered in the year of careful and intensive observation that followed.

Mountain gorillas are ground livers by day, far too heavy to trust their weight to anything but the stoutest branches of the sturdiest trees. But at night, trees provide safety, and gorillas build platforms in the crotched corners of branches to rest their backsides against. They travel in groups that contain anywhere from fifteen to forty-six members. Groups always include a silver-backed male; in fact, several in a group are common. Groups do not always number among their members younger black-pelted males, however. Instead, young black backs often wander about on their own, dropping in occasionally on groups which they encounter. Females have never been seen outside groups. Since adult females unencumbered by pregnancy or children are unknown, it is highly improbable that females ever wander as isolates. An adult and a youngster alone are at a disadvantage, it seems, for a silver-backed male who was followed into independence by a large infant did not manage to survive, and the infant lived only because it was captured. Groups always include adults, juveniles, and infants of both sexes.

At first glance it looks like there are one and a half adult females to each adult male in most gorilla groups. This is considered an "unbalanced" sex ratio. Unbalanced sex ratios are noted most for dimorphic species with large size differences and are usually seen as characteristic of groups of ground-living primates. The idea that sex ratios are unbalanced appears dubious. When age rather than size is used to compare the numbers of adult males and females, it turns out that there are just about as many males as females around. Since sexually mature black-backed males that have not yet reached full growth may be only peripherally or occasionally associated with groups, they are often not counted as either adults or group members. Should they be counted out, however? What constitutes a group, what animals are adult, and what we consider to be group membership are significant issues in a discussion of sex-role behaviors and the part they play in the evolution of sexual dimorphism.

Although it might seem, given the notions about behavior and physical traits that are current, that these marginal males have been driven out of their groups by larger, more powerful, jealous, dominant, leader-protector types and prevented from mating and contributing their genes to later generations, such is not the case. Like orangutans, gorillas behave in ways that contradict this kind of theory. What they do do, and what orangutans do, as we soon shall see, provides us with some clues as to how sexual dimorphism might have arisen among socialized behaviorally malleable higher primate species.

Female gorillas are constantly in the company of silver-backed males and they have a monthly estrus cycle. This means that the possibility for matings are year round. But sexual intercourse is infrequent. The few episodes of intercourse observed by Schaller—two in a year of observation—indicate that silver-backed males enjoy no sexual prerogatives. Black-backed males were chosen as consorts in both instances, and neither had "status." In one case the young male, who was not a "regular" group member, began copulating with a female who had solicited his services. He retreated, discretion being the better part of valor, when a silver back nicknamed Big Daddy approached. The latter, after unsuccessfully presenting himself as a candidate to the mating-minded female, wandered away. With appropriate signals the female encouraged the younger male to return and complete what had been left undone. He did. Such a bland resolution of a potentially conflict-ridden situation may seem out of character in a species in which truly intimidating chest thumping is used for threat. Yet such bland behavior is in keeping with the general tone of quiet tolerance that pervades gorilla interactions. Silver-backed males may lead the group in its day-to-day foraging, but they do so by consensus. They do not enforce compliance. Some of these beetle-browed males even indulge in play with growing active youngsters.

Although silver backs generally set the direction in which groups move, perform the entire chest-thumping threat for which gorillas are famous,[31] and along with other males take positions between the group and danger when the group is threatened, they are evidently not sexually favored. Full size and social responsibility do not assure a male sexual success. (The pinnacle of his sexual activity may be reached, as we shall soon see, earlier in life.) Once again, it seems that dimorphism, sex roles, and sexual successes do not quite confirm prevailing popular theories.

Chimpanzees: Chimpanzees in the wild have been observed in several types of habitats, heavy forests, forests bordering on open ground, and even near cultivated plantations. More numerous than gorillas and orangs, like rhesus they have explored several niches. At least one field worker[32] reported them living as a silent troop-like assemblage. This trooping group, which was found scrounging freely among some fruit trees that a tolerant plantation owner let them harvest, is unlike arrangements found elsewhere. Its members, always moving, were led by an old male, well past his physical prime. Each day he would emerge from the forest, peer about until assured that all was well, and then he would head toward the grove of standing fruit trees. He was followed by romping subadults, male and female, and finally by a sedate "nursery group" of pregnant females and mothers with their young. All activities were conducted in silence. After spending the day foraging and playing (on the ground as well as in the trees), the troop would return to the forest in reverse order. The old male was always the last to leave. He once delayed his forest return, sitting down to stare at a spectacular sunset before going. What the troop did or where they went in the forest was not investigated.

Elsewhere, in the Budongo forest, Reynolds and Reynolds[33] found that the din of chimpanzee vocalization is constant. Here the resident chimpanzees spend most of their time in the trees in roving bands. These groups or bands are so fluid that membership changes daily or hourly. New animals join and other animals leave constantly. The Reynoldses observed very little of the stability noted on the plantation. At any given moment a particular band or group might harbor only mothers and children, or only adult males, or only adults of both sexes. Then, again, it might include individuals of all ages and both sexes. Furthermore, individuals of both sexes and older than about four are seen from time to time outside any group in the Budongo, as elsewhere.

The Gombe Stream chimpanzees, Goodall's subjects, maintain similarly loose group and ranging patterns. Many of them have discovered the advantages of localizing their activities somewhat around strategically placed commissaries where bananas are occasionally made available to them. Since bananas are doled out individually and infrequently, foraging remains a matter of looking around all the time for things to eat. Groupings are, even in the manipulated setting, no more stable than they are in the Budongo. Animals move widely to eat well.

In loose groups which fragment at will, no individual, male or female, regularly acts as leader. There is no place in them for a leader like the one identified on the plantation, for no individual is always setting the direction and establishing the pace of travel. Leaders also have to have followers. Where groups break up and one or several animals can peel off and go their own way, "leadership" is at best only a matter of a temporary and fragile consensus. Leaders, like groups, are constantly being redefined in the Budongo and Gombe. Territoriality, in the form of defending or maintaining a piece of space against conspecifics, simply does not exist. Ranges or areas within which animals interact more with one another than with animals from surrounding areas can be mapped, but even these have open "borders" which are constantly crossed.

In the popular ethological literature, leadership is associated with "dominance." Kortlandt's silver-backed chimpanzee "leader" is reported as enjoying a "dominant" position. Evidently other group members, male as well as female, treat him as a dominant. They regularly present their backsides to him (a position that allows an animal to run off if it is received hostilely). They groom him and solicit grooming from him. They give way before him, and allow themselves to be displaced by him. So, on the grounds of this one case, it would seem that dominance and leadership do go hand in hand.

But what of dominance in more fluid chimpanzee aggregated arrangements? Which animals are dominant and what (if any) advantages do they enjoy? What (if any) special roles do they play? In Kortlandt's plantation study, young black-backed males give way to the old silver-backed leader. At Gombe, as in the Budongo, black-backed gray-rumped young adult males regularly displace all other animals. Older silver-backed males give up their places to them. Those black-backed males higher in the displacement hierarchy are not group leaders. Nor are they particularly privileged in other respects. They do not, for example, have any priorities over food, even special foods.

Meat is special. In Gombe, chimpanzees "hunt."[34] Every so often a young colobus monkey, bush pig, or unwary baboon is killed and its meat is eaten. The successful hunter, whether male or female, is surrounded by wheedling, begging chimps as soon as they discover that a kill has been made. They whimper and make soft cooing sounds while requesting tidbits. They remain relaxed and do not fret with one another.

Since observers recognize a stable dominance hierarchy at Gombe, with a chimp they've named Mike at its apex, one might expect that Mike takes a leader's role in coordinating hunting. One might expect that he gets a lion's share of the kill and that he is a favored recipient when he begs for meat from the chimpanzee that has taken the kill. Mike, in fact, has no particular advantages in any of these situations. It is especially interesting that his success in begging is

A chimpanzee holding an infant baboon he killed. Other chimpanzees may beg for bits of meat from the successful hunter and even occasionally receive some. Photo by Geza Teleki.

average and that he on occasion gets nothing. His "status" is irrelevant. When a group is hunting, stalking, and chasing, whoever is in front is leader; the taker of game, whoever that may be, hangs on to it and eats most of it. This owner gives out pieces of meat at his or her discretion. Hunts are not uncommon at Gombe, and careful counts have been kept of who gets what. Dominance gives Mike no special access to scarce and desirable foods as hunter or beggar.

"Dominance" does not even assure its possessor a favored role in the sexual sweepstakes. Among chimpanzees, intercourse is initiated by females, who solicit whom they wish. Males, regardless of their position in the dominance hierarchy, amicably await their opportunity, neither harrassing each other nor the interested female. Dominance as displacement is evident but does not assure its possessor privileges. Subordinate animals experience stress but are not so excluded from the necessities that they are incapacitated. They may even rise in the dominance hierarchy if the chance for inflicting stress on others falls to them. Mike did. He moved up the hierarchy by the simple expedient of clanging large empty cans and intimidating everybody.

In all wild chimpanzee populations, activity differences between the sexes are to be found: on plantations, in the forest, and in the provisioned free zoo at Gombe. Behavioral sex differences in activity profiles appear most forcefully when females become mothers. A newly matured female becomes less wide-ranging, less playful, and less aggressive than her male peer as soon as she becomes involved with pregnancy and birth. This occurs at just about the same age as maturing males are experiencing rapid growth and are very active and mobile. Behavioral difference between the sexes become dramatic at the same time that differences between their growing bodies become evident and hormonal changes occur. Nevertheless, the physical differences between male and female chimpanzees are not associated with the kinds of specialized role behaviors to which they have been attributed. Once again it seems that notions of the social significance of sex differences do not reflect chimpanzee social realities. Why, then, is it that human sex differences are said to reflect the social adaptations of our primate ancestors? Chimpanzees, clearly, do not provide the model used.

Baboons: Baboons, the sexually dimorphic dog-faced monkeys of Africa, often live in the kind of environment to which early hominids adapted. Because of their terrestrial habits, and the fact that many live on the savanna, their social patterns have been seen as a likely model of humanity's earliest social circumstances. Their big canine teeth, which are used in aggressive displays, suggest to some that at least a few of their adaptations are shaped along "apish" lines. How distantly they are related to us tends to be minimized in the search for a social model.

In the 1920s, the early days of primate behavior studies, zoo colonies of baboons played a part in speculative reconstructions of humankind's past.[35] In zoos, baboons are bad-tempered. They are competitive, likely to be easily aroused sexually, bare their teeth often at each other, and they are often dangerous to their keepers. It was not until recently that we learned that troops in the wild, on the other hand, lead rather tame lives. Cynocephalous baboons (chacma, yellow and olive) find safety in numbers. When living on the open savanna, they stay in large troops and serenely graze alongside keen-eared kudus. Cautious about interlopers, they rely on their own sharp eyes and the kudus' sharp ears. Each species stays alert for the approach of predatory lionesses and leopards.

Early research showed that on the savanna, baboon troops move as units. They pull out and break off grass shoots with their hands for food. They browse quietly, loosely dispersed and slow moving if undisturbed, and tightly knotted when moving rapidly or threatened. The young adult males play and roam on the edges of the group but avoid wandering off alone: it's too dangerous. Mothers with their young stay close to the center of the moving mass, near those few senior adult males to whom other animals regularly defer. These dominant or "alpha" males are reported by Washburn and Devore[36] to act as leaders and protectors, rushing to meet threatening situations when they occur but placidly ruling the roost from their central position when peace reigns. On the perimeter, then, are the young active explorers; in the center are the older, more dominant males.

Alpha males were seen as the chief inseminators of females, yet within the troop there are no permanent pair bonds. Females solicit multiple mates, but upon reaching full estrus they may be party to a special relationship. At the height of estrus, which coincides with ovulation, females are reported as confining their interest to a dominant senior male who therefore seems to have a reproductive advantage over the less dominant males. This "consort pairing," as the relationship is called, presumably results in a dominant male's sperm reaching the egg. But nobody knows how long a baboon's sperm remains viable after intromission. Human males produce spermatozoa that retain their motility for varying lengths of time, sometimes a week or more. Baboons probably are similarly constituted. The sperm that succeeds may not be that of the male of the ovulatory moment. Even when consort pairing occurs, its effects are not readily predicted. There are no data on which of the many males a female solicits succeeds in impregnating her.

This patterned adaptation to grassland living can be used to account quite nicely for the development of sexual dimorphism. It presents strong evidence that male–female physical differences are tied to differences in sex roles. It clearly intimates that "dominant" males dominate the gene pool. Unfortunately, long-term observations reveal that even on the savanna, things are more fluid than they at first seemed. Marginal subdominant males may, over time, become alphas. Large troops split up, and subdominant males are often the central characters involved in establishing new, independent groups. Over long periods of investigation it has also become evident that consort pairing is not as universal a pattern as first observations suggested it to be.

In forested regions, where forests abut grasslands and clearings, and in farming areas adjacent to government roads there are baboon groups with other kinds of social organizational patterns.[37] Troops do not move in massed formations with adolescent male sentinel scouts on the outside. Instead, they string themselves out along a line of march. At Ishasha there is a great deal of movement between such moving groups. Not only adult males but, in one instance, some adolescent females, as well, have been seen changing groups. With frequent moves between troops, males do not establish among themselves any rigidly maintained rank order or hierarchy. Conflicts between males are rare, and the few aggressive encounters observed reveal no consistent pattern of attack and avoidance or displacement between individuals. In the forest, as on the savanna, males do not groom each other much, but, on the other hand, they do cooperate in mutualistic activities.

Big males often "police" the groups to which they become attached, sitting on comfortable vantage points that permit them to keep an eye on things. If any animal is disturbed, it barks. A big male will investigate, and, if the situation warrants, will take up a position that puts him near the disturbance. He issues other warning barks if necessary. After a while, a second male moves. He goes off in another direction, away from the danger, and he barks. Carefully, looking away from the site of anticipated danger, the other baboons in the group slip away toward him, disappearing into the forest nearby. When only the watching male remains, he too silently exits.

Ishasha baboons always react to imminent danger by flight. Whole troops flee. No big males stand to threaten or fight. The males with their longer legs are first out of sight and the females carrying the heaviest infants vanish last. As protectors, big males are far from adequate.

In the normal line of single-file march each day, an adult male leads the group and another closes it. Are these males "leaders"? As it turns out, it is usually an adult female who chooses the direction of movement. In the morning, as group members get themselves together, scratching and stretching themselves slowly into wakefulness, a neat little charade is played out. First, one male tentatively moves out. No one follows. He returns. Then, after a while, another sets off. And again no one follows. Back he comes. Until one of the older adult females picks herself up and sets off after a male explorer, the group stays put. But once a female is in motion, movement becomes general and off they go with a male in front, one at the end and no particular order in the middle of the moving line.

At Ishasha, no permanent, long-enduring pairing was found. Sexually receptive females solicited mates, usually several each day, and males responded, if so inclined. No pattern of mate preference, as reported for the cynocephalous baboons on the savanna, appears. Evidently, baboons do not conform to a single mode of social behavior, even in their sex lives.

Hamadryas baboons, whose activities in zoo settings caused one observer to call them sexually promiscuous,[38] are perhaps the least promiscuous of baboons in the wild. Field observers report them as living in jealously guarded monogamous-like relationships. Their behavior as we shall see, is such that the origins of the nuclear family among humans is supposed, by some, to have arisen out of a hamadryas-like adaptation.

The hamadryas baboons find themselves in the chronically dry Ethiopian highlands.[39] There they sleep on cliffsides in aggregations of up to 700 individuals. These massed aggregates leave their cliffside sleeping places each day and break up into smallish bands. These bands further separate into smaller units to forage. The foraging group has been called a "one-male unit." In it an older male, often with a young male companion, jealously herds one or several females. The younger male, as time passes, will take over herding and mating as the aging male begins to spend more and more time with other older males.

The small hamadryas group is obviously an adaptation to a desiccated environment in which food is scattered, predators infrequent, and dispersal to take advantage of scarcity is critical for survival. In Ethiopa, cynocephalous baboons living under similar circumstances also forage in small groups. Under extreme circumstances, groups cease to exist. Trapped on an island in the flooded Zambezi, with food growing ever scarcer and nowhere to go except into the surrounding waters, baboons took to competitive individualized foraging.[40]

At first glance, it seems that among baboons group size and group structure are straightforward adjustments to ecological circumstances. The troops on the relatively rich savanna are, after all, large, and where scarcity is great or starvation threatens, baboon groups are small or nonexistent. But there are indications that other factors are implicated in what forms groups take.

The hamadryas one-male small-group pattern is *not* the same kind of small-group arrangement adopted by the cynocephalous baboons in the dry uplands of Ethiopia. On the other hand, the one-male group is evidently a pattern pursued by the baboons (*Papio leucophaeus*) of the lush forests of the Cameroons, where food is easily obtained. Why do baboons in the same kind of environment differ socially and others in very different kinds of circumstances socially resemble each other?

There are, clearly, differences in the physical appearance of these various populations, differences that are great enough to lead to species distinctions being made between them by some authors, and it is quite possible that the genetic variations that are responsible for these physical differences also account for the fact that hamadryas baboons act one way and the cynocephalous baboons behave in another way, even in identical situations. It might be that cynocephalous types simply are not genetically disposed toward the behaviors that characterize the one-male unit in hamadryas. However, in the cynocephalous troops at Gombe, jealous males sometimes "herd" females in heat (rather than just consorting with them as on the savanna). Some older Gombe baboon males seem also to develop hamadryas-like associations with juvenile males. It looks rather like they can, at least sometimes, do the things hamadryas do.

It may also be, however, that the hamadryas pattern is not particularly ingrained in the hamadryas genetic code. That the latter is likely to be the case is suggested by studies of a captive hamadryas baboon colony.[41] Adult males reared in the colony herded females very imperfectly and very infrequently. Raised in the colony, their genes were wild, but their experiences were not. An old female, one of the original captives, apparently ill-disposed to lapses from the old familiar ways, chased and bit quarreling females in the way only an adult male would in the wild. Her genetic predisposition to being herded apparently was sublimated and she herself became a herder. Perhaps she had a little cynocephalous in her for, as it happens, where cynocephalous and hamadryas ranges overlap, the two "species" interbreed freely. However, the colony-bred males of pure hamadryas parentage did not conform to species pattern either. How much in the way of behavioral variations between baboon population can we attribute to differences in specific behavior-controlling genes?

As we look back over these various types of baboons and the way they behave, it looks like species-wide standardized stereotyped sex-role behaviors are hard to find. Whether genes, or modifications on customary patterns, or both lie at the root of social behavioral differences between populations of baboons is very important when we realize how often baboon behaviors are used as models for early human adaptations and baboon sex roles are characterized in terms which imply that they are somewhat stereotyped. For the moment, for my discussion here, it is most important that physical sex differences persist as role behaviors vary. When baboon adaptations in all their variety are laid out side by side and compared with those of anthropoid apes, they are illuminating; they raise some interesting questions about the relationship between sex-role behaviors and physical sex differences.

RETHINKING THE EVOLUTION AND SOCIAL SIGNIFICANCE OF PHYSICAL SEX DIFFERENCES IN PRIMATES

How can we explain the evolution of human physical sex differences if among our primate relatives, those close to us geneologically and those living where our ancestors lived, sex differences do not correlate with the social-role behaviors to which they have been attributed? Can we say that the greater size and big canine teeth of orangutan or chimpanzee or baboon males are a direct result of selective forces that favored bigger males, who were well equipped for protection, leadership, combat, and sexual athleticism? Obviously not, if big males are not necessarily protectors, leaders, combatants, or very active sexually. Can we say that the physical sex differences among humans reflect these sex-role distinctions when human groups vary a good deal in the way the sexes are called upon to fulfill their roles? Human beings, male and female alike, as we shall see in later chapters, exhibit an amazing ability to participate in a variety of roles and social arrangements, as do most of our primate relatives. If sex roles vary so much and individuals of either sex are able to adapt their behavior without being bound to genetically programmed patterns, to what factors can we tie the kind of sexual dimorphism we are heir to? Let's look at physical sex differences among primates from a perspective that ignores role behavior.[42]

Since the big teeth or hairy mantles or threatening crests of the primates we have discussed do not necessarily accompany nasty tempers and protective roles, these awe-inspiring male traits may be accidental or marginal aspects of a more basic condition of maleness. Among dimorphic primates, these male traits occur in conjunction with a maturation rate which is slower for males than for females. Simply put, males take longer to grow to their full size than females do. Females experience little growth after their reproductive organs become fully functional. At sexual maturity,[43] the organs associated with reproduction are fully elaborated, sometimes quite obviously. Although males reach sexual maturity at the same age that females do, they continue to grow. It is during this later growth that in dimorphic primate species males develop crests, mantles, throat sacs, big canines, and/or other secondary sex traits. Since activity levels go down as the growth rate declines, males tend both to be more active and to stay active for a longer time than females do, before assuming fully adult social behavior patterns. If most secondary sex differences in dimorphic species boil down to a basic differentiation of growth and maturation rates, we should ask: what advantages accrue to primate males that end up larger than females of their species, with big teeth and hairy manes and threatening crests? Why should smallish females (often those with elaborations of their reproductive organs) who share the same environment be favored?

Environment seems to be a very important factor in whether dimorphism develops in a species. Most of the dimorphic primate species spend all or a significant part of their time on the ground. Dimorphism is commonest in terrestrial or semiterrestrial situations where predators threaten. Although sex differences in terrestrial primates have been attributed to the protective roles larger males fulfill against predators, we have already found that largish males are not necessarily protective at all and rather various and variable in how they relate to danger, to each other, and to their groups.

The environmental setting nevertheless seems to be implicated in the problem. Most arboreal primates are not dimorphic. Few exhibit much in the way of sex differences, although when they do differences may be dramatic.[44] The most notable example of size differentiation in an arboreally inclined primates is that of the orangs. Free from predatory harassments, totally free of the stereotyped sex roles relating to protection, sex differences are still large. What is it about the orangutans that makes them so like more terrestrial primates? Interestingly enough, it seems to be that orangs, like more terrestrial primates, must range widely in the search for food.

For most arboreal primates the ranges they exploit are three-dimensional. Animals move up and down through the forest canopy, as well as horizontally, and they do so with relative ease. The gallery forest is diverse and rich. Leaping, swinging, clinging, and climbing with the aid of gravity requires skill rather than effort. The nutritional needs of a female may go up during pregnancy, but meeting these needs in a three-dimensional range does not call for much additional work or heavier energy expenditures on her part. Remaining smallish has no particular energy advantage. Thus, most arboreal primates seem to live in an equal-opportunity environment—but orangutans do not. For them, food is scarcer and more spread out.

The dimorphic terrestrial and semiterrestrial primates (as well as orangutans) face a different kind of problem. They must range over large, two-dimensional areas to eat properly both in the trees and on the ground. Much of their movement is horizontal. Since gravity is no aid in getting about, traveling requires relatively more in the way of energy outlay than swinging around. It is in this kind of setting that we find the early female maturation and delayed male growth cycle that underlies marked sexual dimorphism. Why? First, there's the food search. Pregnant and nursing females who are eating for two need lots of food and must work relatively hard to get it. They are under real pressure to conserve energy. Anything that makes pregnancy or nursing easier is an advantage. Smallish females who need less food to stay healthy and are not forced to scramble for sustenance while they succour and suckle their young have some advantage over larger females. Small females simply do not have to eat as much or to search as widely as larger ones. On top of which, where predation is a threat to ground-foraging primates, safety lies in numbers, and there are usually other animals (mostly females and their young) browsing close by. Even if a food resource is rich, getting a lot of it at the center of a cluster of animals can be difficult. Where resources are scattered, as is most often the case on a plain or savanna, food is, in effect, scarcest at the center of a browsing group.

Those females whose metabolism permits them to make the most efficient use of what they actually get to eat in this pressured situation are likely to be healthy and to have healthy infants. Eating enough to stay well and strong during a first pregnancy ensures that a female will have another infant, and as long as she stays safe and well, yet another, and perhaps another. In the long run, the smaller, less mobile female can end up living longer and having more infants than her large sisters. Early cessation of growth is reproductively advantageous for females on the ground where foraging in the safety of a group requires work and pregnancy and nursing increase the work necessary to stay well.

How much food a male needs varies with his size and activity levels. A male may need no more food than most females. However, he is in the position to move around to get it and is encouraged to do so. In the "crowded" center of a terrestrial or semiterrestrial aggregate, there is often chronic low-level quibbling, if not keen competition, over food. Moving out a small distance can successfully reduce stress. Growing males with hearty appetites and youthful energies are likely to find the food search less stressful if they go off where they do not compete with less mobile animals (and where they sometimes, as reported for baboons, eat things females never get to taste). Unimpeded by a growing infant, they can wander widely while foraging. Undrained by the demands of pregnancy or nursing, there is little need to be economical about investing effort. So males are able simultaneously to move around more than females and support a larger body size on equivalent food intakes.

It seems that the conditions of social terrestrial foraging can lead to at least some sex differentiation in a species. However, the males of some primate species get to be much bigger and more imposing than females and—evidently—much hungrier. Bigness is helpful for covering distances. Bigger animals take fewer "steps" to get from one place to another. This undoubtedly helps in the food quest, and some of the larger primate males move well beyond the edges of female–child-centered groups. In terms of just ranging habits, I suspect (but would be hard put to demonstrate) that in species where males travel much more widely than females (as seems to be the case among gorillas and orangutans), they are much larger and more rugged than females. Where males range over areas only a bit more extensive than those females cover (as seems to be the case in the fluid chimpanzee aggregations), sex differences are smaller. Even if there is a correlation between range area and body size, diet is probably only part of the picture, since where males go off as isolates or in groups of two or three, separating themselves from the security and safety of social groups, other factors come into play which would favor further and sharper differentiation from the females typical of their species.

89

If newly maturing males become free ranging, and travel alone or in small groups for a while, larger size, intimidating bony crests, showy mantles, booming voices, and prominent canine teeth—all aspects or by-products of continuing growth—can afford significant survival advantages. What better equipment is available to them for warding off predators? There is no doubt that "the bigger they are, the harder it is to make them fall," so one might well imagine that it would be the bigger males who wander off that are the most likely to survive long enough to ultimately meet up with females with whom they may mate. These secondary sex-linked traits not only work to arm them against predators but make them recognizable to cospecies members. Where moving in and out of groups is easy, these threatening appurtenances seem to have little use in intraspecific intimidation but, as among baboons, they may serve to ensure successful reentry into a group, which of course affords mating opportunities that might otherwise be unused. In the final analysis, the secondary elaborations that occur in conjunction with continuing male growth have a competitive advantage in the reproductive arena, whether or not they are used as weapons in intraspecific conflicts, because a free-ranging male has more opportunity to inseminate females than does a male who stays put.

Ultimately, then, the reproductive advantages that have fallen to larger males and led to varying degrees of sexual differentiation in terrestrial and semiterrestrial primate species do not have to be accounted for in terms of a stereotyped male social role. The evidence indicates that there is no single kind of role these primate males play. Rather than rigid role patterns being involved, it appears that because pregnancy and motherhood prevent females from coming into estrus often, a male who moves around visiting for a while increases his chances of running into a female who is in a state of sexual receptivity. It follows that an active, mobile male is going to have more opportunities to father more infants than a less active, less mobile, and probably smaller male. Getting bigger as a result of a delay in the cessation of growth affords reproductive advantages to males even if they are never called upon to use their size in a battle for sexual rights (although size is useful even there). They do not have to get into fights with other males, become leaders, or act as protectors.[45] They simply have to get around a lot, and each has to inseminate more females than his peers inseminate.

It would seem, then, that we can explain the evolution of many key features in primate sex differences by arguing that adaptations that involve a wide-ranging food search select for different male and female body types. In such settings reproductive advantages have fallen to males who are active enough to move around, big enough to do so safely, and also versatile enough to exploit alternative food resources and a variety of social situations. For males, behavioral plasticity is clearly a part of the picture. By contrast, reproductive advantages have fallen to those females with body types that make them the most efficient in using their limited food intakes for reproduction and nurturing regardless of which male is their mate of the moment. Since primate females without offspring exhibit the same general behavioral repertoires males do,[46] in a challenging terrestrial setting females as well as males must be able to adapt behaviorally. Physical sex differences can be explained without associating them with particular social roles. Considering that there is little to indicate that sex roles among dimorphic primates are stereotyped or standardized, such an explanation has the virtue of not violating or contradicting field data on primate behavior.

SUMMING UP PRIMATE SEX DIFFERENCES

Where does this examination of primate sex differences and social behaviors and this model of the evolution of sex differences among primates bring us in a search for the roots of the human institution of family? While we have seen that occasionally nonhuman primate populations have social arrangements that resemble one or another human family form, we have also seen that the behaviors of some primate species are various and variable as regards sex, sex roles, and social groupings. Apparently many nonhuman primate species, although dimorphic and but distantly related to humans, rely very little (if at all) on stereotyped species-wide behavioral patterns. This suggests that in dimorphic species of higher primates, males and females are endowed genetically with similar capacities for learning social behaviors. However, in the arena of parenting behaviors, the evidence so far presented leaves room for the idea that there are indeed inborn, native differences between males and females. In the wild females inevitably become involved in prolonged infant care while males are more likely to expend little time and energy on infants and remain free to wander. Is this an indication that primate males and females are born with different behavioral aptitudes? That they are endowed differently with regard to parenting abilities? That differences in behavioral capacities inevitably shape the roles of the sexes in human family arrangements? Before addressing this problem in the next chapter, which deals with what laboratory and field studies have further revealed about parenting behavior in primates, there is one other "sex difference" that deserves mention—a difference between humans and other primates that has been made much of.

Human beings are often said to be much more interested in

sex than other primates are, given to extraordinary indulgences because of their sex drives. Much, including the origins of the family, has been attributed to this appetite for sex. It is true that many cultures, including our own, are sex-fixated. Yet the contemporary Chinese regard sexuality as a minor force in society. The Dugum Dani of highland New Guinea[47] conveyed to Karl Heider that they do not think of intercourse or sexuality as passionate necessities, and the Arapesh,[48] who were made famous by Margaret Mead, give little thought or effort to satisfying sexual cravings, which to them are not driving needs. Actually, humans are unique primates in that they are the only species that regularly manages to postpone pregnancy in females so that females spend some time as sexually mature adults without young. In some instances the postponement of pregnancy may be the result of adolescent sterility, a delay between the onset of menstruation and the beginning of ovulation. But cultural norms that call for postponing marriage or mating customs and result in limiting births are common, occurring most often in technologically simple collecting–hunting societies[49] and in technologically advanced industrial ones. (Early marriages and high birth rates are favored mostly by societies with subsistence and production techniques calling for easily trained work groups.) In the light of this unusual pattern of postponing pregnancy, it seems dubious that human beings have a difficult time keeping their sexuality under control or that they are innately sexier than other primates. Such a "sex difference" between human and nonhuman primates seems to me more important in understanding the nature and origins of the uniquely human institution of the family than does our so-called "sexiness."

NOTES

1. See, for example, Talcott Parsons, *Societies: Evolutionary and Comparative Perspectives* (Englewood Cliffs, N.J.: Prentice-Hall, 1966).

2. See Marvin Harris, *Culture, Man and Nature* (New York: Thomas Y. Crowell, 1971).

3. John Buettner-Janusch, *Physical Anthropology: A Perspective* (New York: John Wiley, 1971), examines this and other debates about primate classification.

4. Unless otherwise specified, the information on the physical traits of the small primates and larger monkeys (mandrill, baboons, macaques,

etc.) is taken from Thelma Rowell, *Social Behavior of Monkeys* (Harmondsworth, England: Penguin, 1972), an excellent book that ably conveys the social and physical variability of many species of monkeys.

5. Rowell, *Social Behavior of Monkeys*, p. 122.

6. George B. Schaller, *The Year of the Gorilla* (Chicago: University of Chicago Press, 1964). An informative, charmingly written, and illustrated volume, full of personal comments as well as descriptive data.

7. David Agee Horr, verbal communication.

8. Jane Van Lawick Goodall, "Chimpanzees of the Gombe Stream Reserve," in *Primate Behavior*, ed. Irven DeVore (New York: Holt, Rinehart and Winston, 1965), pp. 425–473.

9. Bjorn Kurten, *Not from the Apes* (New York: Random House, 1972). See also how various authors classify relevant early primate fossil in John Pfeiffer, *Emergence of Man* (New York: Harper & Row, 1972), Chap. II.

10. Desmond Morris, *The Naked Ape* (New York: McGraw-Hill, 1967), pp. 64–76.

11. Gina Kolata, "!Kung Hunter–Gatherers: Feminism, Diet and Birth Control," *Science*, *185*, 1974, pp. 932–934. See also Leona Zacharias interviewed by Richard A. Knox about her report in the journal *Obstetrical and Gynecological Survey* in the Boston Globe, March 26, 1976, pp. 2, 33.

12. Philip Morrison, "Books," *Scientific American*, *227*, no. 4, 1972, p. 124. Data on pelvic variability in modern populations appear in Duncan E. Reid, Kenneth J. Ryan, and Kurt Benirschke, *Principles and Management of Human Production* (Philadelphia: W. B. Saunders Company, 1972), Chap. 24, "The Normal and the Abnormal Obstetric Pelvis," pp. 448–466. The controversy surrounding the sexing of fossil skeletons is addressed in James V. Neel, "Lessons from a 'Primitive' People," *Science*, *170*, no. 3960, 1970, pp. 815–822.

13. "The Third Sex," *Science News*, *102*, December 9, 1972, p. 376.

14. Victor A. McKusick, "The Mapping of Chromosomes," *Scientific American*, *224*, no. 4, 1971, pp. 104–113.

15. Recently, an outstanding athlete was prevented from participating in the Olympic games. Her physical examination revealed she had two X chromosomes and a y. Because of her y chromosome, she was deemed to have an unfair advantage over the other women athletes on

the grounds that male chromosomes assure greater athletic proficiency than female chromosomes. According to J. H. Wilmore of the University of California at Davis, however, the superiority of men over women in sports may be due more to "social or cultural restrictions imposed on women, rather than to true biological differences in performance potential between the two sexes" (*Science News*, *104*, 1973, p. 347). The female's physical capacities are not as inferior as some believe, says Wilmore. The strength of the lower extremities, when related to lean body weight, is slightly greater in the female. Endurance capacity in the highly trained female distance runner approximates values obtained in the highly trained male distance runner, when the values are expressed relative to lean body weight. And as women are encouraged more to participate in sports, their true potential also becomes more evident. In the 1924 Olympic Games the winning time for men in the 400-meter free style was 16 percent faster than for women. In 1972, the world records for the two sexes differed by only 7.3 percent.

16. M. Kay Martin and Barbara Voorhies, *Female of the Species* (New York: Columbia University Press, 1976), pp. 84-107.

17. Clarence R. Carpenter, "Life in the Trees: The Behavior and Social Relations of Man's Closest Kin," in *A Reader in General Anthropology*, ed. Carleton S. Coon (New York: Henry Holt, 1948), pp. 2-45.

18. Clarence R. Carpenter, "A Field Study in Siam of the Behavior and Social Relations of the Gibbon," in *Naturalistic Behavior of Nonhuman Primates*, ed. Clarence R. Carpenter (University Park, Pa.: Pennsylvania State University Press, 1964), pp. 145-271.

19. Charles H. Southwick, Mirza Azhar Beg, and M. Rafiq Siddiqi, "Rhesus Monkeys in North India," in *Primate Behavior*, ed. Irven DeVore (New York: Holt, Rinehart and Winston, 1965), pp. 111-159.

20. Descriptions of the parenting behaviors of the species named appear in articles by Phyllis Jay, Paul E. Simonds, Jane Van Lawick Goodall, and George B. Schaller in *Primate Behavior*, ed. Irven DeVore (New York: Holt, Rinehart and Winston, 1965), and in John Frisch, "Japan's Contribution to Modern Anthropology," in *Readings in Anthropology*, eds. J. D. Jennings and E. Adamson Hoebel (New York: McGraw-Hill, 1966), pp. 121-129.

21. Sheo Dan Singh, "Urban Monkeys," *Scientific American*, *221*, no. 1, 1969, pp. 108-115.

22. Carpenter, "Life in the Trees," p. 44.

23. Carpenter, "A Field Study in Siam," is the primary source for the data presented.

24. David Agee Horr was kind enough to tell a class at Northeastern about the results of his field work in the fall of 1972. My notes on his presentation are confirmed and supplemented here by the observations in Birute Galdikas-Brindamor, "Orangutans, Indonesia's People of the Forest," *National Geographic, 148*, no. 4, 1975, pp. 444-472.

25. Robert Meier, Indiana University, letter, March 11, 1976.

26. The reference is to David Horr's work.

27. The observer is Galdikas-Brindamor, "Orangutans, Indonesia's People of the Forest," p. 460 (see note 24).

28. Nevertheless, Galdikas-Brindamor sticks with a more-or-less traditional interpretation of the evolutionary basis for the sex differences among orangs, modifying it only slightly. The traditional view is that bigger males succeed most often in the mating game because they are able to intimidate or overcome smaller competitors. Galdikas-Brindamor says, instead, that sex differences in size have evolved because females prefer the larger males as mates. That big males were reproductively most successful is thus attributed to a competition between males in physical attractiveness. Yet Galdikas-Brindamor tells of Mute, a sub-adult male who is unusually active, mating several times, despite being of relatively small size and despite the fact that the females he mated with resisted his advances. She also notes the sexual triumph of another male, Throat Pouch, who drove off a larger male in a confrontation over a female named Priscilla in the only fight she saw take place between male orangs during a four-year period. These episodes hardly indicate that reproductive success falls to the biggest males around. Her evidence does not jibe with the way it is interpreted.

29. The tradition of the unarmed naturalists was established by Carl Akeley. He believed that an observer with a gun is likely to be unnecessarily provocative. He argued that an observer with a gun would be inclined to use it when faced with trouble. An unarmed observer, he noted, must work to avoid trouble and establish rapport. Such an observer, to survive, must learn the signals that frighten and antagonize the species being studied, and those that assuage their fears. An observer whose presence is not disturbing sees more. Akeley's approach has proved to be most rewarding.

30. Schaller, *The Year of the Gorilla*, p. 17ff.

31. George B. Schaller, "Mountain Gorilla Displays," *Natural History, 70*, no. 7, 1963, pp. 10-17.

32. Adrian Kortlandt, "Chimpanzees in the Wild," *Scientific American, 206*, no. 5, 1962, pp. 128-140.

33. Vernon Reynolds and Frances Reynolds, "Chimpanzees of the Budongo Forest," in *Primate Behavior*, ed. Irven DeVore (New York: Holt, Rinehart and Winston, 1965), pp. 368–424. See also Vernon Reynolds, "Some Behavioral Comparisons Between the Chimpanzee and the Mountain Gorilla," *American Anthropologist*, *67*, 1965, pp. 691–707.

34. Geza Teleki, "The Omnivorous Chimpanzee," *Scientific American*, *228*, no. 1, 1973, pp. 32–42.

35. Solly Zuckerman, *The Social Life of Monkeys and Apes* (London: Routledge and Kegan Paul, 1932).

36. Irven DeVore and Sherwood L. Washburn, "Baboon Ecology and Human Evolution," in *Readings in Anthropology*, eds. J. D. Jennings and E. Adamson Hoebel (New York: McGraw-Hill, 1966), pp. 147–156.

37. Rowell, *The Social Behavior of Monkeys*, pp. 26–45.

38. Zuckerman, *The Social Life of Monkeys and Apes*. The allegation of promiscuity is repeated so often that it is not worth noting a page reference.

39. Rowell, *The Social Behavior of Monkeys*, pp. 46–66. See also Hans Kummer and F. Kurt, "Social Units of a Free-Living Population of Hamadryas Baboons," *Folia Primat*, *1*, 1963, pp. 4–19.

40. Bernard Campbell, *Human Evolution* (Chicago: Aldine, 1966), p. 280.

41. Rowell, *The Social Behavior of Monkeys*, p. 81ff.

42. This orientation is also presented in Lila Leibowitz," Perspectives on the Evolution of Sex Differences," in *Towards an Anthropology of Women*, ed. Rayne Reiter (New York: Monthly Review Press, 1975), pp. 20–35.

43. "Menarche might be considered onset of sexual maturity but not onset of fertility due to adolescent sterility," Robert Meier, Indiana University, letter, March 11, 1976.

44. It is well to point out that the onset of menstruation is usually taken as an indication of a female's "maturity." Males producing viable sperm, on the other hand, may be considered subadult before they stop growing. Actually, females continue to grow physically for a while after menses has begun, and fully mature or adult behavior is established after, sometimes long after, the birth of an infant. Experimentally it has been shown that baboon females continue to grow larger and play

longer if prevented from becoming pregnant at or soon after menses. Rowell, *The Social Behavior of Monkeys*, p. 38ff.

45. In the context of these remarks it is interesting to note that Rowell reports that among baboons "in the wild, 33 percent of seventy-six mating attempts by adult males were avoided by swollen females" while "Only one out of twenty-nine attempts by large juveniles was avoided." Thelma Rowell, "Female Reproductive Cycles and the Behavior of Baboons and Rhesus Macaques," in *Social Communication Among Primates*, ed. Stuart A. Altman (Chicago: University of Chicago Press, 1967), p. 24.

46. Sharlotte Neely Williams, "The Argument Against the Physiological Determination of Female Roles," *American Anthropologist*, 75, no. 5, 1973, pp. 1725–1728.

47. Karl Heider, *The Dugum Dani, A Papuan Culture in the Highlands of West New Guinea* (New York: Wenner-Gren Foundation for Anthropological Research, 1970).

48. Margaret Mead, *Sex and Temperament in Three Primitive Societies* [New York: William Morrow (Mentor Edition), 1953].

49. Neel, "Lessons from a 'Primitive' People," p. 816.

3

Primates as Parents:

Some Data and Analyses

Reconstructing how families arose as subunits of larger populations involves trying to figure out how and why individual males got linked to specific females. Linked to particular females, males also became tied to the youngsters they gave birth to. Whether family is seen as originating out of precultural pairing or as arising postculturally in flexible, open, social aggregates, inevitably theorists end up having to confront issues related to parenting. That the human species is sexually dimorphic and that sex differences also are characteristic of many other primate species contributes to how parenting is usually viewed.

We have already discovered that among primates sex differentiation is marked in species where newly adult males wander far afield, but females who become pregnant early do not roam as much. Sex differences in activities are accompanied by sex differences in growth and maturation patterns. Differences in adult activity levels also coincide with differences in the boundaries and types of social relationships that the sexes become enmeshed in; females normally interact with infants intensely, males interact with infants far less or hardly at all. Because sex differences in growth patterns and physique occur in conjunction with these distinctive social patterns, it is tempting to conclude that the sexes differ genetically in their behavioral potential, especially with regard to parenting. Maternal behaviors appear to be "natural." An inclination to "mother," it follows, can be interpreted as a solidly entrenched genetically based attribute of female primates. The "paternal" behaviors of men in families, on the other hand, can be interpreted as a not altogether successful cultural modification of a genetically based male proclivity (e.g., indifference or outright hostility toward infants). It is not surprising, then, that even theorists who see family as a cultural innovation often believe that the roles and activities of men and women in families and other social institutions were and are shaped by sex differences in behavioral predispositions.

A rhesus mother and child. Although male–young interactions rarely receive attention, maternal behaviors have been studied extensively both in the laboratory and in the field. Photo by Lynwood Chace from National Audubon Society; Photo Researchers, Inc.

Some of the ways in which contemporary human family arrangements depart from a universalistic pattern of sex-role structuring are dealt with later when we examine family forms in non-Western and industrialized Western societies. This chapter is concerned only with whether male and female primates, human and nonhuman, are differentially endowed with regard to their potential for parenting. In it will be described laboratory studies and field observations which cast doubt on this proposition. As it happens, most of the available work on maternal and paternal behavior among primates has been done with dimorphic species of monkeys that are further removed from the human ancestral line than the specialized apes who diverged from the human line more recently. Since a capacity for social flexibility characterizes many species and is presumably quite ancient in the primate order, the evidence that parenting is "learned" or socially acquired by rather more distant relatives of ours than the apes is especially significant. If contemporary humans and those nonhuman primates with whom they shared a common ancestor long, long ago are similarly dependent on social experience for developing appropriate parenting behaviors, the notion that proto or early humans were behaviorally programmed and sexually differentiated parents is very questionable. "Mothering" as well as "fathering" behaviors among higher primates, human or otherwise, whether they occur within a family framework or without one, are acquired, we shall see, by females as well as males, during the course of the individual's development.

RESEARCH BIASES
ABOUT PARENTAL BEHAVIORS

When I first started thinking about writing this book I decided to include a chapter focusing on fathering rather than mothering behaviors because I had run into little that could be called research on male–young interactions. Yet my children were enjoying the ministrations of a father who refused to fit into the then-current notions of what fatherhood was about. I knew my husband was not particularly unique, although I rarely saw men diapering or calming, soothing, and otherwise coping with a squalling infant. As park bench acquaintances with neighborhood mothers ripened into babysitting exchanges and family friendships, I got to see other fathers in action with youngsters, theirs and ours. By the time our kids were toddlers, it was perfectly clear that along with their little friends, they expected and got a good deal of care and attention from their fathers, men who were as charmed by children and babies as my husband was. Like him, most kept their fascination to themselves and enjoyed children in private, playing with them well away from prying eyes, and talking "children talk" out of public earshot.

When we moved to a community where we had access to a school swimming pool with a Friday "Family Night," I discovered one of the few public places where men felt free to fondle and fool with their children. An injury put me into the balcony as an onlooker one Friday and I got a fresh view of things I had barely been aware of when I was in the water with everybody else. As fathers went through the gymnastics and gyrations of teaching youngsters of assorted sizes to swim, they not only maintained close bodily contact with their little students, they often comforted or rewarded them with hugs, kisses, and pats. These were awarded in the pool as well as immediately outside of it. Up to the moment that people disappeared into the locker room, touch contacts between father and child continued. A transformation took place in the locker room, however, for as people emerged in street clothes onto the campus, babies appeared only in their mother's arms. Infrequently, a suddenly awkward male would hold an infant as his wife stooped to tie a child's shoe or button a button. Normal public forms of male–young interactions got put on with street clothes.

As women's liberation became a serious movement, a lot of young fathers freed themselves from fettering their displays of affection, so that young men with babies in their arms, or on their backs, or holding their children's hands have become more common-place. Paternal tenderness is more public than it used to be and fathering has become a legitimate research concern. Male–young interactions and the male potential for playing nurturing roles, it would seem, deserve special attention in any discussion of the origins and shape of human family arrangements. But investigations into these subjects have barely begun. Most discussions of nurturing in the family disregard men entirely, and focus on motherhood. That "maternal behavior" has been studied *ad nauseum* whereas "paternal behavior" has not been studied at all until recently is a reflection of the long-standing Western sanctification and enshrinement of motherhood. Motherhood, in Western tradition, is idealized in paintings, sculptures, photographs, and films. Father is attached to the Madonna image only as an absentee impregnator. Rarely is a man memorialized with a child in his lap.

The notion that childbearing and childrearing are the God-given duties and domain of womankind is locked into Christian belief, although the Catholic Church permitted women to have abortions up until the 1870s (it was permissible to abort a male fetus up to the third month of pregnancy and a female fetus up to the fourth month[1]) and although unmarried British Christian mothers did not have to care for their infants until the Poor Laws saddled them with this responsibility.[2] Motherhood was nevertheless regarded as the ultimate rationale for a woman's existence. In the late nineteenth century, this view of motherhood was translated by scientists into the concept of "maternal instinct," a subject that promptly became a target for investigation. There is, consequently, a rather large literature on human behavior dealing with mother–child relationships, exploring and sometimes challenging the notion that women are born with this instinct. Although until recently students of human behavior did not deal actively with men as fathers, as evidence on human mothering accumulated, some began to entertain the idea that neither fatherly indifference nor motherly love are inborn human instincts. But, as we shall see, more evidence to support this view has come from studying women in other cultures, and rhesus monkeys in the laboratory, than from studying human males who take charge of children. Because of these old research biases, then, it has proved easier—and ultimately more illuminating—to look at what experimental and social scientists have learned about both sexes, and deal with parenting per se, rather than just with male fathering.

Social Scientists and Human Mothering

It was inevitable that anthropologists, social workers, and psychologists studying family situations would eventually find themselves challenging the notion that "maternal instincts" determine mothering behavior. Their research brought them into contact with women whose cultural and social circumstances obscured or denied the traces of such an instinct. Many social workers and psychologists at first tended to mark off as biologically "defective" those occasional mothers in our society whose lapses in motherliness failed to meet middle-class standards, and social workers ended up implying that the instincts of such defective mothers had gone awry presumably because of genetic abnormalities. From the 1920s on, as the influence of Freud increased, the view grew that these mothers were themselves a product of defective mothering, a view that subordinated "instincts" to the influences of circumstance, but nevertheless assumed that "good" mothering is a woman's natural inclination. Anthropologists, however, were encountering whole societies in which all or most of the women were not given to the types of behavior that Westerners expected of them. (See Chapter 5 for examples.) In these societies the ideals of what women and mothers are supposed to be like contrast sharply with Western values. Since it was perfectly evident that babies were born, raised, and became adults and parents in these societies without grossly adverse effects on themselves or their societies, the idea that socialization and experience shaped mothering behaviors and women's roles became current. (See especially the works of Margaret Mead and of John and Beatrice Whiting.[3]) While few data were taken on males as regards fathering behavior, the idea that socialization affected adult social-role behavior was extended to include men. Still, theoretical discussions of family continued for the most part to treat family structures as if the mother–child relationship is fundamental and the role of father peripheral or even antithetical to male instincts.

Social scientists in general began stressing socialization over instinct and the part played by tradition and experience in shaping human sex-role behavior, but remained convinced that the human dependence on social stimulation and learning is unique in the animal kingdom. Human mothers might have to learn appropriate mothering acitivities, but, it was believed, nonhuman females were dominated by their maternal instincts, which, after all, are "part of nature." Since nonhuman species were supposed to "know" how to go about mating and mothering automatically, few researchers were prepared when laboratory experiments uncovered the embarassing absence of appropriate inborn sexual and maternal "instincts" in rhesus monkeys.

Experimenters and Nonhuman Primate Mothering

The experiments that turned up these unexpected results began about fifteen years ago, when Harlow and his staff[4] took some newborn rhesus monkeys from their mothers. They placed each infant by itself in a sterile cage, and provided it with nourishing bottles and excellent waste-disposal services. A few infants, in a later stage of the experiment, shared their cages with a terrycloth, button-eyed "surrogate" mother, a doll to which they could cling. These isolated babies were left very much alone. The results? Some strangely behaved adult monkeys who proved sterile in more ways than anticipated! The animals indulged in idiosyncratic, self-destructive, and repetitious behaviors, some rocking back and forth incessantly, others huddling apathetically in a corner of their cages ceaselessly sucking on one or another portion of their bodies.

Upon reaching sexual maturity, attempts were made to mate the isolation-reared animals, and the females when in heat were introduced to the adult males who were intended to be their mates. To everyone's surprise, females at the very peak of physiological receptivity evinced little interest and no "know-how" about mating, while the physiologically mature males, who certainly should have been interested, were not. In fact, the animals indulged in self-biting and fear rather than intercourse and sexual passion when they were paired off with one another in cages. Eventually a few isolation-reared females were successfully mated to socially reared, sexually experienced, and gentle males. Some became pregnant. A few managed to give birth to live infants. What happened then was even less anticipated. The infants were promptly either "man"-handled or rejected outright, and many infants had to be rescued quickly from their mothers. Not only did the isolation-reared monkeys lack social experience, they also obviously lacked "programmed" patterns to tell them how to proceed with mating and mothering.

The accumulated expertise of zookeepers surely should have forewarned scientists, for zoo employees have been playing adoptive mothers and nurses to deserted infant mammals for many years. Newspapers are constantly reporting zoo abandonments as "human interest" stories. Since I grew up near the Bronx Zoo and spent a lot of time roaming it, for years I kept up with news items about the trials and tribulations of Mr. and Mrs. Martini (I think he was a curator), whose home became a nursery for every infant lion, tiger, monkey, or other animal deserted at birth. Tales of events at the Bronx Zoo were much like tales from other zoos. There was, for instance, the unpleasant story of the female gorilla housed in Bukavu, Congo.[5] Not knowing what to make of the strange wriggling object that appeared in her cage one day, she bit it. It died. It was her newborn infant. Or there is the more recent item about the orangutan at the Phoenix Zoo who ignored the 4½-pound baby she had just given birth to. Her keeper retrieved it as he went by on his rounds.[6] I remember also a charming account of a cage-reared chimpanzee who had spent her life in a colony of adult chimpanzees. For safety's sake she was isolated during and after giving birth. Evidently her social experiences were such that she took to her baby but was ignorant about handling it. Until returned to her cage and shown by a cagemate how to hold the baby upright, she allowed her infant to cling to her any which way. Similarly, a first infant was poorly cared for but a second well-tended by a gorilla mother in the Basel Zoo.[7] Since zoo reports bandied about in newspaper columns are seldom seen as particularly worthwhile scientific data, they were ignored or were seen as insignificant. Only a laboratory report raised the possibility that some of the higher mammals are notably lacking in "maternal instincts."

SEX DIFFERENCES AND BEHAVIOR: HORMONE STUDIES

The Wisconsin Primate Laboratories, where the rhesus isolation study was conducted, continues to pursue lines of research opened up by that experiment. Now one of many centers studying nonhuman primate behavior, workers there focus particularly on the relationship between social experiences during growth and adult behavior patterns. Sex and sex differences are of major concern. Three of the questions being asked at Wisconsin are: If complex behaviors such as mating and mothering are not preprogrammed and stereotyped in upper primate species, how do behavioral sex differences in adult males and females of these species develop? Are subtler aspects of adult sex differences in behavior (such as aggressiveness) related to physical factors? If so, how? Underlying the investigations of these questions is the apparent conviction that sex-based physical factors, although subject to modification by social inputs, nevertheless contribute heavily to the development of sex differences in adult behaviors. In line with this view of the relationship between physiology and behavior, experiments involving the manipulation and modification of normal hormonal and physiological characteristics have been devised. Presumably these experiments have helped identify the effects of sex hormones on sex-role behavior, because in theory the experimental animals have been subject to the same sorts of socialization as the animals they have been compared with.

One such study focuses on the effects of the "male" hormone androgen.[8] Now, rhesus (and human) females produce a limited quantity of this "male" hormone normally. In fact, if females fail to produce any androgen, or produce too little, they are not interested in sex or sexual encounters of any sort. They do not solicit males when they come into estrus and do not respond to the overtures of males (or females) at any time. While males normally have somewhat higher levels of the hormone than females, androgen has been identified as a male hormone primarily because it plays a part in the prenatal development of the male genitalia. The production of a high level of androgen early in pregnancy permits a fetus to develop male sex organs.[9] The experiment designed to test the effects of androgen on behavioral development involved administering extra quantities of androgen to fetuses whose sex was already established as female. Androgen was introduced to female fetuses while they were still in their mothers' wombs, but before they were born in order to watch how a genitally female animal with male hormonal balances would act. The procedure is both complex and time consuming and only a few female fetuses have been so treated.

The androgenized female infants created at the Wisconsin Primate Laboratory were housed with their mothers and were reared with other animals, participating in the usual social interactions of a laboratory colony, playing with animals of their own age. What the experimental females did was carefully watched and recorded, as they grew up, and the summary of their activities indicates that they were more inclined to rough-and-tumble play, mounting, thrusting, and threatening behaviors than were untreated females. They did not, however, go in for quite as much of these sorts of things as growing males. Some researchers feel the results of this experiment show that male hormones are directly responsible for heightened activity levels and the frequency of the activities considered to be "male" ways of behaving. Others are not so sure.

Studies by Mitchell and Brandt[10] indicate that infant monkeys of both sexes have comparable activity levels when caged only with their mothers or alone. When the same infants are caged in pairs—male/male, female/male, or female/female—and separated by a transparent plexiglass screen from a mother infant pair in an adjacent cage, the activity levels of male infant pairs are higher than those of pairs of mixed sex or females. In this setting the behavior of male infant pairs involves a greater number of threats toward one another and more imitative play. Apparently, social settings have their effects on the way male and female infants react, suggesting that it may be wise to look again at the behavior patterns of the androgenized female rhesus.

Not only do rhesus males have penises rather than vaginas, they grow at a different rate to a different size than females. One of the effects of the prenatally administered hormone was a physical masculinization of the experimental females. Even though the infants had the ovaries, wombs, and orifices that make them functionally female, their vaginas developed prominences resembling testes and penises. Now, one of the first things socially reared rhesus mothers do is inspect their infant's sex organs, and they keep on inspecting them from time to time. In fact, rhesus infants and youngsters undergo a good deal of inspection by other species members all the time. Since no one knew at the time of the experiment that rhesus mothers tend to treat male infants differently than they do female infants, pushing them off sooner, discouraging them from clinging, and encouraging them to interact more with other animals, no one took notes on what kind of "mothering" the androgenized females experienced. Nobody, as far as I know, has done the experiment over again since it has become evident that even among rhesus monkeys, males and females are differentially socialized. The intermediate-type sex organs and modifications in growth patterns of the experimental animals might well have elicited responses from mothers and peers that encouraged intermediate-type behaviors. We simply do not know yet whether raised androgen levels masculinized the behavior of these "females," or whether the increased androgen masculinized their bodies enough to change the social milieu in which they grew up.

Laboratory work has, however, shown that the relationship of a rhesus mother to her male offspring has an effect on his development of "male" behaviors. [11] Young rhesus, whether male or female, attempt to mount each other at a fairly early age. As long as there are mothers around, they manage to acquire a preference for opposite-sexed animals and appropriate sex positions during their first year of life. Males separated from their mothers at three months of age and allowed limited access to monkeys their own age show less-than-normal sexual activity. As juveniles, they display no real preferences for either male or female mounting partners, or for male or female sexual positions. Without tampering with hormonal levels, the behavior of growing rhesus males can be quantitatively "feminized." It seems that mothers and peers exert a profound effect on the development of a male's aggressiveness and sexuality, subtly inhibiting and directing his sex play.

Some students of primate behavior believe that sex-hormone levels are seriously affected by social forces. It has been demonstrated that among rhesus a male's hormonal balance is directly related to his social circumstance.[12] Testosterone (another male hormone) levels correlate absolutely with an animal's immediate social dominance position and aggressiveness. But what causes what? Does a high testosterone level cause aggressiveness, or do social circumstances cause changes in testosterone secretions? Four rhesus males were tested. If four rhesus adult males are enough to draw conclusions from (and many primate behavioral experiments from which grand generalizations are drawn involve even fewer animals), then social factors account for hormonal levels more than hormonal levels account for social placement. All four males tested went through the same experiences with the same results. After each spent two weeks as the only male in a compound with 13 females (a period during which his testosterone secretion rose to nearly twice previous levels) each monkey spent a brief (fifteen minutes to two hours) period with a well-established group of thirty adult males. During this brief but traumatic episode the testosterone levels of each of the tested males plummeted (by 80 percent). Levels remained low for up to sixty days, rising again only after each, one by one, was reintroduced to the female group.

Does this sort of hormonal responsiveness to social circumstances by rhesus monkeys reflect much about the conditions under which humans operate? It is hard to generalize from these monkeys to humans without further work. For one thing the data we have on humans is contradictory. For another, the data on humans are neither comparable nor complete, although some work has been done. For instance, the testosterone levels of human males have been looked at. Thirty human male homosexuals were found to be significantly lower in their testosterone levels than were fifty heterosexual males,[13] but the hormonal balances of forty-two members of a lesbian organization were identical with those of nonhomosexual women.[14] Although these data on human males could be taken to indicate that homosexuality among males is induced by hormonal conditions, the evidence on female homosexuality can be interpreted solely in terms of social factors, yet in neither case was there any attempt to alter either the social contexts or the hormonal balances of the subjects under investigation. It is perhaps presumptuous to argue from such meager information that social forces affect the sex-hormone secretions of humans as they do of rhesus. It is even more presumptuous to argue, however, that a man or woman's hormonal levels are responsible for his or her sexual orientation, maternal proclivities, or social-role behaviors, although many biobehavioral studies of monkeys, men, and mothers do just that.

Biologically oriented studies of behavior raise more and more questions as one study or experiment leads to others, and differences in their interpretation lead to yet others. Motherhood was a beginning issue to be dealt with. The discovery that monkey mothers are social products and not born "motherly" stirred up investigations into the biological components of behavior, encouraging experimenters to manipulate biological conditions and determine the behavioral effects of their manipulations. But they also generated laboratory work on behavioral development in which the only thing manipulated is the social situation. Monkeys are now being observed in ways that parallel the way humans growing up have been observed for awhile. Monkeys are being studied in terms of how they develop in different social settings. Scientists are consciously creating alternative and sometimes extreme situations for infant monkeys. In these, they observe the effects of such situations on behavioral development, and, as we shall see, the findings parallel observations on human infants.

SEX DIFFERENCES IN BEHAVIOR: STUDIES OF SOCIALIZATION

Isolation-reared monkeys are crippled, socially and emotionally, unable to partake in normal activities. They are withdrawn, self-destructive, and given to idiosyncratic behaviors. Does this result from an absence of mothers and mothering? Playmates? Other animals generally? To find out, infant rhesus have been reared in a variety of ways. Some were allowed carefully controlled allotments of time only with their mothers. Others were permitted scheduled times only with infants their own age, and still others had access to both mothers and peers.[15] Controlling the amounts of social interaction, and the number and types of animals with whom youngsters interact at various stages of their growth, makes it possible to get some idea of what kinds of socialization experiences engender what kinds of behaviors. Again somewhat surprising results are encountered. In the laboratory (although never in the wild, where there are no bottle-bearing experimenters), monkeys raised only with peers do as well in acquiring effective social behaviors as those raised by hovering mothers. When experimenters separate strongly attached peers, it turns out, the monkey gets just as depressed and withdrawn as infants taken from mothers.[16] (Separated mothers do not do well either.) Significantly, infants taken from their mothers and housed alone remain depressed and withdrawn. Their development seems to grind to a halt. Those housed with peers after being taken from their mothers recuperate and are only slightly retarded in their development.

When it was realized that the effects of separation shock are reduced in "normal" monkeys if they have active peers around them, it seemed logical to explore whether an isolation-reared monkey could benefit from an enriched social situation. Putting emotionally crippled isolates with healthy peers had disastrous consequences, however. Isolates proved to be unresponsive victims of their peers. Easily pushed and picked on, incompetent to handle normal social interactions, they got little warmth and remained withdrawn. But social, pokey, active infants, who persist in grooming and cuddling and continue to make approaches again and again to unresponsive elders, are effective therapists. Even if the unsocialized animal was a juvenile male, a trusting, playful infant could win its attention and produce healing changes in its behavior. Putting isolates with infants resulted in a kind of obverse mothering. The infants, in effect, socialize the older crippled animals, reversing expected adult-young roles and favorite precepts of what is involved in the parent-child interplay. This turnaround was extremely suggestive to some researchers.

PEOPLE AND OTHER PRIMATES:
STUDIES OF SOCIALIZATION AND MALE PARENTING

Gary Mitchell is one of several who worked on a number of team studies of maternal behavior at Wisconsin, getting a degree in comparative and physiological psychology. Shortly after being awarded his doctorate and becoming a father for the third time he became interested in studying paternal behavior. Recognizing that there just are not many studies of male-young interactions around, and being fully aware of what has come to be seen as "the infant therapist" phenomenon, he and some coworkers at a California laboratory decided to look into how a normal adult male rhesus and an infant would respond to each other when left alone together. He argued that if infants could help "bring up" juvenile male isolates, infants might be able to induce healthy males to "mother" them. Interestingly enough, the experimenters believed that rhesus males might prove to be successful socializers of infants because they were familiar with some observations on human babies that had been done many years before.[17]

Well before the discovery that isolation reared rhesus infants became incapacitated rhesus adults, psychiatric case histories showed that human children who for one reason or another grew up without contacts with other humans suffered similar effects. In the mid-1940s it was pointed out that babies left to be taken care of in foundling homes do not do particularly well either. Many die, despite receiving what appears to be adequate attention. Those that survive are often retarded and disturbed. To discover why, Spitz[18] did a pioneering study of two institutions with almost identical facilities. One was a foundling home with a high infant mortality rate and many retarded and emotionally defective children, and the other was a nursery affiliated with a home for delinquent girls, where few infants died and the older children were healthy, active, and normally bright. In both institutions babies were breast fed only until their third month. After that the nursery infants continued to be handled, dandled, and fondled when their mothers visited them, while the foundlings got little further attention from nurse helpers, who cleaned, fed, and sparsely ministered to their physical needs. Differences between the institutions in infant mortality rates and the growth and development patterns of children were attributed solely to what mothers do for their babies. Yet in a third institution infants paired with older inmates, adolescent boys and girls, got enough emotional warmth to sustain normal growth and development without "mother." This limited evidence suggested that any individual can successfully nurture a human infant. Mitchell and his colleagues reasoned that the same might be true with respect to peer-raised rhesus monkeys. Thus rhesus male adults could quite possibly succeed as parents.

Most of the available literature did not support the likelihood. Field and laboratory reports indicated that adult male rhesus show little interest in newborns, and often react to an infant's approach aggressively. Occasional references to males romping with immature monkeys, or grooming the infants of familiar and friendly females, offered some encouragement to the researchers, but not much. Still, as we have seen, monkeys in the wild vary a lot with respect to male and female roles in infant care, both within and between species. The idea of giving an adult male an infant to take care of was pursued.

Since males have been known to kill infants, special precautions were taken from the outset. Each of the four adult rhesus designated to become a father was visually introduced to "his" infant. Each infant (two males and two females) was placed with its mother in half of a large indoor cage. A clear plexiglass barrier separated them physically but not visually from the father-to-be. For a month the adult male was allowed to observe a mother and "his" infant-to-be together, without being able to come into contact with either. The mother and infant were finally separated from one another out of the father-to-be's sight in another room. Out of sight is not out of hearing range, however, and when an infant named Pierre was taken from his protesting mother, their distressed outcries so upset Pierre's soon-to-be-father, Mellow, that he bit himself repeatedly, wounding himself slightly several times. A week later, weaned to the bottle, Pierre was placed in a small steel cage which was introduced into Mellow's larger cage. What happened thereafter between the two of them was typical of all the male–young pairs that the experimenters created.

Mellow sat himself next to Pierre's little cage, resting his arms on top. When Pierre was taken out of his cage, Mellow approached him and touched him. Then both animals independently began exploring the area. After a bit, Mellow began grooming the infant. Finally, Pierre turned around, reached for Mellow, clung to him, climbed on his head, hung on to his ears, and generally took infantile liberties. After six minutes of tolerating this unfamiliar treatment, Mellow's anxious restraint gave way. He threatened, with open mouth, his tiny tormenter. Pierre screeched. Mellow pushed him away. Pierre fled up the sides of the cage hastily, then descended to huddle in a corner and suck his penis. When Mellow saw this disturbed behavior, he sat down to groom him.

In the next seven months, Mellow groomed the infant often, and Pierre occasionally groomed Mellow. At first, if Pierre's activities became annoying, Mellow would threaten the youngster. After a while Pierre's rambunctiousness was met less emotionally, and Mellow would simply push him away. Often Mellow's brief aggressive outbursts got converted into roughhousing, although Pierre was the one who initiated contact most often. The two indulged in much more rough-and-tumble play than is seen in mother–infant pairs, and whereas infants reared with their mothers grow more and more independent and come into contact with their mothers less and less frequently as time goes on, the episodes of physical contact between Mellow and Pierre grew longer and less rough over time. Their attachment to one another got so intense that when they were briefly separated after seven months, Mellow's rage was uncontrollable. He bit himself severely, cutting several major blood vessels. Without prompt surgery he would have died. He was reunited with Pierre very quickly, to prevent a depression that could impinge on his recuperative powers. Mellow continued to be an exemplary father, while Pierre continued to develop normally.

The attachment between Mellow and Pierre, as measured by reactions to separation, is matched by the attachment between the other adult male–male infant pairs. Far less emotional energy was expended in reactions to being separated and reunited by two male–female infant pairs. In general, the male–male pairs roughhouse with one another more often, for much longer periods of time, and with greater abandon than the male–female pairs. Nevertheless, the female infants, like their male counterparts, develop normally.

Bonnie, a female infant, was almost denied the adoption opportunity at the very moment of initial contact with her father-to-be, Clyde. Unlike Mellow, Clyde was a male raised in isolation. Although Clyde had observed Bonnie and her mother through plexiglass for a month and had done nothing untoward, isolation-reared rhesus monkeys are unpredictable. The experimenters—exercising great caution—tested how Clyde might treat the baby just before releasing her from her little steel cage into the larger one she was destined to share with him. To do so, they threatened Bonnie. Clyde's reaction *was* ♦ strange. He hit out at Bonnie's cage. If someone had not accidentally failed to lock the barrier that kept them apart, the two would never have been permitted to get together. But Clyde pushed aside the barrier under the eyes of the alarmed experimenters, and the two animals approached each other. Despite administering a few cuffs to the curious Bonnie, Clyde did little else. In fact, nothing much happened. Three days later the two were sleeping curled around one another.

Bonnie probably would have been given alternative social opportunities, but Clyde surely would have been marked off as intractable if someone had not neglected to lock the lock. Instead of the next months marking an end to Clyde's experimental career, they turned out to be a beginning. Clyde's idiosyncratic behavior typical of isolate-reared animals steadily grew more normal as his aggressive responses to Bonnie's overtures decreased and were replaced by vigorous play. Although Clyde continued to bite himself, and to sway back and forth alot, Bonnie picked up none of his odd patterns, and developed normally. Bonnie has shown that infant therapists can benefit an adult male reared in isolation, and Clyde has demonstrated not only that infant care is possible for a male rhesus, but that even an emotionally crippled male can provide enough warmth and social experience to ensure an infant's healthy physical and social growth. Evidently human infants and rhesus infants need much the same thing, warm social contact, and the sex and age of the individual or individuals who provide it is less important to their development than that contacts be maintained.

Although providing evidence to challenge those who doubt that adult males—even rhesus monkey males—can become attached to and care for infants or who believe that it is only the exceptional or feminized male who can do so, the researchers who worked on this experiment nevertheless conclude from their data that male–young interactions and female–young interactions are intrinsically different. Their prior experiences with laboratory animals had shown that rhesus mothers deal with their young somewhat differently than these adoptive rhesus "fathers" treat "their" infants. Normally if an infant is threatened a mother will scoop it up and retreat. Adopted fathers, with the important exception of the deviant Clyde, threaten those who threaten the infant. Mothers hardly ever get into rough-and-tumble play sessions with their charges. "Fathers" often do. Mothers get less and less attached to their infants. "Fathers" don't.

All in all, it looks like adult rhesus males are malleable enough to undertake parental behaviors barely hinted at in the wild, but these researchers argue they are still so differently constituted from females that maternal and paternal behaviors inevitably remain distinct. Two things prevent me from feeling that such a conclusion is warranted: Clyde's peculiarities; and the fact the comparisons being made between males and females center on mothers that nurse and "fathers" with bottle-fed infants.

In conjunction with another experiment (the last I'm going to cite before turning to the field observations again to see what monkeys and men do when left to themselves), Clyde's somewhat idiosyncratic responses suggest that more may be involved, once again, than genetically distinctive male–female responses. Chamove, Harlan, and Mitchell[19] took 30 adolescent rhesus (15 male and 15 female), introduced each individually to a one-month-old infant, and noted the responses. For statistical purposes they matched each male with a female reared similarly (reared in isolation, reared only with peers, reared by its mother), and analyzed the material to identify how much and in what ways male and female rhesus differ from one another in their reactions to infant rhesus. Typically, males reared by mothers displayed hostility toward an infant (one bit off an infant's finger) 10 times more frequently than similarly reared females, while the females groomed and hugged infants four times as often as the males. The differences between the reactions to infants of adolescent males and females reared in the company of rhesus their own age are less dramatic, and differences between male and female reactions vanish altogether among isolation-reared adolescents. Clyde's idiosyncratic responses to Bonnie may be due to his socially deprived upbringing, but they may be the same kind of reactions an isolation-reared female would have to an infant.

Which brings me to the second reason I question whether the data being used imply that adult males and females respond differently to the parental role because of basic biological differences in their behavioral-control mechanisms. At least some of the sex differences between "maternal" and "paternal" behavior the experimenters are explaining away can be traced to a single situational factor: nonnursing males are being compared to nursing females. This introduces a variable the experimenters did not consider. Nursing may well consume the energies and provide the body contacts involved in roughhousing. Furthermore, as infants grow older, they grow larger and hungrier, literally draining more and more resources from their food supply. The rhesus males and females being compared are not in truly comparable situations, because the females are food suppliers and the males are not. It seems highly likely, therefore, that a breast-feeding female will roughhouse less and grow less and less tolerant of a growing infant in her charge than a male who is merely caring for or interacting with an infant. Although the experimenters have ably demonstrated that male rhesus have the potentiality of becoming fine fathers, they have not demonstrated that the differences they identify between maternal and paternal behavior are due to intrinsic differences in the behavioral potentials of males and females. To do so requires that comparisons be made between males and females standing in an equivalent relationship to infants. We need some nonnursing "mothers" to compare with our nonnursing adopted "fathers." Until we get them it is premature to conclude that rhesus males and females respond differently to the parental role because of gene-based differences in their psychological makeup.

If, indeed, an experiment with nonnursing mothers is set up, since socially reared rhesus males and females are subjected to somewhat different socialization experiences by their socializers, it might be well to choose a female or two reared in isolation like Clyde for the experiment. Although rhesus females reared in isolation proved to be such inept and dangerous mothers that we had to reinspect the notion that nonhuman species harbor well-elaborated "maternal instincts," Clyde, it seemed, was a worse candidate for parenthood than any of them. (After all, he is male.) Because females reared in isolation are known to beat, bite, and reject their own newborns (usually when they encroach on their mother's bodies in unfamiliar ways, and attempt to nurse) is no reason to assume that isolation-reared females are any less able than Clyde to rear infants, if they do not have to nurse. Certainly, such an experiment would go a long way toward clearing up questions about whether the rarely realized potentialities for paternal behavior that male rhesus have differ fundamentally from female behavioral potentialities. Since the experimental studies of Chamove's group and Mitchell's team are open to rather contradictory interpretations, it is obvious that much more experimental work has to be done.

Field Studies of Paternal Behavior in Primates

It is in the laboratory that male potentialities for paternal behavior are being recognized as real and will be analyzed as to their parameters. However, it is in the wild that the male potentialities for paternal behavior were developed. It could be (and has been) argued that since laboratories are not "real life," the information on animal behavior we garner from experimental work cannot explain evolutionary events. I do not accept this. At any rate, the fact that primate males in the wild sometimes play paternal roles should certainly dispel the notion that paternal behavior in the laboratory is per se "unnatural." It should also suggest that the human male's capacity for interacting warmly and positively with infants and youngsters (or the human female's capacity for not doing so) are part of the primate heritage of behavioral plasticity. It is all too easy to mark off behavioral potentials that are not often realized as evolutionary "accidents," as having little significance for survival. A potentiality for male "mothering" could be treated as an evolutionary accident except for the fact that male primates who care for youngsters are far more frequent than most people realize. If rhesus macaque males rarely display paternal behavior in the wild, other primate males, including human ones, do so often. But rhesus males do have this potential, occasionally exercise it in the wild without benefit of human intervention, and contribute to their species survival in so doing.

Let me not, however, overstate the case. We can find killers of infants as well as caretakers of infants among nonhuman primate males. The range of variation in primate patterns is extremely wide. Some primate males have no contact at all with youngsters; others may be hostile or indifferent to them. Some groom and play with them, babysit them, and even adopt them. In some New World species males spend more time and effort in nurturing them than females. Hanuman langurs males who kill infants when they take over a harem are certainly no more helpful for explaining human male behavior and family institutions than babysitting Barbary macaques, considering that human males are as capable of killing infants as caring for and about them. Male–young interactions vary between primate species. They also vary within some primate species, as is the case among humans. It makes little sense to pick out a single aspect of human male behavior and trace it back to some single langur-like or baboon-like or macaque-like ancestral social arrangement, especially since the males of some species of these primates are as plastic and variable about the way they interact with youngsters as men.

Some of the clearest evidence for species plasticity in male/young interactions is found among macaques. Enough has already been said about rhesus macaques to illustrate that rhesus males are capable of varying their behavior in different environmental settings (see Chapter 2) as well as in controlled laboratory settings. What is known of the male/young interactions among Barbary macaques is perhaps even more illustrative of within species male plasticity of behavioral potentials. But so much has been made of male indifference and aggressiveness toward infants that we are far more likely to run into an analysis of the evolutionary significance of the infanticide practiced by a male Hanuman langur when he takes over a harem than of the male babysitters found among Barbary macaques. Local populations of Barbary macaques exhibit different patterns of male–young relationships, and none of these patterns came about because humans intervened to elicit them. One field report[20] notes that in one locale an infant Barbary macaque spends about 8 percent of its time with dominant males during its first twelve weeks of life. In another field population, each male protects one infant and continually ignores the other infants around.[21] In this group a mother never objects to the male's attention and takes her infant back at any time. In yet a third colony—in Morocco[22]—a baby is moved from male to male, returning to nurse on its (presumed) mother. Here, a male carrying a baby may approach or attract other males, adult and subadult. Together they often examine, groom, mouth, and fondle the infant. What rhesus macaque males can be induced to do in the laboratory Barbary macaque males practice, with some interesting social elaborations, in the wild.

Chacma, yellow, olive, and hamadryas baboon males all go in for babysitting young juveniles. Sometimes they "adopt" orphaned youngsters. Hamadryas males do so regularly. A male hamadryas will capture a juvenile female. When she grows up, she becomes part of his "one-male" group (just like the juvenile male that is usually attached to such a group), and his mate. It has been suggested that primate males who adopt infants are actually sexually motivated. This seems to be the case among Hamadryas. But a macaque (*M. fuscata*) named Boris who took charge of a female infant confuses the issue. Although she grew up to become sexually receptive, Boris never mated with her. Furthermore, he continued to care for her and for the infant she bore.[23] Boris' behavior has been held to tell us something terribly important about the origin of the incest taboo.[24] Since there are a number of theorists who believe that the institution of family arose out of an inherent human aversion to mating with familiars—siblings and parents—Boris' actions seem very significant. Interpreters of the hamadryas males' habit of adopting their mates-to-be argue that paternal behavior among primates has its origins in anticipated sexual access. Not only do these explanations conflict with each other (paternal behavior is sexually motivated, a paternal relationship leads to sexual aversion), they also do not come to grips with why the behavior of one primate species or group or individual is more relevant than that of another for understanding the backgrounds of "human nature." These explanations barely acknowledge that among nonhuman primates male–young interactions are varied, or that within the diversity characteristic of human adaptations men relate to children in diverse ways.

Research into paternal behavior is benefiting from past neglect. Awareness of the biases that prevented earlier investigators from paying close attention to the ways in which male mammals interact with the young of their species has made investigators self-conscious, cautious, and careful about their observations of animal behavior. They are trying to avoid grand and inaccurate generalizations, and are as concrete and detailed as possible. In a sense, those who are studying paternal behavior among animals are starting out with a clean slate, unencumbered by an accumulation of misinformation. Students of human behavior are not nearly so lucky.

Studying Human Fathers, the Neglected Area

Social scientists have been studying child care and childrearing for some time now. Presumably there should be a lot of detailed information available on how men interact with children. Yet the data we find more often involves broad categorical generalities than detailed observations of real events. And those broad generalities tend to distort both the quantity and the quality of the interactions between men and children. For instance, the characterization of infant care as a woman's province suggests that men are nonparticipants or incompetents in its execution. Undoubtedly, many Western fathers who have never been exposed to the ideals of participatory parenthood are unable to do much more with a baby than hold it. Nevertheless, I was taught how to diaper a baby by a doting father long before changing Western values allowed that men might or even ought to know how to diaper a baby. Few social science texts, or baby manuals, drew or draw men as normally capable of child-care activities. There are occasionally books that admit of the possibility. Occasional exceptions like the novels *Heidi* and *Silas Marner* deal with adoptive fathers who are well past the age when their masculinity or motives might be misconstrued by a public prejudiced against accepting males who involve themselves with child care. Although sentimental, and even saccharine, these novels do little to dispel the notion that it is abnormal or unusual for a man to be involved in child care.

That some real live men, neither widowers nor grandfathers, take part in baby and child care was extremely apparent to me in the ethnically mixed neighborhood in which I grew up. It was just as apparent that some parents beat their children and others do not. Because my experiences told me that there are ethnic and individual differences in both fathering and mothering, the popular American ideal or image of fatherhood did not strike me as applying to all males everywhere. But when I got to be an anthropology student my neighborhood and my experiences began to appear extraordinary, as, over and over again, the accounts I read of childrearing in other cultures mentioned men rarely (if at all) and usually only in conjunction with teaching older boys male skills. Why?

Although social anthropologists are trained to keep an eye on everyday events and report them in careful detail, they also learn to deal with social behaviors and social institutions under categorical headings. If one looks up child care in an index, or in the great compendium of cross-cultural data which is the Yale Human Relations Area Files (HRAF), one discovers summary accounts of responsibilities and obligations rather than of real events. Sometimes if one reads closely, men appear as actors in episodes which make it clear that in cultures in which anthropologists report that child care is women's work, men are by no means free of child-caring obligations. One reads, for instance, how Mbuti pygmy fathers comfort their sons during somewhat unpleasant and painful initiation rites.[25] One can discover that Ojibwa women, when they are absorbed in time- and attention-consuming tasks, like scraping and curing hides, are aided by their husbands, who take on the ongoing domestic tasks. (A husband in an emergency, it is said, even managed to nurse an infant.[26]) One finds that in multihusbanded Marquesan households, where women are encouraged to be as sexually attractive and adept as possible, babies are breast fed but briefly, and then given over to be cared for by anxious and attentive fathers.[27] Sometimes photographs and films depict paternal behaviors that are slighted in written texts. That Bushmen males care for their infants or cradle their sleepy or sleeping youngsters while they chat is clearer from photos than from the accompanying descriptions. What these males are doing is "child care," but it is rarely so characterized.

A Bushman father and his infant son. The activities men engage in with children are rarely viewed or classified as "child care." Photo by Richard Lee, Anthro-Photo.

In the anthropological literature male–young interactions

have been neglected as well as misrepresented. Anthropologists have been party to biases which contribute to the view that human males are "by nature" ill-equipped to deal with nurturing. These reports encourage the belief that men lack or rarely indulge a potential for assuming the highly lauded but poorly rewarded role of nurturer. Although anthropologists often recognize that what is "womanly" and "motherly" is subject to social and cultural modification, that goddesses of war and death, like Kali and Astoreth, represent women who are capable of being aggressive and bloody minded, they seem to be loathe to acknowledge that men participate actively in the tenderer human relationships *as men*. The idea that men might even be consciously socialized to do so seems to be downright subversive or contrary to the natural order.

How can we account for the neglect and distortions of male potentials students of human and animal behavior have been guilty of? Inevitably what a social or behavioral scientist sees and reports is colored and shaped by what he or she expects to see, knows about, and is encouraged or required to write about. Like everybody else, social scientists are subject to the traditions in which they grow up. The exigencies of Western industrialism gave rise to family forms and arrangements which are adapted to it. The family unit, in its several forms, is legally assigned unequivocal and ongoing responsibility for child care. Ideally, the Western family has clearly structured highly contrasting sex-role demarcations. Behavioral scientists brought up in the shadow of such ideals are prone to perceive these sex-role assignments as "natural" or at least as more natural than others. Yet many of the more familiar attributes of the tradition are not very old, nor are they characteristic of family units, in all social classes or ethnic enclaves. Nevertheless, most scientists are either born into family arrangements that approximate the ideal, or are reared and trained in settings in which the ideal is frequently realized.

FATHERHOOD, MOTHERHOOD, AND CHILDHOOD IN WESTERN CAPITALIST TRADITION

What is that ideal Western family arrangement like? It includes a father (one), a mother (one), and—if all goes as expected—one or more children. They all share a shelter. Father is supposed to be breadwinner, protector, leader, and sometime autocrat. [About twenty years ago he became (ideally) more of a handyman, pal to his son, and democrat, however.] In terms of a socioeconomic system in which few people have direct access to resources that can help to maintain their shelter, provide warmth, food, and other necessities, one or more individuals in such a unit must work to earn money to buy these things. Working (which nowadays is more likely to mean doing something to earn money than to mean expending labor and energy productively) requires that individuals leave their families to go to a workplace. There they sell their labor to get money which buys the goods and services that ensure the well-being of the members of the family. Workplaces are organized for efficiency. They do not usually provide space for or easily accommodate nonworking members of the family. Whoever works inevitably has to spend a great deal of time away from his or her family. He or she is unavailable for normal daily maintenance tasks, and is often unable to take time off to deal with crises without cost to those depending on his or her earnings. The person or persons faced with earning a living for self and dependents is in a peculiarly conflict-ridden position under these circumstances. If sentimental attachments and personal emotional responsibilities receive priority over work, those to whom the earner is bound by sentiment may suffer serious economic losses. For a variety of historical reasons, which we shall look into shortly, adult males have come to be designated as the permanent earners and breadwinners for a family. With the father role "set" in such circumstances, it is not in the least surprising that a concept of fatherhood that stresses tenderness and strong attachments in male–young interactions is viewed with suspicion. Ideals that play down a man's need to exhibit or feel warmth and involvement with his dependents reflect the realities of the amount and kind of interactions with youngsters that circumstances actually permit. Such ideals undoubtedly reduce the conflicts that men are likely to feel when forced to make difficult choices. Men must walk a line between loving their wives and children enough to support them but not so well that the attachment to the workplace is disrupted.

Subsistence needs alone do not shape sex-role ideals. There is more to the foundation of our image of maleness and fatherhood than an accommodation to the way a great number of people in our society secure economic survival. If what it takes to secure an adequate income were all that shaped and colored our role models, our role models might well be different. After all, a great many women work. Indeed, women make up around 45 percent of the work force and contribute to or are the main support of many family units. While presumably poorly equipped by nature to deal with complex machinery, women have "manned" typewriters, sewing machines, and switchboards in low-paid women's occupations for years. And if, after a day or week's work, they act toward children as working men and fathers are (realistically) expected to act, they are condemned as failed mothers, and unwomanly or unnatural. Our sex-role models mock rather than mimic these realities. They make a mockery of the lives of underpaid and underemployed men who are demeaned as failed breadwinners, looked upon suspiciously if they take on domestic and childrearing tasks, and accorded respect as men only for sexual successes that, if productive, worsen their economic condition. Our ideas of what men and women are, or are supposed to be, are not solely accommodations to subsistence realities. To what, then are they related?

We live in a highly competitive socioeconomic system. People compete for property, power, and prestige as well as for just the jobs that are needed to secure a livelihood. The nature of that competition and the uneven distribution of resources in which it is rooted are what shape our models of manhood and womanliness. The resulting model is a simplistic one. Men are, it is said, inevitably the providers, as well as protectors and aggressors. Even among early humans, this model argues, these responsibilities fell to males. Men's ineptitudes in childrearing were encouraged by their need to compete as hunters, while women, who were good with kids anyway, were too busy taking care of the domestic hearth to take on much else, became more and more motherly. Although those who wish to rationalize a social order often try to trace that social order back as far as possible, the evidence from living collecting–hunting societies is that in most, subsistence goods are provided primarily by women. The model of the adult male as sole or preeminent provider and breadwinner reflects the norms and measures of success in our own very recent socioeconomic system, and has little relationship to what happens in collecting–hunting, horticultural, or peasant societies. The model is, in fact, not a model of what real people even in our own society do. It is, instead, an ideal, a credo glorifying succinctly what it takes to achieve or maintain success and status in our market-oriented industrial–commercial upper and middle classes. The ideal of males as inherently unsuited for feeling or displaying tenderness toward youngsters while women are so suited promotes and perpetuates the legitimacy of that social system, and of the kind of family arrangement that people with a modicum of property, power, and prestige adhere to. Our notions of what men, women, and even children are naturally capable of are actually of shallow historical depth.

The idea that children are nonproducing dependents, to be cosseted, nurtured, and trained within the confines of a small family unit is a relatively recent one in Western tradition. It is less than a century since Sarah Claghorn wrote:

> *The golf links lie so near the mill*
> *That almost every day*
> *The laboring children can look out*
> *And see the men at play.*[28]

While grown men and women might suffer the ravages of exploitation, without undue popular concern, by the time she wrote public sensibilities were outraged that children should suffer so, although at first mill work was regarded as the salvation of poor children. The relatively recent laws governing child labor and woman's working conditions were motivated by the belief that children are not fit for productive work, that childhood is playtime and should be spent at home, that the proper place for a child is with its mother. Phillipe Aries traces the emergence of this view in his study of the transition from medieval to modern family arrangements, *Centuries of Childhood.*[29] Aries intimates that the transition began in the mundane decisions of successful merchants when they refrained from sending their sons (and daughters) into aristocratic circles as pages, and handmaidens. The children learned nothing as apprentices in aristocratic households that would help them perpetuate the mercantile fortunes they were destined to inherit, and contracting a marriage to a noble family became costly enough to wipe out such capital-based "family" fortunes. Consequently, the education and training of the sons of successful merchants was privatized and tutors were brought into the home. Dowered daughters were also kept at home to meet eligible merchants, since home was where business was conducted, at first. While poor people and landed nobles bid their children goodby at an early age, rich merchants made sure theirs could maintain the new wealth they commanded, and kept them close at hand.

The complexities of business were soon transferred to special workplaces, separating family affairs from business affairs. The world well-to-do merchant's wives inhabited became a purer domestic sphere. Daughters were trained in the management of elaborate households, in the virtues of sexual restraint, and to be an ornament among the many a successful entreprenuer might acquire. Sexual virtue, however, was more than ornamental. For whereas there was a good deal of room for illegitimate offspring in the open households and estates of the land-based medieval lords, legitimacy was all-important in the inheritance and transfer of fluid mercantile wealth. In the process of elevating the value of sexual virtue in females, the women of the merchant classes were systematically desexualized. Whereas the wandering medieval estate owner acknowledged the sexual proclivities of his spouse by locking her in a chastity belt to prevent her from going astray, the woman of the rising merchant and middle classes was told that the joys of the matrimonial bed lay in bearing the babes conceived therein, and not in the bed itself, although her brothers, husbands, and sons found those joys to be so satisfying that they were permitted to continue to make bastards where they could among the less civilized poor, or the more decadent rich. In any case, it was the sexual event her aggressive, go-getting brothers, husbands, and sons were preoccupied with, and not the offspring of their efforts. While having legitimate children became the justification for the existence of the woman of this class, with many servants around she might or might not spend much time with the children. It did not matter.

Truly professionalized "natural" mothering places the responsibility for a child's psychological well-being squarely in its mother's hands. It means more than arranging for meeting a child's physical and educational needs. This image of motherhood appeared, interestingly enough, when the labor market made it more and more difficult for hard-working and reasonably well-to-do merchants, managers, and professionals to get household help for their wives. It used to be possible to find poor women glad to get a domestic position in which they performed as a part-time or stand-in mother (just as male domestic servants were glad to get jobs as combination fathers, male models, and lackeys). Changes in the labor market and hard-won improvements in working conditions made this difficult. The moderate well-to-do wife, like her less well-to-do sisters, found herself alone and on her own at home. Advised of her natural bent for motherhood, the middle-class mother became an avid purchaser and reader of books (usually by men) that instructed her on the care and rearing of children. Because her husband earned enough to live well on and because she was both literate and did not have to work, her situation was idealized as natural, true, beautiful, and the measure against which normalcy is determined. Her late-to-get-home-for-dinner husband, in the meantime, equally assured that the aggressiveness needed to "get ahead" in the world of the employed male was his natural style, either cuddled and coddled his kids on the sly, or believed what he was told about his natural unsuitability for dealing with infants and children and kept his hands off them.

The challenge to such limited and limiting visions of what men and women, males and females, are capable of is recent. If comes at a time when the domestic lives of those trapped on the treadmill to success are undergoing yet a new upheaval. Researches into whether males can take care of babies got started after the relatively benign problems of relatively affluent women were voiced. When articulate, educated women began to object to the apparent arbitrariness of their role assignments—to being indentured into unpaid jobs for which they are overtrained—to being restricted to motherhood, or overworked and underpaid in the business world—or doubly overworked if they chose to be both professionals and mothers—middle-class researchers lent an ear to their outcries. Few noticed the earlier outcries from women of lesser social stature. But the treadmill to success is stuck. If there was little or no research on human and primate male–young interactions when this chapter was first conceived, some is now available and hopefully more will be forthcoming in a time when more and more middle-class men may find themselves staying home while their wives compete with other men for scarce jobs in a tightening economy. Studies of male–young interactions may be of more than academic concern.

THE GENERALIZED PARENTING CAPACITY: ITS SIGNIFICANCE

There is already enough data available on the subject to reject the easy assertions that males are ill-equipped to handle the domestic scene. The behavior of nonhuman primate males and females as regards child care, protectiveness, aggression, and food getting is demonstrably more diverse, flexible, and subject to circumstantial shaping than many have alleged them to be. That humans are behaviorally less adaptable than monkeys is hardly a tenable proposition. The man left in charge of the domestic arena may find the house husband's job either more or less worthwhile than he has been led to believe it is. Nevertheless, the primate and human behavioral evidence indicate there is no "natural" reason why he cannot do the job well.

Cultures outside our own tradition make excellent use of the flexibility of the parenting capacities of both men and women. In the next chapter we will see how much so as we examine some of the various ways in which sex roles and tasks are structured to accommodate to local circumstances in non-Western societies. By viewing patterned arrangements and structures which are rare, but nonetheless real expressions of human variability and potentials, the minimal common denominators that characterize families everywhere and define family will become clearer. From the descriptions that follow we will see that social definition of sex roles and the social assertions of parenthood are more critical in the establishment and shaping of family subunits than putative programmed sex differences in parenting capacities or actual biological parenthood.

NOTES

1. I owe special thanks to Janice Raymond of Hampshire College, who drew my attention to Pius IX's Constitution *Apostolical Sedis* (1869), which made a sharp change in church law by eliminating any distinction between the animated and unanimated fetus, and meted out the penalty of excommunication for all abortions. Until this document appeared there was evidently no consolidated "Catholic" position on abortion and considerable differences of opinion regarding the morality of abortion in early pregnancy. For further information, see Bernard

Ransil, *Abortion* (Paramus, N.J.: Paulist Press, 1969), especially Chapter II, and Daniel Callahan, *Abortion, Law, Choice and Morality* (New York: Macmillan, 1970), especially Chap. XII, p. 413.

2. Herma Hill Kay, "The Family and Kinship System of Illegitimate Children in California Law," in *The Ethnography of Law*, ed. Laura Nader, American Anthropological Association publications, vol. 67, part 6, December 1965, pp. 57-81.

3. See, for instance, Margaret Mead, *Male and Female* (New York: William Morrow, 1949) and *Sex and Temperament in Three Primitive Societies* (New York: Mentor, 1950) or Beatrice B. Whiting and John W. Whiting, *Children of Six Cultures: A Psychocultural Analysis* (Cambridge, Mass.: Harvard University Press, 1974).

4. Harry F. Harlow, "Love in Infant Monkeys," in *Psychology—The Biological Bases of Behavior*, readings from *Scientific American* with introductions by James L. McCaugh, Norman M. Weinberger, and Richard E. Whalen (San Francisco: W. H. Freeman, 1966), pp. 100-106.

5. George B. Schaller, *The Year of the Gorilla* (Chicago: University of Chicago Press, 1964), p. 213.

6. "U.S. Orangutan Population Gains Bouncing Boy," *Boston Globe*, December 28, 1972, p. 8.

7. Schaller, *The Year of the Gorilla*, p. 212.

8. Robert W. Goy, "Hormones and Psychosexual Development," in *The Neurosciences*, ed. F. O. Schmidt (New York: Rockefeller University Press, 1970), pp. 203-218.

9. John Money and Anke E. Ehrhardt, *Man and Woman, Boy and Girl* (New York: New American Library, 1972).

10. Gary Mitchell and E. M. Brandt, "Behavioral Differences Related to Experience of Mother and Sex of Infant in the Rhesus Monkey," *Developmental Psychology*, *3*, July 1970, p. 149.

11. "Mothers and Sexual Development," *Science News*, *102*, October 28, 1972, p. 282.

12. "Social and Sexual Influences on Testosterone," *Science News*, *101*, April 29, 1972, p. 281.

13. Robert C. Kolodny, William H. Masters, Julie Hendryx, and Gelson Toro, "Plasma Testosterone and Semen Analysis in Male Homosexuals," *The New England Journal of Medicine*, *285*, no. 21, 1971, pp. 1170-1174.

14. "Female Homosexuality," *Science News*, *102*, July 22, 1972, p. 84.

15. Harry F. Harlow and Margaret Kuenne Harlow, "Social Deprivation in Monkeys," in *The Nature and Nurture of Behavior; Developmental Psychology*, readings from *Scientific American* with introduction by William T. Greenough (San Francisco: W. H. Freeman, 1973), pp. 109-116.

16. Robert J. Trotter, "Human Behavior: Do Animals Have the Answer?" *Science News*, *105*, April 27, 1974, pp. 274-276.

17. Gary Mitchell, William K. Redican, and Jody Comber, "Lesson from a Primate: Males Can Raise Babies," *Psychology Today*, 7, May 1974, pp. 63-68.

18. René A. Spitz, "Hospitalism," in *The Family: Its Structure and Functions*, ed. Rose L. Coser (New York: St. Martin's Press, 1964), pp. 399-425.

19. A. Chamove, H. F. Harlow, and G. D. Mitchell, "Sex Differences in the Infant-Directed Behavior of Preadolescent Rhesus Monkeys," *Child Development*, *38*, 1967, pp. 329-335.

20. R. K. Lahiri and C. H. Southwick, "Parental Care in Macaca Sylvana," *Folia Primate*, *4*, 1966, pp. 257-264.

21. M. H. MacRoberts, "The Social Organization of Barbary Apes (Macaca Sylvana) on Gibralter," *American Journal of Physical Anthropology*, *33*, 1970, pp. 83-100. See also Frances D. Burton, "The Integration of Biology and Behavior in the Socialization of Macaca Sylvana of Gibralter," in *Primate Socialization*, ed. F. E. Poirer (New York: Random House, 1972), pp. 29-62.

22. John H. Crook, "The Socio-Ecology of Primates," in *Social Behavior in Birds and Mammals*, ed. J. H. Crook (New York: Academic Press, 1970).

23. B. K. Alexander, "Parental Behavior of Adult Male Japanese Monkeys," *Behavior*, *36*, pp. 270-285.

24. Seymour Parker, "The Precultural Basis of the Incest Taboo: Toward a Biosocial Theory," *American Anthropologist*, *78*, no. 2, June 1976, pp. 285-305.

25. Colin Turnbull, *The Forest People* (New York: Simon and Schuster, 1967), p. 217.

26. Ruth Landes, *The Ojibwa Woman* (New York: W. W. Norton, 1971), p. 141.

27. Marquesan household arrangements are discussed in greater detail in the next chapter.

28. Sarah Claghorn, "Through the Needle's Eye," in *A New Anthology of Modern Poetry*, ed. Selden Rodman [New York: Random House (Modern Library), 1938], p. 148.

29. Phillipe Aries, *Centuries of Childhood: A Social History of Family Life* (New York: Random House, 1962).

4

The Human Family Arrangement:
Themes and Variations
Among Food Growers

ADAPTABILITY AND VARIATION
IN FAMILY ADAPTATIONS

The biologically based behavioral adaptability of many higher primates, the capacity to be socially flexible, is clearly a heritage shared by human beings and evidently, the background against which human family arrangements must be understood. Flexibility and great variability characterize the most basic aspects of human behavior. We have seen that men and other primate males are much more capable caretakers of infants and children than most biological interpretations of family and its origins would have us believe. We have also discovered that women and other primate females are by no means intuitively motherly. Even the mating behaviors of higher primates are malleable, subject to shaping by social experiences.

Most of us recognize that humans are generally more sexually innovative than other creatures. The most behaviorally malleable of our free-living primate relatives do not persistently pursue sexual partnerships that are reproductively dead ends as some humans do, nor do they indulge much in sexual positions and activities that are reproductively unproductive, as we sometimes do. Most of us do not realize, however, that humans are so flexible that while some peoples view sexual activity as a joy in its own right, there are others who deem it of little importance and refrain from it for prolonged periods with ease. Herein lies an example of a major difference between the sex lives of humans and other primates which plays an interesting part in varying the shape of human family arrangements. Direct control over reproduction is not possible for the females of other primate species. Refraining from intercourse is but one of many methods humans have long used to free women from being tied down, at least for awhile, from the impediments of pregnancy and nursing.[1] What women and men are called upon to do, then, as regards mating and marriage and the number of children they have and how—or if—they care for them, is subject to manipulation, and is not determined by purely biological considerations. This chapter deals with some of the ways that humans define sex, sex roles, and sex behaviors as they go about building on their rich and flexible behavioral capacities, adapting their goals and social organization to local circumstances.

The peoples whose customs are described in this chapter were selected from a rather large number of possible examples. They were chosen as deserving attention here because the sex roles, marriage rules, and family arrangements they find reasonable and which have proved to be adaptive are, from our point of view, particularly odd, and pose problems for defining family. The six social situations described all involve peoples who raise food for a living. Their social systems, however, are not "typical" of gardening or farming societies. All involve populations whose descendants, ancestors, or close relatives conform to other arrangements so that it cannot be held that any of the populations discussed are genetically isolated and genetically programmed for an odd social adaptation. Four of the social systems presented are embedded in state societies. The Marquesans, with whom we shall begin, and also the Irigwe, are less directly articulated to state systems. All but one of the peoples described here accommodated their family arrangements to the circumstances they found themselves in. The sixth case, that of the Kibbutzim of Israel, involves a conscious rebellion against the norms of Western industrial capitalism and an effort to eliminate "the family" from society.

BASIC FEATURES OF THE FAMILY
IN ALL SOCIETIES

The inspiration for the kibbutz experiment came from the examples offered by societies outside the European tradition to which the kibbutzniks were heir. Many non-Western societies had arrangements quite different from those with which the rebellious experimenters were familiar. These varied arrangements not only indicate that alternative forms of family are possible but also suggested that family is a social invention which might well be dispensed with. Seeing family as an aspect of an exploitative system based on private property, the kibbutzniks sought to dispense with both institutions simultaneously. In their imaginative efforts to rid themselves of oppressive social forms, the kibbutzniks substituted new arrangements for old ones, believing they were eliminating "the family" per se from their outposts on the frontiers of a new society. What they consciously devised shows that there was little clarity as to what in fact constitutes family. Despite a superficial knowledge that humans have varied their family arrangements, little was done before the kibbutzim were set up to identify or conceptualize the features of family that are common in all cultures. Lacking an adequate definition of the family, the kibbutzniks created a form of family that is but a slight departure from that which they attempted to eliminate.

The common denominators underlying the institution known as the family and uniting into a single institution the unusual family arrangements described in this chapter with the more familiar ones described in Chapter 5 were examined in the Introduction and are, in brief, the following:

1. Every social entity that is recognized as a "family" is a subunit of a larger social aggregate, and its members can be identified as belonging to it by the people around them, whether or not they interact as a group.

2. These subunits are a regular feature of the social landscape. There are always some of these subunits in the social aggregate, although death or divorce may dissolve or disband one or another of them.

3. In all cases the subunit defines the statuses of children born or adopted into it, allocating them to a place in the larger social network and restricting them, via incest rules, regarding whom they are permitted to have intercourse with or marry.

4. While there are other sorts of societal subunits imposing incest restrictions that define a child's status and place limitations on whom it is permitted to marry or mate with, membership in them is determined by descent. These units (lineages, clans, moieties, sibs, etc.) endure over many generations. Family differs from these in that the "family" subunit is *generated* by the public acknowledgment of a "contract" and endures only as long as there are parties to the contract alive to maintain it.

5. The publicly recognized contracts that generate family subunits can unite as spouses, however briefly, people of the opposite sex, of "opposite" or different subunits or groups, or, as is usually the case, people who are opposites in both respects—males and females belonging to different groups.

6. Although marital contracts which link spouses may

convey a variety of rights and obligations, they invariably involve the minimum condition of a public acknowledgement that the two parties to the contract share a joint status as regards the children who fall under its jurisdiction.

7.   Marital contracts name names; that is, the two parties to the contract are either specific individuals or are represented by specific individuals.

With these common denominators in mind, the family is here viewed as simply a regularized subunit of a larger social entity, generated by a contract linking specific individuals and establishing with whom the children included in the subunit are permitted to marry and/or mate. The unusual family arrangements described below are variations on this theme. In each instance the social form represents a response to a particular combination of historical, ecological, and economic factors. Therefore, each description emphasizes those factors that appear to have played a significant part in the development and continued functioning of the local social system. The data are presented to illuminate these factors and are not organized to fit a standardized descriptive format.

THE MARQUESAN ISLANDERS[2]

The Marquesas are an island group in the Pacific lying 10 degrees south of the equator. The islands are rugged volcanic peaks rising precipitously out of the water and lack the surrounding barrier reefs that make fishing easy and rewarding on other Pacific islands. The location of the islands on the very edge of the rain-rich tradewind belt means that periodically the winds fail, and severe and prolonged droughts occur. The islands are warm year round, have very good soil, and are rich in the timber and other resources that make an elaborate material culture possible. Yet the islands pose some serious problems for subsistence and survival.

Narrow valleys with steep slopes washed by erratic rains, from downpour to drought, make the typical Polynesian garden of yams and taro difficult to maintain and an uncertain investment of labor at best. The Marquesans rely on fruiting trees (when a child is born several are planted to feed it for life) and breadfruit, coconut, and bananas, which supply the staples, require little work and take well to hillsides. In good years trees produce three or four harvests, in bad ones none. The first breadfruit crop in a good year is communally harvested, cooked, wrapped in leaves, and stored in vast pits dug into the rocky soil. Under the aegis of a local leader it is reserved for distribution in feasts and famines. The second and later harvests are handled by individual households, some of it set aside and drawn against when needed.

The Marquesans fish from the streams. (Some stream fishing sites are forbidden to women.) Periodically, local leaders who "own" canoes also organize deep-sea-fishing expeditions—dangerous and often unproductive undertakings. The fish and fruits the Marquesans depend on require brief spurts of intensive activity and little more.

Most of the rest of their time is spent in elaborate craft work, which ranges from making small personalized objects to canoe and housebuilding. The latter two occupations are intimately bound up with the competition for manpower that makes deep-sea fishing and large storage facilities possible.

The French, who planted their flag over the islands in 1842, brought little change in the traditional technology of the islanders, who resisted French intrusions into their valley strongholds as much as they resisted each other's incursions. The French did manage, however, to introduce new diseases which decimated the island populations. Whether an imbalance in the sex ratio is the result of this devastation or of other forces is unclear. That men seriously outnumbered women at the end of the nineteenth and beginning of the twentieth century is evident in the social structure described here.

Marquesan society, as it was observed, recorded and reconstructed from native accounts, developed ideals and norms of sex roles and social behaviors almost diametrically opposed to ours. These ideals and norms were reflected in several sorts of marital and household arrangements; households with just a husband and wife; households in which a wife has several husbands; households in which a married man marries a married woman who brings along her previous husband; and a variation of any of these three types to which unmarried men, "secondary husbands" who are free to leave, are attached. In all these instances the woman or women in the household share the services, sexual and economic, of whatever males, except for brothers and fathers, are around. Sexual activities also extend well beyond the household, however, for both men and women, and they begin well before marriage. Yet sex *is* a key to household formation in the Marquesans, although this generalized open sexual accessibility contrasts sharply with what we think marriage, families, and households are about.

There are yet stronger contrasts with our values and customary views of households in Marquesan domestic arrangements. Women do little in the way of subsistence or domestic work, and contribute hardly at all to child care. Babies are weaned from the breast between two and four months of age and fed and cared for casually both before and after weaning by men. When a child is big enough to get about and cadge food for itself, it does so in the company of other little children. From the detailed descriptions of Marquesan life garnered by Ralph Linton in the early 1920s we learn that women play an unusual—and surprisingly important—role in the organization of an economy to which they make no significant productive contribution. Erotic skill and sexual stamina are raised to high art and, as the sole preoccupations of women, demonstrate the importance of women as the center around which are organized the cooperative men's work groups, which keep people fed and housed.

The narrow valleys of the islands are dotted by well-made rock platforms, some 50 to 60 feet long, which form the base of house sites. Many homes stand vacant. Near an occupied house there is always a cooking house, storage pits, a special storage house in which are placed goods and foods tabooed to women and men who have recently had intercourse, and if a woman of the house is about to or recently has given birth, a temporary birth hut. These structures require a great deal of heavy labor to build and together constitute a property that is passed down to the first child born into the household as soon as it is born. In other words, children "own" these properties, and actually can, as Linton one day saw a nine-year-old do, force everybody to camp out. The person who actually manages the household, the adult who supervises and recruits both man and womanpower, is only a steward.

Since each and every Marquesan owns a breadfruit tree and a coconut tree to supply life's staples, and gardens are minimal management problems, stewardship involves supervising the first annual harvest, storaging and distributing jointly worked supplies, arranging for the building of canoes, and organizing occasional deep-sea-fishing expeditions. Stewardship entails recruiting, sheltering, feeding, and entertaining manpower to do all this. A successful steward is one who can attract household members, and organize their activities well enough to attract yet others.

People have to remain fairly close to the trees planted for them at birth, but unless they are firstborn children, they are encouraged to leave the house of their birth. Consequently, populations remain rather localized. Married adults usually stay put in the households of their marriage partners. The excess unmarried males are free to move from one local household to another. Children's groups roam freely through their home localities. Each local group has a distinct identity and commonly builds a dancing ground as a community project, as evidence of its unity.

A dancing ground is an extremely large rock platform, a place to gather informally in the evening, especially for teenage groups; it is also a place to stage formal entertainments, frequently for other local groups. Entertainments include feasting and erotic songs and dances.

133

These entertainments are supposed to culminate in public mass sexual exercises in which all share. Girls and women take pride in the number of men they can sexually satisfy. The imbalance of the sex ratio does not deprive anyone, guest or host, of satisfaction. Because local groups specialize in particular kinds of products (one group supplies yellow dye, another makes canoes, etc.) interlocal feasts often accompany or are part of trade exchanges, and while there is a good deal of hostility and warfare between local groups in the competition for scarce resources, letting a group one is trading with go away hungry or unsatisfied sexually is bad business as well as bad manners.

The organization of local feasts and entertainments requires a kind of super supervisor, a prestigious position that big households compete for. Important households rise and fall, people change their allegiances, local groups sometimes coalesce or break, depending on the abilities of household stewards to attract and hold contributing members or to broaden the groups they control through alliances.

Hostilities between local groups disappear when marriages with elaborate gift exchanges are arranged between the firstborn children of important and rising households. At such times new house platforms, calling for much joint labor, are built before the marriage. The original house sites of the newly joined groups are deserted after the marriage and left vacant. To move to a vacant house site is a sign of poverty and low status. Uninhabited platforms, deserted before the diseases Europeans introduced took their toll, stand as mute evidence that traditionally a pattern permitting shifting alliances and changing allegiances is old. The pattern probably developed out of the need for mobility when devastating droughts could reduce the population by a third in a short time.

Whether the strategies controlling the distribution of population and limiting births and thus controlling population growth were built around the highly developed sexual expertise of women in precontact times is not recorded in rock platforms, however. It can only be guessed at. When an aged and respected women takes pride in recounting how as a girl she was able to sexually satisfy the entire crew of a whaling vessel long at sea, one begins to suspect that the tradition of applauding a woman's erotic achievements has old roots. Linton notes that the Marquesans evidently knew more about birth control than their European "conquerors" and that while they were materially rich, they suffered from periods of severe starvation and population pressure. Thus lauding eroticism as independent from childbearing was both possible and advantageous, and using women as sexual specialists might well have been central to ancient shifting land-tenure patterns. In any case, whether ancient or recent, from birth onward the Marquesans emphasize sexuality as the focus of a woman's role.

Although Marquesans deny practicing female infanticide,

apparently few firstborn children are female, since Linton found only a small number of households "owned" or led by women. It might be, however, that few firstborn females survive the rather casual, and somewhat rigorous, care infants receive. A newborn baby is immediately washed in an icy stream and for a few months thereafter dipped in the stream several times daily. This washes off the dirt the baby acquires from lying on a floor mat that is changed only when noticeably or offensively fouled. It also removes the remnants of chewed shrimp and coconut milk poured on the baby's mouth as nourishment. Mothers don't like to breast feed their infants and cease to do so as soon as possible, leaving the baby to the constant ministrations of a male, usually its biological father, the male who was granted the privilege of inseminating the woman during intercourse, or to one or another "secondary husband." A petulant or restive child is quieted by masturbating it, and in female infants and little girls masturbation is used to elongate the vaginal labia, a sign of beauty. Toddlers are watched over because of the danger of kidnapping and cannibalism. To lose a child this way is an affront to the prestige of a household. By the age of eight or so, boys and girls are free to roam in unsupervised gangs, stream fishing and raiding for food together, sleeping in whatever household they find themselves at evening, snuggling down there among the adults. Prepubertal sex play and intercourse, a common gang activity, is open, with onlookers waiting or resting as the boys take their turns with the girls.

At adolescence, before the girls are married and settled into a household, these gangs become entertainers, decorating themselves for public performances of singing, dancing, and sex. Training in other adult crafts and skills begins at the end of the teens. It is then that young men learn everything from housebuilding to cookery and young women learn how to make mats, baskets, fans, and barkcloth. A man can only wear the barkcloth made by the woman of his kin group and cannot have intercourse with a woman whose barkcloth he may wear. By the end of their teens all women are married, either in elaborate exchange ceremonies or by simple agreements. Once married, a woman is expected to provide sex for her husband and whatever other males, husbands, or visitors he or she manages to attract to the household.

A woman's major concerns are her attractiveness and sexual skills. She has a long apprenticeship acquiring the latter, and plenty of free time to work on the former because her major job in the household is to attract and hold men. Good and ample sex, provided by women, and good and ample food supplies, provided by men, bring other men, increasing the size of the work force. A good woman for a household is an adept and accommodating sex partner.

Pregnancy, which ruins the figure just as nursing does, offers a woman one advantage. She is awarded the constant companionship of a man who serves her whims, and eventually may help her deliver the child. (The presence of another woman at birth is considered dangerous.) Otherwise, to a woman pregnancy is simply on onerous duty that is required of her by the household. Her baby may be given to an adopting household, which expects payment for rearing the child in order to cement an interhousehold alliance. For a woman sex is primarily worthwhile for its own sake, not for begetting babies, an orientation admirably suited to keeping population pressures down.

Interestingly, the difference between a woman's public and private sex life mirrors this emphasis on erotic satisfaction for its own sake. While public sexual service is a day-to-day part of a woman's life, her demands in private affairs focused on cunilinguis, breast play, and penetration when *she* gives the signal. In this hypersexual atmosphere, which deemphasizes affection yet provides for gratification, it is ironic that suitors can be turned away, and the denial of sexual access can lead to threats of suicide. A suicide for unrequited love poses real threats to the well-being of a household, and the threat of suicide is likely to lead to household support for the rejected lover.

Marquesan household and family life in no way resembles what we are accustomed to think of as "family living." The Marquesan way of controlling population (and they consciously nearly controlled themselves out of existence under French domination) is unusual in that it considers respectable erotic but unproductive sexuality. This is a very different approach to the problem of population control than that of the Dugum Dani or Jale, who simply refrain, without evident stress, from intercourse for as long as four to six years after a child is born, a degree of restraint Americans view as unhealthy and unnatural. Marquesan family arrangements are strange to us, but no stranger in most respects than those of the Irigwe, who have had to adapt to different sorts of conditions. While an Irigwe woman, unlike a Marquesan woman, is valued as a mother, a good woman is expected to leave her children.

THE IRIGWE OF AFRICA [3]

On the Benue Plateau of Nigeria, about 17,000 Irigwe-speaking people live in clustered settlements of extended family compounds. Each compound, large or small, has a number of garden patches and seedling starter beds near it. Scattered fields as much as six or seven miles from the compound receive these seedlings, and in them with the help of traditional hoe agricultural techniques, most of the vegetable foods on which the compound depends are raised. Men do a fair amount of hunting to supplement the diet. Although the average compound includes thirty-five or so members, all of them are rarely at home there at the same time.

The Irigwe are neither hierarchically organized nor subject to any centralized "chiefly" authority. Rather, they are divided into two main divisions: a "parent" or older division, and a "child" division. These are further divided into 24 subdivisions or sections, each of which has a centralized shrine and ritual responsibilities. There are "male" sections and "female" ones in both major divisions. The "male" sections regulate rituals associated with the dry season and hunting, "female" sections regulate those of the wet season and planting. The most senior male hunting section, that is, the one that is recognized as being oldest, presides over the three-day all-Irigwe hunt, which is the highpoint of the dry season.

The sections are made up of patrilineages whose members cannot marry one another. Marriages are also prohibited between those who have a common great-grandparent and between persons born into the same compound regardless of kinship. Thus Irigwe marriage rules cast a wide net over the countryside, binding it together in a complex system of exchanges and interchanges.

There are two types of marriage, and everyone is expected to marry not just once, but several times. First or primary marriages are different from later secondary ones in that the contract is initiated by the boy's family. The boy is usually very young, or even an infant at the time he is "married." His father approaches a friend who has a daughter of the same age and asks if the girl's father and mother agree to an engagement between the children. If both her parents consent, the girl's mother receives a gift of a white hen, or a new calabash, or, recently, cash. And that's that for a while. When the boy is big enough to do a good day's hoeing he is assigned some fields to prepare by his "wife's" family. Since a boy's relatives may contract more than one such marriage for him, he may have several parcels of fields to work when he comes of age. He, along with a dozen or so of his lineage brothers, puts in time preparing the fields assigned at the start of the next few rainy seasons. After three or four years of performing this service, the bride, who is well into puberty by this time, moves to her husband's compound and the marriage is finally consummated. From this point on, he owes her family no further work.

While Irigwe girls are not given in this sort of primary marriage to more than one youth, they are encouraged to become linked to several other men even prior to the consummation of a primary marriage. In secondary marriages the suitor himself makes all the arrangements. If a girl encourages him, he must seek out her father or marriage guardian to ask for her. The marriage guardian usually agrees to a marriage after checking with the young woman and making sure that she is not already pledged to a member of the suitor's section, or to a man of the suitor's mother's section or from his mother's natal compound. A secondary marriage is formally concluded when a payment is made to the girl's guardian, and then the girl is committed only to spending a single night with her secondary husband at his compound. She may, if she chooses, stay longer. Since girls are committed to living at least briefly with their primary husbands, and delaying the consummation of a primary marriage too long can produce a serious conflict of interest, a fair amount of juggling is involved in deciding on when a primary marriage is to be consummated and the labor of a primary husband dispensed with. An Irigwe mother of a bride, although not technically her daughter's guardian, often receives a substantial gift from a primary husband's family to ensure that a marriage with a secondary husband is postponed. Once a girl moves to a husband's compound, her agricultural labor and the children she bears to the husband offset the payments in kind, cash, and labor that were already made for her.

When a woman goes to a husband, whether primary or secondary, she normally can be counted on to remain at least from planting time through harvest season. On her arrival the husband gives her grain and a granary in which to store it. When she uses up this grain supply and can get another elsewhere, she may decide to move on, but when a woman moves, she keeps only the clothing and jewelry she is wearing. Everything else, including her children, she leaves behind. The husband she leaves may fetch her back the morning following her departure. She may if she wishes remain with him because she is not obliged to sleep with any spouse more than one night. Or she can choose to return again and again to her new husband, ultimately staying on with him. Since there is no such thing as divorce, a woman's former marriages are never terminated by her switches in residence. Thus a woman not only gets to choose all but her first husband, she can decide which of her spouses she wishes to live with.

Cowives as well as parents are proud of a woman who has a lot of marriages. Each of her marriages brings them goods or prestige or both. The pressures toward marrying again and again are enormous. By middle age most women have borne children for at least two and sometimes as many as six husbands. In order to accomplish this feat, women move around a lot while men stay put in their compounds with whatever wives happen to be there.

Despite the impetus for moving, women settle down for protracted periods with husbands for whom they have borne a child because a child's illness or death is attributed to witchcraft incurred by the desertion of a mother, the desertion not of her child but of her obligations. In old age women actively seek a permanent home, trying to return to a compound in which they have a grown son. Inevitably, the others in the compound are strangers.

The marriage-go-round that keeps Irigwe alliances, exchanges of goods, and kinship networks in motion discourages deep or affectionate relationships. An idiosyncratic couple, who wished to live out their lives in one another's company and surrounded by their children find themselves bucking pressures almost too difficult to endure. The woman's marriage guardian aggressively promotes alliances, she avoids them. The death of her infant and the fear of further witchcraft by her guardian against her other children finally forces the wife to go, although briefly, to another husband.

Ideally, Irigwe men and Irigwe women marry often. Economic transactions accompany each marriage and bring goods to the relatives of the bride and groom. Children are an important commodity in marriage and their patrilineage membership is secured and confirmed through rituals, which, in effect, ignore biological paternity. While great care is exerted to see that men and women marry people unlikely to be related to them and from many groups, the resulting network of relationships is sometimes a tangled one. An error in choosing a husband too closely related encouraged one young couple like the one described above to challenge the woman's marriage guardian and reestablish a monogamous household. But Irigwe husbands are usually polygynous. Simultaneously, their wives are polyandrous. A man's several cowives and a woman's several husbands never come from the same marriageable group.

There is no special anthropological term for marriage and household arrangements such as those of the Irigwe. Yet the pattern is not unique. Although recognized only recently, it occurs in a slightly different form elsewhere, among a collecting–hunting people, the Tiwi, who will be described in the next chapter. It is a system admirably suited to establishing and maintaining widespread flexible contacts and interchanges.

WEST AFRICA:
WOMAN MARRIAGES

As hoe agriculturalists, the Irigwe, with their farflung fields and significant emphasis on hunting, seem to be newcomers to investments in permanent and stationary property. This is by no means the case in West Africa, where a reliance on agriculture is much older. At the base of the bulge marking the continent's profile, a long tradition of fruitful cultivation, craft specialists, and extensive trade routes made possible large and complex states long before European colonizers made their way along the coasts and inland. Trade and capital cities were backed by hinterlands filled with villages and hamlets populated by food producers. In them proprietors of large gardens and compounds were sometimes—like aristocrats—polygynous. Multiwived well-to-do males participated in family arrangements different from our own but not so foreign to those familiar with the Old Testament as another form of arrangement that grew up alongside it. Polygynous marriages are described extensively in the literature.[4] Here I have chosen to discuss what is known as "woman marriage" because it better reveals the structural principles on which family is built.[5]

The family arrangements linked to West African woman marriages, a term that describes the sex of the parties to a marital contract and implies nothing more, are probably less startling to Euro-American eyes than the patterns of sexual relationships and childrearing in the situations we have already looked at. Woman marriages, in which a woman "husband" takes a woman wife, have a familiar quality in the way they are linked to individualized property ownership. A woman husband takes a wife in order to have children who will perpetuate the name and wealth she owns.

She provides her wife with a place to live. She supervises her wife's sex life, as she is able to. She is close at hand and involved in the household in which the children her wife bears her are reared. She can demand that her wife perform the usual domestic functions wives are supposed to perform, and she must provide for her wife in ways husbands in West Africa are expected to. The relationship between a woman husband and her wife is not a sexual one. It is, however, linked to the disposition of wealth and to the use and productivity of land holdings.

Land is not owned individually. Individual wealth is not derived from privately holding, renting, or selling land. Traditionally, men related to each other agnatically (through the male line) shared a common residence or compound and farmed an estate or land area with the help of their wives. As a group they prevented others from encroaching on the lands they customarily worked. The members of the group farmed where they wished on this land, moving their gardens around from year to year and using as much of it as they needed or wished at any particular time. Nobody "owned" anything, but everybody had a right to a farm sufficient to support the members of a family group.

In recent years laws transformed these informally recognized land-using kin groups into land-owning communal corporations with well-defined holdings. With changing opportunities for making a living in urban centers the kin-group estates have become sort of kinship-group community centers and provide the members of a kin corporation with a form of social insurance. They can fall back on farming it when other ways of making a living fail, joining those who have remained. Little has changed in the way individual rights to use it are allocated.[6]

Individualized wealth is measured in movable property. An individual owns what he or she produces, earns as wages, or gains from trade. Women and men traditionally raised different crops and made different items. Women were responsible for a number of things that were important in the traditional markets that dotted the countryside. Many of these marketable items became increasingly valuable as foreign trade expanded. A woman kept and still keeps as her own the profits she makes in the markets.[7]

Women are in the position of accumulating the kinds of goods, including cash, called for in the paying of a bride price. Land is not one of them. Neither a man or a woman can give land to gain a wife. Nevertheless, land access plays a part in marriage. A bride comes to live at the kin compound of her husband, doing most of her gardening there. As a resident she gains access to land neither she nor her kin group have access to otherwise. In the areas in which we find woman marriages, there are also men with several wives. Their wealth is evident in the fact that they have the ability to pay many bride prices and that their kin groups control land enough for them to use. Women who take a wife or several wives have to be able to pay for them in cash and kind, and keep them in a style to which they soon become accustomed since women husbands often take wives from land-poor lineages.

One of my Ibo students, the granddaughter of a woman "grandfather" describes with admiration the ingenuity of her widowed grandparent, who held on to her independence and kept her extensive and profitable gardens intact by taking a poor young woman to wife. The bride taken by the widow bore children (by whom my student did not tell me) to the dead man's lineage, since the widow did not wish to relinquish what she had gained through her dead husband. Rather than marrying another man, with the proud consent of her dead husband's kin, she exercised her considerable entrepreneurial skill in building up her already impressive wealth, keeping intact what she had gained by hiring help and using relatives to work lands whose produce she sold in the circulating women's markets which are spun like spider's webs over the area in which her estate rights lay. This African woman's efforts subsidized an American college education of not one but several of her wife's children's children.

A female husband need not be a widow. She may herself be a wife who has accumulated enough capital to establish a compound of her own. Obviously, the wife or wives a woman takes are impregnated by males. Sometimes these are trusted employees, sometimes they are the woman "husband's" sons. The compounds headed by a woman husband are not very different from those run by a man husband, except that a wife's "extramarital" affairs are conducted within full view of the consenting "husband." Otherwise, domestic activities, gardening, cooking, eating, childrearing, etc., are pursued in much the same way in both. The confidence of affluence pervades a woman husband's family and, if my student's childhood is an example, offers a pleasant atmosphere to grow up in.

A marital contract between women is, at least in one respect, traditionally more explicit than a man–woman marriage contract. Under a man–woman contract where the children will inherit rights, who they can and cannot consequently marry are customarily clear-cut. The children automatically are entitled to membership in the husband's patrikin group. By contrast, a woman husband can arrange for her wife's children to be assigned membership in either of two patrilineal kin groups: the one she herself was born into, or the one she married into. While West African woman marriages at first glance appear odd to Westerners inclined to suspect that when women marry children are not an issue, like marital contracts everywhere they are instruments for placing people in a social network of obligations and exchanges. The family and household subunits they generate are not particularly perverse. In fact, they differ hardly at all from the family arrangements generated by male–female marital contracts among other well-to-do farmers in the surrounding society.

FAMILY IN INDIA: THE NAYAR CASE

Into the complex tapestry of preindustrial Indian state societies were woven family arrangements of many sorts. Most depart drastically from Western middle-class norms and bear little resemblance to arrangements in West Africa, where women could often actively control their destiny. Differences in placement in the social hierarchy, regional variations in environment and technological and social adaptations to it, differential inputs from an assortment of invaders with various economic, moral and religious codes are all juxtaposed in a subcontinent that was divided, before colonialization, into small competitive states. Throughout the subcontinent were scattered populous administrative, religious, and trade-oriented urban centers. As a result of this diversity, in any one locality there often coexisted— side by side—a number of family arrangements, calling for entirely different behaviors. Some of the women in a particular caste were called upon to go to their deathbeds unmarried and virginal, while their married sisters were expected to throw themselves on the funeral pyres of their dead husbands. In other caste groups all the women might be married before puberty and expected to do no more than sacrifice something small on the death of a husband. Some old arrangements continue despite the impact of Westernization, but some are gone. We will look at only two of these many "family" arrangements, two that pose special problems in understanding what family is.

The family arrangements of the Nayars of the Malabar Coast of southern India (now part of the state of Kerala) are the subject of much debate and discussion. A complicating factor in much of this debate is that these arrangements no longer exist. They were reconstructed, by the anthropologist Kathleen Gough,[8] from the memories of talkative informants and from documents. Historical reconstruction, a common anthropological undertaking, is never more suspect than when it turns up the unexpected—social forms that cause problems in theory building. Gough turned up material that was both unexpected and problematic. Her description of Nayar life is viewed suspiciously by some authors,[9] who apparently mistakenly assume that firsthand on-the-spot reporting is qualitatively better than what an eloquent "native" recalls. It is viewed as accurate by others, who have sought and found confirming evidence.[10] As we shall see in considering family arrangements elsewhere in India, Gough's reconstruction appears to be a valid one. The pattern she discerns seems to be nothing more than a variation on a widespread Indian theme, one of several adjustments to the exigencies of the economy of caste, and intercaste relationships, unique in only some of its details.

The background against which the Nayar arrangement has to be placed is that of a hierarchical caste system. Rights to the ownership of land, to the practice of various skills or professions, to the gods one worships, to what one is permitted to eat as well as with whom one is permitted to take food, are all tied up with rules of marriage. The caste "system" insofar as it is systematized (its applications are far more flexible and locally adaptive than the ideology of caste suggests) is built around the notion that marriage and mating appropriately occur strictly within segments or sectors of the population which are essentially alike in social position and customs. (A certain amount of flexibility in the system is inherent in the fact that the caste affiliation of a particular localized descent group can be loose and subject to change.) People who are alike in what they own and what they do and which gods they worship are supposed to marry each other. Crossing caste lines in certain kinds of social intercourse and, under most circumstances, for *any* kind of sexual intercourse endangers an individual's social position and affiliation in this life. Violating the rules can bring about the "outcasteing" of an individual—removing him or her from the supports of caste membership. In the long run, violations of rules of sexual and social conduct also endanger one's future lives, the reincarnations of the individual, who may return to a life on this unpleasant earth as a member of a group in a lower and more exploited social position.

In the nineteenth century some Nayars played a specialized role in the caste hierarchy as manifested on the Malabar Coast. They were members of landowning warrior subcastes ("jatis" or localized extended lineage groups) ranked beneath and subordinated to the Brahmins and royal subcastes that dominated the region. Internally rent by internecine strife and competition, there was also chronic competition with neighboring groups that were similarly organized. The effect of all this conflict was that the services of men-at-arms were required. Adult Nayar males, warriors, were constantly "on call" and supposed to be "ready for duty" in these conflicts. In many ways Nayar men resembled the knights of medieval Europe, around whom grew up the ideals and poetry of Love and Romance. Like them, many remained technically bachelors. In Europe this bachelorhood was related to the fact that knights had no source of income other than court and war service. The promiscuous knight bachelor lived an itinerant life, wending his way from court to court, seeking favor, kingly and female, whence he could. Fiefs or landed domains were occasionally awarded a successful knight. On the Malabar coast the Nayar warrior was better off. He had something more concrete to fall back on.

Nayar warriors were the sons of landed matrilineages which maintained "taravads," estates to which they remained attached all their lives and to which they could always return. A rather special form of bachelorhood was the destiny of a Nayar male. He might or might not become a bridegroom or husband. If he served as a "tali" or ceremonial husband for a woman of his own caste, his life was no different than if he did not. As a ceremonial husband his relationship to his "wife" was a nominal one. He neither slept with nor supported her. In fact, he never saw her again after the marriage rites were conducted. Although it was understood that his sex life was not pursued in the marriage bed, if by the time he was thirty or so he had not established a more-or-less permanent relationship with a woman of his own caste, he was suspected of being promiscuous, seeking sex outside his caste. Most Nayar males evidently found more-or-less permanent lovers in taravads near their own, or near those where they were "stationed." This sort of bachelorhood, which was hardly more celibate than that of European knights, was enforced by Nayar marriage rules, not by the lack of resources to fall back on. Nayar warriors were not compelled to seek their fortunes. They simply had to provide services, and did so.

The taravads, or landed estates, on which Nayar men and women depended for their guaranteed livelihood were matrilineally inherited household properties. Among those who were well-to-do, as on the plantations of the American South and medieval fiefs, the landowners did not work the land. Much of the heavy labor that produced the goods and provided the services which the Nayars consumed was performed by tied laborers. The Nayar women remained on the taravads they were born to all their lives. There they entertained visiting lovers and "sambundhan" husbands from the time they were "married" to a tali husband (just before puberty) until they were no longer able to attract them. They performed no heavy labor outside of that involved in giving birth to the children they bore to their matrilineage, nor did they involve themselves in managing the estate. That job fell to the most senior male of their matrilineage.

The oldest surviving male of a matrilineage was expected to take charge of a taravad. He was given the title karnavan, gave up the life and obligations of a warrior, and acted as overseer of the estate for the lineage. He supervised the day-to-day drudgery and year-round work of the dependent and exploited lower caste peoples who were bound by obligations to their Nayar master's just as the Nayars were bound by obligations and birth to their superordinates, the Nambudiri Brahmins. While a karnavan might be a tali or ceremonial husband, the fact that he controlled a considerable economic enterprise in no way affected the fact that he owed nothing to a tali wife. The fact that his marriage to her served in part to legitimate the children she bore in no way intruded on his obligations to his own taravad and lineage group, or to his Nambudiri "lords." A karnavan was no more or less a husband than other Nayar males.

While matrilineal descent reckoning and inheritance kept Nayar properties intact and, through the karnavan, functioning, the Nambudiri Brahmins with whom the Nayar were associated reckoned descent and inheritance patrilineally. Nambudiri estates were kept intact by means of primogeniture. The oldest son of an oldest son automatically inherited the estate, preventing his younger brothers from vying with him for property rights or the allegiance of retainers. The Nambudiri attached a rather extreme clause to this system of inheritance. Only an oldest son, an inheritor, was permitted to marry, and obviously, according to caste rules, he could only marry a woman of his own caste. This meant that there were a lot of unmarried Nambudiri Brahmins, male and female, left. Their sustenance was not a problem. The patrilineal estate provided them with what they needed. Their sex lives were another matter.

Unmarried Nambudiri women were kept in closed households to protect their virginity and maintain the purity of their caste. Keeping them under surveillance at home was undoubtedly less difficult than keeping tabs on their much more mobile brothers. These unmarried Nambudiri males were not only permitted, they were expected to establish liaisons with Nayar women. While the pregnancies caused by

145

Nambudiri males among the matrilineal Nayar did nothing to upset the status quo of Nambudiri inheritance, an illicit pregnancy in an unmarried Nambudiri woman was a challenge to the social order and cause for outcasteing, even if the impregnator was of her own caste.

With this background in mind, Nayar family arrangements begin to make sense. Briefly, they consisted of the following. A Nayar woman was married in a ceremony to a tali husband before she reached sexual maturity. He left. (A tali husband, like a "woman husband," is not a sexual partner to a wife.) She remained in her taravad. There she entertained lovers and more permanent husbands with the approval of the karnavan. Sometimes she had several visiting husbands simultaneously, who carefully respected each other's rights. (A spear left by the door of her quarters signaled a prior visitor and that an intrusion would be impertinent.) When she became pregnant, it was usual for one or another of her sambundhan husbands to publicly present her and the baby with small gifts. If no gifts were offered, it might be construed that a lower-caste male, who dared not reveal himself, was her lover. Aside from the token gifts her lovers and husbands (ceremonial and temporary) gave her, men outside a woman's matrilineage contributed nothing to her upkeep or that of her children. As long as her children were acknowledged by a male of her own or a higher caste, her life on the taravad remained secure.

In quite another caste context elsewhere in India, although the rules of marriage again grant women legitimate sexual access and accessibility to several men, and men access to several women, the household and domestic situations differ markedly from those of the Nayar. Among the Pahari the concepts of "husband" and "wife" also take on unexpected meanings which illuminate what family is about.

INDIA:
THE PAHARI PEOPLES[11]

The lower ranges of the Himalayas from southeastern Kashmir across northernmost India and through Nepal are inhabited by groups of Hindu-speaking people collectively known as Paharis—"of the mountains." In the western part of the region polyandry is reported in several districts. In the central and eastern Pahari areas polyandry is evidently not customary. Gerald Berreman carried out studies among the central Pahari-speaking peoples of the district of Garwhal and also among adjacent groups to the west of them in Jaunsar Bawar. The physical circumstances in both places are virtually identical, the cultures of both groups derive from a single source, and in both areas the high-caste populations depend primarily on an agricultural economy and secondarily on animal husbandry. The high-caste working agriculturalists travel considerable distances to tend lands and cattle, while lower-status artisan castes rely on specialized crafts for a living.

As in most of northern India, land is not scarce but is valuable. It is owned jointly by men of a patrilineal, patrilocal extended family. Inherited lands are commonly divided between the males of a patrilineage who are "cousins" (the sons of brothers). Normally, brothers continue to hold and work their properties jointly. Women work, too, and contribute as much to subsistence as men. If divisions are made among brothers, the shares are usually equal. While a joint family is dominated by the oldest active male in the household, he cannot compel younger men to remain in it.

Marriage partners are chosen from within caste groups, and from outside father's and mother's clan. Fraternal polyandry is the common or preferred pattern in the Jaunsar Bawar district. Fraternal polyandrous unions involve a ceremony in which the eldest of a group of brothers marries a woman. The man represents his brothers, all of whom, after the ceremony, become the woman's husbands. If subsequent wives are taken, each woman is individually married to the eldest brother, with the same stipulations. No brother can remain a member of the joint family and claim exclusive rights to a wife. A woman considers all the brothers "husbands." Children recognize them all as fathers, and inherit from all without regard to paternity or maternity. If one or more of the brothers wishes to break away and the joint family is divided paternity can be assigned by lot, or a mother can designate to whom the child will be assigned, or the oldest child can go to the eldest of the brothers, the second oldest to the second brother, and so on. This form of polyandry (which is also found in central Kerala, nearer the Nayar) is readily acknowledged by the people of Jaunsar Bawar and regarded in a positive light.

The *idea* of polyandry, fraternal or otherwise, is rejected by Garwhal residents. In one typical Garwhal village of 300 marital unions, 85 percent were regarded as monogamous. The remaining 15 percent were polygynous. Every Garwhal family is careful to secure at least one wife for each of its sons, and each is ceremonially married to a bride. Yet sexual relationships are much the same as in Jaunsar, despite the avowed dislike for polyandry. Brothers in Garwhal have sexual access to one another's wives, just as is the case among their polyandrous neighbors.

The major difference between the fraternal polyandry of Jaunsar Bawar and the monogamous unions recognized by the Garwhal lies in the way children are viewed. In Garwhal every man not only has "his" wife, but he also has "his" children. The title to a woman's offspring is not shared. Nevertheless, despite this difference in values and the way marital contracts are viewed, household arrangements in both areas remain essentially the same. The joint family holding is an economically viable unit, and a child's caste and clan memberships remain the same under both kinds of marriage contract. For the property-sharing cooperating joint households in polyandrous Jaunsar Bawar and ostensibly monandrous Garwhal, life is very similar despite opposing ideals of what consitutes a "proper" marriage.

The subsistence conditions against which marriage contracts are set shape the realities of domestic and family relationships. The marriage contract itself appears primarily to be an economic device. In all of the situations that we have looked at up to this point—none of them resembling the nuclear family household we are accustomed to—a marriage cements ongoing economic interdependencies between groups in the community. Some sort of ritual or real exchange of goods and services normally distinguishes a marriage, which places children into an exchange network, from a love affair. Since love and marriage do not necessarily go hand in hand, since humans are evidently capable of living with all sorts of mating and nurturing arrangements, and since the family units generated by marriage contracts are frequently exploited and in some situations exploitative, social reformers have on numerous occasions experimented with modifying or eliminating marriage and the family. The kibbutzim of Israel were built on attempts to eliminate both. The unusual arrangement that emerged, the last family arrangement to be described in detail in this chapter, lays bare most of the essential traits that underlie the institution of family among humans.

A WESTERN EXPERIMENT:
THE ISRAELI KIBBUTZ

In Israel today there are some 93,000 people living in over 220 kibbutzim, collective settlements based on communal principles.[12] There is considerable variation in practically all aspects of the social life of the kibbutzim, but they are historically united by common roots and a common set of goals. Although the kibbutz is part of contemporary Jewish life, it owes more to the development of various sorts of communistic ideologies among the displaced Christian Eurpoean peasants of the eighteenth and nineteenth centuries than it does to early Jewish tradition. The same conditions that brought the Oneida colony into being, that gave birth to Brook Farm, Shaker celibacy, Mormon polygyny, and Amish fundamentalism affected nineteenth-century village and urban European Jewry, whose rights to land were also severely restricted. Like their Christian counterparts, they sought a land-based economy without private property in a distant, promised land. For Jews that promised land was Israel, and their rationales were, by the end of the nineteenth century, not Christian communal ideals but Marx's concepts of scientific socialism and the Zionist goal of reconstructing a Jewish state in Palestine.

Some of the early (1882) Jewish immigrations to a Palestinian farming life were subsidized by wealthy coreligionists. But the farming life lent itself as easily to cooperative management as to capitalist investment and bureaucratic management. Since private funding was viewed with suspicion, it was quickly dispensed with. By 1921 the ideal of the collective land-based communal settlement in which all work is valued, all work is shared and rotated, and all members are equally "owners" was turned into an articulated Zionist goal. The Twelfth Zionist Congress granted permission for the establishment of experimental kibbutzim and legitimized their right to exist alongside the private properties and cooperative enterprises also being undertaken in the emerging national homeland. Kibbutzim today are home to between 2 and 3 percent of all Israelis.

Like some of their Christian counterparts who settled in the Americas, the young Jewish communards found the sexual mores of Europeans to be built on "false" and discriminatory morality. Their rebellion against a double standard, and against the discrepancies between the romantic ideal of love and marriage and the realities of marriage brokers, dowries, and the commercial dickering for spouses which prevailed, was declared in no uncertain terms. Things were going to be different in the new world they were establishing. Nevertheless, their rebellion was grounded in a ghetto tradition, which emphasized that Jewish survival was dictated by sexual loyalty between Jewish partners as well as by a parental investment in children. Unlike the Christian Shakers, who saw in all sexual relationships the impulse to private ownership and chose celibacy as the road to true economic egalitarianism; unlike the members of the Oneida group, who chose sexual communism and group marriage as the antidote to concepts of private ownership; and unlike the Mormons, whose rebellious model of family derived from the Old Testament multiwived patriarchs, the young kibbutzniks emphasized the individual's freedom to exercise his or her sexual preferences. They rejected Victorian prudery about the naked body and at the same time embraced the view that sex play among children is not particularly desirable, so that children were brought up with a "look but don't touch" approach toward their age mates. The kibbutzim were organized around these sexual values as well as around the principle that economic equality is the result of communal endeavors and shared resources. All members of the kibbutz community are entitled to support no matter what their contribution. Children born on the kibbutz were originally regarded as the children "of" the kibbutz.

The young people who settled the early kibbutzim viewed the institution of "marriage" with a jaundiced eye. Since the sexes are equal, and both are or should be equally free, partners chose each other in the early days. Whenever a woman and man "agreed" on it, they simply requested a double room to share. When the community at large granted their request, they became a "couple" or pair. A couple wishing to discontinue their relationship simply requested single rooms again. Few did so, for although sexual relations between one of the pair and an outsider were not forbidden, they were strongly frowned upon and "divorce" was rare. The public acknowledgment of such unions and separations is no more and no less elaborate than what is regarded as marriage and divorce in many societies. By 1948 Israeli state law insisted on the registration of all marriages and required that a valid religious ceremony be performed, doing away with what appeared to outsiders as casual liaisons, and making divorce, rare to begin with, rather more difficult to achieve.

Early kibbutz settlements conformed to a general model. The communally owned, cooperatively worked fields lay spread out around the buildings where farm equipment was kept and in which the members of the community slept, ate, and generally looked after their domestic needs. Jobs in a communal kitchen, dining room, and laundry were rotated, ideally irrespective of sex, among communards, as were the field tasks, like running a tractor, which required but one or two persons to perform them. All able-bodied adults who were free of such jobs were expected to participate in the daily farm work. Meals were taken together and the dining hall often served as a meeting hall for discussions of kibbutz business, and as a social hall. Whenever possible single and double rooms provided sleeping quarters for adults. Children, at first only a few, were housed in their own dormitory-like quarters and infants in a nursery. Children ate, bathed, slept, played, and learned together in groups under the supervision of adults drawn from the community's membership. The tasks associated with caring for youngsters were among the first to involve more or less permanently assigned personnel and, significantly, it was considered unacceptable for men to care for young children.

In those kibbutzim that retain the original ideology of kibbutz life, children are still housed separately from their parents. In their separate quarters they are as lavishly cared for as the sometimes extensive facilities permit. The four-day-old infant is brought from the hospital to an Infants House on the kibbutz, where, with no more than fifteen other infants, it is cared for by full-time nurses until it is one year old. Then it is moved to a Toddler's House, in which no more than eight youngsters live. Boys and girls still eat, sleep, play, shower, and learn together under constant adult supervision. Between four and five years of age, toddler groups are combined. Groups of sixteen

On the kibbutzim men, women, and even children may participate in agricultural activities but men and women are commonly assigned different tasks. Photos by Louis Goldman, Rapho/Photo Researchers, Inc.

or so youngsters remain together under the devoted guidance of "metapalets," adult specialists-in-charge, until they enter high school. The children attend the kibbutz school, which is run by kibbutz teachers, and when they reach high school age may find themselves bussed to a regional school. Most of the day growing youngsters are with children their own age and with adults who are not related to them. The evening, however, is special.

In the Infants House, there is a visiting hour for parents when fathers may be present. While a mother is nursing, she shows up whenever called for. The older toddlers visit with their parents in their room for as long as two hours a day. Post-toddlers and pre-high schoolers may visit with their parents for two hours or so after the evening meal. By high school age these visits become less frequent. For most parents, it seems, the entire day is a prelude to the brief period in the late afternoon when they are joined by their children.

The parents, meanwhile, fulfill tasks in the fields, productive facilities, kitchens, laundries, granaries, packing houses, and so on, of and for the kibbutz. Since all adults eat in a common dining room, sleep between sheets laundered in a common laundry, work in commonly owned work places, share equally in the kibbutz income, kibbutzim cannot be said to encourage or further a family-based household economy. (Some less traditional kibbutzim now are permitting couples to have a teapot of their own as well as a radio in their rooms.) Interestingly enough, although a sexual division of labor was spurned as ideologically undesirable in the early days of the kibbutz movement, women have found themselves performing "service" tasks: child care, food preparation, laundry, and so on, ostensibly because they are no longer needed in the fields or for performing heavy labor. This emergent sex division of tasks has been regarded as a natural result of growing productive efficiency rather than as related to the values attached to affluence in the whole of Israeli society. Natural or not, "the discontent of women and the disharmony between kibbutz values and practices would seem to produce a psychological barrier to the open and genuine relationships between the sexes sought for by the pioneers, although the form of dissatisfaction is frequently expressed as a desire for greater "femininity" and familism."[13]

The developing sexual division of labor which keeps women closer to the nursery, and the tendency of youngsters to marry outside the age group in which they have been reared, are interpreted by some investigators as a triumph of inborn human impulses over the irrational "rationality" of the starry-eyed idealists who attempted to flout human nature.[14] It is important to keep in mind when weighing such statements the values of the vastly larger social nexus in which the kibbutzim are embedded and the historical circumstances that colored and still shape the development of work patterns and social relationships. Until Israel achieved statehood in 1948, there were 20 to 50 percent more men than women in kibbutzim, and in some early collectives the membership consisted of one or two women and a dozen men, men who brought with them the values of their culture of origin and "token" women, who sometimes protested their quick assignment to sex-stereotyped roles. Although women worked side by side with men in productive tasks, the ideologically less important service tasks were not considered the province of males. The situation has not changed. Today, no boys of adolescent age are trained in "women's jobs." Girls, on the other hand, are trained for "men's work." Under these circumstances, few women seek a career in "men's work," and the few that do, face the usual consequences of minority status. In the context of limited access to highly valued work arenas, minority men *and* women often are reluctant or wary participants in public forums and women on the kibbutz are no exception. Stuck with demeaning, routinized service and maintenance tasks, workers often wish for independent self-regulated work situations. For many kibbutz women freedom from work in communal laundry, kitchen, or the demanding child guidance jobs evidently lies in caring for their own small family.[15] That mates are sought outside one's own age set and dormitory cohort may involve an effort to escape tacitly understood status differences between peers of the opposite sex as well as reflect the nonsexual atmosphere encouraged in the dormitories, bathing, and play groups age mates share.

Few communalistic rebellions and conscious experimental departures from the monogamous nuclear family norms of Western industrialized countries have managed to survive or maintain themselves in confronting the hostile societies around them. Those that have survived like warts or beauty spots on the body politic are those which mimic most closely the sexual mores as well as the laws of the nation-state in which they occur. Antiestablishment rebellions are not always free of the influence they seek to escape. What is desirable, what is possible, and what is probable as regards family arrangements are by no means the same thing.

SUMMARY

The variations on the theme of family arrangements we have looked at cover a wide range. They are based on a number of different kinds of marriage contracts, from a simple informal consensual union between opposite-sexed partners to a formal ceremonial contract between spouses who never sleep with each other yet whose marriage allocates to children a place in a marital network. A variation on "family" arrangements not described here in detail is that involving brother–sister marriage or parent–child marriage. Both have been documented for royal lines in a number of places (among the Azande, Inca, Egyptians, and Hawaiians) and brother–sister marriages are also on record for affluent commoners in Roman Egypt, as are the property rights that went with them.[16] What living arrangements went along with these brother–sister marriages we do not know. However, even without detailing them, we can see how great is the diversity of domestic, household, sexual, and child-caring arrangements humans thrive on.

Marquesan households are built around women who contribute little direct work to the domestic economy—a few weeks unwillingly spent nursing a child—but who play an important role in bringing together male work groups. By contrast, a Nayar woman's husbands have nothing to do with the economy of the household she lives in with her children. Her limited household duties evidently include child care, but like the other women of her matrilineally organized household, she relies on her needs being met by peoples of lower castes, who perform the basic subsistence work. Among the Irigwe a woman is encouraged to contract many marriages, to contribute labor and children to the households of at least some of her husbands, and to leave children behind as she moves from one to another. West African women who take wives maintain stable households much like those of the polygynously married men of the society. Women, whatever their status, play an active role in producing both subsistence and market goods. In Pahari households both men and women work hard. Whether marriage is "monogamous" or "polyandrous," households are often joint, mates numerous, and child care shared. Monogamy on the kibbutz is maintained within the framework of a collective "household" in which men's and women's tasks are divided along traditional Western European lines although children are housed separately from their parents. Although the jobs associated with domesticity are organized in a manner quite similar to that found in commercial laundries and cafeterias elsewhere in Western industrial countries, they are performed by commune members, women, rather than hired help.

With these materials before us and keeping in mind that people don't always end up (or begin) as members of a family, the notion that humans have an inborn predisposition to the family or to one or another mating and nurturing pattern is clearly untenable. It is also apparent that while defining "family" in such a way as to encompass all the familial arrangements human beings have devised is fraught with difficulties, it is yet possible to isolate in the midst of diversity the several underlying common denominators enumerated earlier that unite these arrangements.

The peoples discussed in this chapter derive all or part of their subsistence from raising food. Some do so only to meet their own needs. Others garden or farm for sale on a local market which is indirectly affected by international trade, or for sale on an international market (the kibbutzim). Although the family arrangements they have made are all more-or-less affected by a tie to the land, they face different problems and have solved them in different ways. The solutions they have come up with as regards structuring the relations surrounding such fundamental things as having and raising children or working together or in competition with one another are uncommon ones. Their social adaptations show how flexible the family subunit is, and how the family subunit can serve a variety of social needs and function in a number of ways. It is evident from these few cases that the family can be the means by which properties are conveyed from one generation to another, or it can serve as the instrument for forging bonds between groups or both. The family may be no more than a legal entity, or it can be the focus of intense personal involvements and the unit held responsible for breeding, raising, and nurturing children. Family among these food growers serves these ends and more. Extremely adaptable to social exigencies and local circumstances, it is clearly shaped by cultural forces and built around common features that are grounded in culturally based forms of interaction.

The cultural foundations of family are equally evident, although not always recognized or acknowledged, in the diverse arrangements of populations that are not involved in plant and animal husbandry. The family arrangements of "simple" collector–hunters today (whose adaptations are far from simple) and those found in different classes of complex industrial settings, although statistically predominantly nuclear, are not as uniform as is often believed. The varied forms that family arrangements take in the collecting–hunting and industrial situations discussed next, and the similarities between the social ends they sometimes serve, are especially significant in a discussion of the origin of family since it has been argued that the nuclear family form is one to which humans are genetically predisposed even though humans sometimes have to overcome that predisposition, as, for instance, in the societies that we have seen. The argument holds that the male–female–young group is frequent among collector–hunters today because it was adaptive for societies organized around a foraging subsistence base, that a genetic predisposition toward this family form was consequently selected for during the three to five million years or more when humans subsisted solely as foragers, and that with the advent of industrial societies, our biogenetic predisposition has been able to assert itself because industrial technology has eliminated the need to modify what was natural for so long. That family arrangements are both various and responsive to current and local circumstances in technologically simple as well as technologically complex societies will be evident in the next chapter.

NOTES

1. Herbert H. Aptekar, *Anjea: Infanticide, Abortion and Contraception in Savage Society* (New York: W. Godwin, 1931) and George Devereaux, *A Study of Abortion in Primitive Societies* (New York: Julian Press, 1955). Daniel F. McCall at Boston University tells me that abortifacients and pregnancy preventives are also discussed by Virgil Vogel in a book on American Indian medicine published by the

University of Oklahoma Press and a book on African medicine by George Harley. The Birifu women Barbara Hagaman interviewed consistently claimed they could prevent pregnancy although they were not specific as to their methods. Birth-control practices are substantiated by the reports of Richard B. Lee (in Lee and DeVore's *Man the Hunter*) and Patricia Draper (in Reiter's *Towards an Anthropology of Women*) on the successful pursuit of family planning among the !Kung.

2. Ralph Linton's description of the Marquesas, which appears in Abram Kardiner (ed.) *The Individual and His Society* (New York: Columbia University Press, 1939) is the source of the descriptive data presented here.

3. Walter Sangree's article "Going Home to Mother: Traditional Marriage among the Irigwe of Benue-Plateau State, Nigeria," *American Anthropologist*, *71*, no. 6, 1969, pp. 1046-1056, and "Secondary Marriage and Tribal Solidarity in Irigwe, Nigeria," *American Anthropologist*, *74*, no. 5, 1972, pp. 1234-1243, as well as his paper, "Monogamous Hangups and Complimentary Filiation in a Polygamous Society," which was presented at the meetings of the Northeastern Anthropological Association held in Buffalo, New York, in April 1972 are the sources for the information on Irigwe life and social structure.

4. See George Peter Murdock, *Social Structure* (New York: Macmillan, 1949), pp. 26-44, for a general overview of polygyny and references to specific ethnographic examples.

5. The Ibo student informant who supplied the information on day-to-day life and the social structure surrounding woman marriage did so in a series of informal presentations to my class in 1969, and returned to her homeland the following year.

6. Paul Bohannon, "The Impact of Money on an African Subsistence Economy," in *Tribal and Peasant Economies*, ed. George Dalton (New York: Natural History Press, 1967), pp. 123-135.

7. For an interesting discussion of the power women derive from their market activities and other sources, see Robert M. Netting, "Women's Weapons; the Politics of Domesticity Among the Kofyar," *American Anthropologist*, *76*, no. 6, 1969, pp. 1037-1045; and Barbara Hagaman, "Beer and Matriliny; The Power of Women in a West African Society," (Ph.D. dissertation, Northeastern University, 1976).

8. Kathleen Gough, "The Nayars and the Definition of Marriage," in *Cultural and Social Anthropology*, ed. P. B. Hammond (New York: Macmillan, 1964), pp. 167-180. See also David M. Schneider and Kathleen Gough, *Matrilineal Kinship* (Berkeley, Calif.: University of California Press, 1961).

9. William N. Stephans, *The Family in Cross-Cultural Perspective* (New York: Holt, Rinehart and Winston, 1963), pp. 18ff.

10. Joan P. Mencher, "The Nayars of South Malabar," in *Comparative Family Systems*, ed. M. F. Nimkoff (Boston: Houghton Mifflin, 1965), pp. 163-191.

11. Gerald D. Berreman, "Pahari Polyandry: A Comparison," *American Anthropologist*, *64*, no. 1, pt. 1, 1963, pp. 60-75, is the source of the descriptive data.

12. William F. Kenkel, *The Family in Perspective* (Englewood Cliffs, N.J.: Prentice-Hall, 1973), pp. 126ff.

13. Kenkel, *The Family in Perspective*, p. 148.

14. Lionel Tiger and Joseph Shepher, *Women in the Kibbutz* (New York: Harcourt Brace Jovanovich, 1975).

15. Rosabeth Moss Kanter, "Interpreting the Results of a Social Experiment," *Science*, *192*, May 14, 1976, pp. 662-663.

16. Russel Middleton, "A Deviant Case: Brother–Sister and Father–Daughter Marriage in Ancient Egypt," in *The Family: Its Structure and Functions*, ed. Rose L. Coser (New York: St. Martin's Press, 1964), pp. 74-92.

5

Family in Industrial and Foraging Societies:

Nuclear and Other Groups

We can see from the situations already described that the independent nuclear family, a woman and man sharing a common residence and cooperating economically while caring for "their" children, is but one of many kinds of family arrangements, although its bilateral form, in which children are considered blood relatives to the descendants of both their mothers' and fathers' ancestors, is the arrangement with which we are most familiar.

In Chapter 4 we examined some horticulturalists with unusual family arrangements. In point of fact, 83 percent of the societies in which gardening (horticulture) is the dominant means of subsistence favor some sort of nuclear family arrangement,[1] and of these 68 percent reckon kinship, bilaterally.[2] Nevertheless, theorists who regard the nuclear grouping as part of a genetically based behavioral heritage make more out of the occurrence of the form among collector–hunters because the latter live—ostensibly—closer to humans' "true" nature and our ancestral roots than do horticulturalists. The majority of contemporary collector–hunters with technologies analogous to those of late prehistoric human hunting populations do indeed favor monogamous unions, nuclear family households, and bilaterality. The percentages—58 percent with nuclear households[3] and 68 percent with bilaterality[4]—are, however, far from overwhelming. That 42 percent of collecting–hunting societies do not favor nuclear households has not deterred theorists from arguing that the independent nuclear family form common in industrial societies represents a return to a basic "natural" adaptation.[5]

THE NUCLEAR FAMILY
AS AN ANALYTIC PROBLEM

Since the similarities between some of the family arrangements among peoples with simple and with very complex subsistence technologies are given a great deal of weight in recent theoretical discussions, in this chapter we shall examine various family forms in the collecting–hunting and modern industrial settings. The nuclear grouping particularly invites inspection as a social adaptation since anthropologists have expended far less analytic effort on the nuclear family arrangement than on more unusual ones. Family groups based on polyandry, for instance, are the subject of quite a bit of anthropological discussion. Many of the factors (e.g., economic hardship, an imbalanced sex ratio, property rights, tradition, etc.) which encourage people to build family units around polyandry were identified long ago, and at least one anthropologist has gone on to compare polyandrous family arrangements in different societies and reveal that polyandrous-based units are not structurally identical and are adaptive for different reasons in different settings.[6] Yet anthropologists generally take for granted that a nuclear unit built on monogamy is pretty much the same everywhere and tend to echo what sociologists who study Western family situations say about the nuclear group, noting that it is common in societies where people must move to make a living.

The nuclear family has been analyzed over and over again by sociologists and other behavioral scientists. Its manifestations in our society have been investigated from a number of perspectives. In recent years sociologists have been asking: What does the family (meaning the bilateral nuclear unit) accomplish for the society at large? or put another way: What function or functions does the family (meaning the bilateral nuclear unit) serve? Sociologists have had no difficulty agreeing that the kind of family unit we favor is responsible—in our society—for fulfilling some very fundamental societal "functions" (e.g., reproduction, nurturance, socialization, etc.). However, as we have already seen, these "functions of family" are not, as is implied or stated, universally attributable to families everywhere. Nonnuclear family units and, as we shall shortly see, even nuclear family groups vary as to whether or not members of the family are called upon to reproduce, or nurture, or socialize other family members.

The nuclear form of family, although not always recognized as such, was the object of similar nineteenth-century discussion. A few nineteenth-century theoreticians, primarily radical ones, viewed the family everywhere as part and parcel of exploitative socioeconomic systems. Others regarded only its Euro-American nuclear variant as an excresence of capitalism and private property. Many sought to change or abolish the family by eliminating the sexual division of labor and/or private property. The proselytizers of the 1960s and 1970s who are calling for "open marriages" or communal households or recognition of single-parent and homosexual-pair families, or just "alternative-life styles" are their heirs. Generally far less concerned with economic and social structural issues, they tend to focus on problems of psychosexual adjustment and personal fulfillment. They differ from earlier writers in that their rhetoric is usually directed at middle-class sophisticates rather than at the more exploited members of our society, who, as will become clear, often practice alternative life-styles anyway.

It is of interest here that despite the attractiveness of the century-old call for change and sexual liberation in Western society, and despite a number of significant and successful socialist revolutions, the independent nuclear family form remains the prevailing, although by no means the only, form of family household in industrialized and industrializing socialist and capitalist nations alike. The form is also the most frequent, but not the only, family arrangement among recent collector–hunters who occupy areas marginal to expansionist industrial colonization, and are little affected by the norms and laws of the colonizers. By examining various family arrangements in our complex social setting and also those found in the far simpler social networks of collector–hunters, the sorts of economic and social factors that generate independent nuclear families—and other groupings which are expressions of the principal features underlying human family arrangements—will become evident.

Historical data could reveal much about both of these situations, but there are no written records to speak of that could provide details on the former circumstances of recent foragers. Consequently, although this chapter presents an historical overview of the circumstances leading to the prevalence of the independent nuclear family form in Euro-American society, little history is alluded to in the discussions describing the nuclear and nonnuclear family arrangements of the two collector–hunter populations. The distinctively different arrangements among the Andamanese and Tiwi are examined solely in terms of an ecological-functionalist perspective—that is, as to how and why they are adaptive to local circumstances. The discussion is designed to underline the points made in the model of family origins presented in the Introduction and final chapters of this book, which have to do with how and why family as an institution with variant manifestations was adaptive for and adopted by our early ancestors. We begin with the present and its roots, to arrive at an idea of the kinds of social evolutionary factors that probably were operative in the distant past.

FAMILY FORMS IN THE WEST:
THEIR LEGAL BACKGROUND

The nuclear family form is supported by law as well as considered the ideal form of family wherever Western traditions and capitalist and industrial influences have come to dominate. By law, marriages are monogamous and a person is permitted but one spouse at a time. Only a male and female can legally "get married," and then only as long as the two meet certain requirements. The pair, for one

Entrance to a bank in San Diego. The nuclear form of family is idealized in Western industrial capitalist societies. Photo by John Bishop.

thing, cannot be "too" closely related, although the definition of how close is "too" close varies. In the United States it varies from state to state. Some permit a marriage between first cousins or with an uncle or aunt. Others do not. British law once prohibited a woman marrying her former husband's brother and a man marrying a former wife's sister on the grounds that such marriages were incestuous.[7] In all Westernized settings, however, sexual relations and marriages between siblings or between parents and children are not countenanced, nor is marriage or intercourse with a prepubescent child legal. The age at which a child is considered postpubescent or legally an adult varies, however, as do such things as the waiting period between applications for marriage and confirmation of marriage. Blood tests and other such paraphernalia, like religious ceremonies in addition to or as a substitute for state licensing and ceremonials, are matters of local statute, as are the divorce laws, which are changing rapidly and defy summation or generalization.

In industrial societies, when a man and woman get married their parents no longer are legally accountable for maintaining either one of them, and the married pair is put in the position of having to maintain itself in a household of its own. The law confers on the new spouses sexual access to one another and special rights in each other's productivity, excluding nonspouses from making sexual or economic demands on either of them.[8] In law, the married couple is also held responsible for providing for the children recorded as born to them, although it says little about how they fulfill their responsibilities. (Battered and cruelly handled children still have few rights and practically no legal protection from parents.) Furthermore, the inheritance status of children, male and female, firstborn and subsequent, of divorced parents and, in some places, even of unwed parents has been or is being equalized. Thus, the legal systems of Western industrialized state societies call for monogamy, encourage but do not insist on the establishment of permanent independent nuclear family households, and regard all children in a family as being equally entitled to their deceased parents' goods and as responsible for their own support upon reaching adulthood, when they become free to marry without parental consent. By contrast, collecting–hunting societies, of which the two examined later in this chapter are typical in this respect, are not state societies with enforcement agencies that make people obey "the law." Their family arrangements are governed by customary practices and are directly and often rapidly shaped and reshaped to fit changing social realities.

Laws are written and rewritten and accommodate to changing realities, too, but more slowly. In Western societies social realities have been in flux for several centuries. So are the laws that affect our family forms. What were the changing social realities that generated the legal framework of family? Did social patterns established among the rich, or the poor, or those in the middle affect these laws in any special ways? These are the kinds of questions we must ask in dealing with complex, hierarchically ordered social systems.

As Phillipe Aries points out in his *Centuries of Childhood*,[9] the foundations of the modern Western family as a "privatized" entity were laid in the households of well-to-do medieval merchant capitalists. At first the big houses of these merchants emulated those of the aristocracy. Kinfolk, business associates, and domestic staff mingled en masse. But rich merchants, unlike landed aristocrats, derived their wealth and power from business transactions, movable property and money. Better to reinvest the wealth they acquired in their business in order to accumulate more wealth than to distribute it to dependent kin. So the customary support previously owed to peripheral kinfolk ceased being mandated. Better to keep family wealth intact and train sons to take over the business than to let children run free among an array of relatives and hangers on—as did Romeo Montague whilst he pursued Juliet Capulet. So inheritance laws on partible wealth were rewritten. Childhood as a training period for an adulthood devoted to business began to be important for the children of the well-to-do merchants. Special tutors provided the requisite instruction so that sons of merchants came to follow a different trajectory than the children of kinspeople "not in the business;" the children of domestic servants, who remained unlettered; and the children of aristocrats. It was also soon more efficient to conduct business in special work places, where records and goods could be stored and kept track of, than to conduct business affairs within the household. So the place of business ceased to be the businessman's home. In the burgeoning work places merchant capitalists issued orders to male employees. At home their wives and daughters were entrusted with overseeing the male as well as the female servants, and whatever poor relatives remained in residence. Of necessity, civil and corporate law became differentiated. "Family" as owners-inheritors, "home" as the place enjoyed by those privileged enough to be owners, and "childhood" as a clearly demarcated period of training for adulthood emerged in this segment of the population. Yet the households of well-to-do merchants and financiers are *not* the seed bed out of which grew the independent nuclear family group.

Upper-Income Families

Right up to the present day the residences of the well-to-do— although separated from their offices and places of business—are domestic complexes rather than independent nuclear family households. The Kennedy "compound" at Hyannis is an obvious case in point, as are the Rockefeller estates—managed by employees—and the numerous town houses and "country places" of corporate executives and their wives and children. The very young children of the rich are not wheeled about in the supermarket by a mother who shops for the groceries that keep household members fed and clean. They have nurses. When older, they may play touch football on the front lawn with their father during the summer, but they are likely to spend the winter months in boarding schools, and like their parents, be "at home" only during vacation periods. The "family" compound is usually but one of several residences, a temporary one that acts as a community center for an extended kin group. These several residences are not nuclear households in form, nor are they independent entities.

There are a few, possibly very few, younger couples with assured or comfortable incomes and progressive and egalitarian proclivities, who are innovating on this pattern. Liberally minded, well-educated, and well-off, they find employing servants distasteful and living cheek by jowl with parents, even occasionally, uncomfortable. With funds enough to finance a big house (either one divided into separate apartments or one with lots of bedrooms and a large kitchen and dining room), they are experimenting with share-the-work tenancy arrangements. (These, by the way, usually involve tenants who are as well-educated as the house owners, although often not as well-heeled.) A young couple I know owns a two-family house. They live in one apartment and rent the other. They choose as tenants a couple—usually graduate students—with children. In exchange for a low rental fee they ask, and get, free babysitting for their child, and occasional help in household tasks (mowing the lawn, raking leaves, etc.). The tenants are invited to parties, and are treated as equals. Similarly, a friend of mine who is a divorced working mother added an apartment to her old farmhouse. She rents only to couples or singles who can be counted on to work on the house and grounds. (Her latest tenants have a garden and are raising a pig, goats, and some chickens on the old farm property.) They are expected to remain "around the place" as much as possible and provide company and care for her two teenagers. The Jane Fonda–Tom Hayden household in 1975 included, along with the pair and their children, another couple with a child, and the woman who managed the Hayden election campaign. All contributed to the general housework.[10] Evidently those with the wherewithal to do so extend or expand on the nuclear family group in one way or another. The fact that an extended household of some form or other has persisted over time among these well-to-do groups is noteworthy. The independent nuclear family household, the model family and idealized model of family arrangement in industrialized society, it seems, does not have its roots among the rich.

The Family Among the Poor—Past and Present

At the other end of the economic spectrum are the very poor who once could not and still cannot afford the luxury of independent nuclear households or the exclusive sexual bonds associated with it. Tied serfs and peasants of the preindustrial era in Europe,[11] although married monogamously under church rules calling for chastity outside of marriage, often owed their landlord the right to sleep with a bride on her wedding night (droit du seigneur) and were not in the position to contest what happened at other times. Peasant parents who lived long enough to rear a child or two to adulthood made sure their one-room hovels included at least a son or daughter who was encouraged to postpone marriage but had to carry on and perform the tasks and duties owed the lord alongside youngsters apprenticed to the household. On the death of either parent the child married and took charge. The couples' other children were apprenticed at the age of seven or thereabouts and sent off to live with other peasant families or in the workshop homes of village and city craft guildsmen. Few returned as adults to their parental home.

From the beginning of the seventeenth century onward, enclosure acts denying grazing, gathering, and woodcutting rights on common lords' lands, and substituting rent payments for work duties forced many tillers of the soil away from the estates on which they had once provided for themselves and their masters. The estates were turned into ranches and farms, using hired help paid in money wages to produce goods for profitable sale in the burgeoning cities. The evicted men, women, and children turned wherever they could, seeking work in towns and parishes and cities. Parish welfare roles were soon strained. Parishes ceased to provide for the care of illegitimate children, who were, until this period, native born, few in number, easily apprenticed, and not costly. The unwed mother seeking shelter in a strange parish found herself, like all women, excluded from wage work, and in addition found that she was responsible for providing for the children born to her. Among those who roamed the land in search of work, marriage became rare, desertion frequent, and prostitution, child abandonment, and starvation common. The work force could not reproduce itself, and recruits to it were constantly sought from newly landless peoples, immigrants into the industrializing and ultimately industrialized cities.[12] By the early twentieth century most Western European countries had established doles and welfare systems and marriage became possible again for the unemployed and underemployed. Divorce remained out of their reach, however, and desertion the only recourse open to those who were unable to cope with the insoluble problems their marriages were subject to.

The principle was established some time ago that the unwed and deserted mother is responsible for her children. Later, doles and welfare gave poor women with children increased survival chances. The simple fact that these women when helped by stipends from the community could survive with their children permitted this marginal segment of the population to develop "alternative" forms of family. Currently, while mothers are bound to children, fathers under stress are not. This is being viewed as costly to taxpayers. Today in the United States: "Deserting welfare fathers cost taxpayers $1.3 million a year . . . . New rules require states to begin establishing the paternity of welfare children born out of wedlock and locate deserting parents and collect child support payments . . . . Welfare mothers will be entitled to collect a bounty [sic] of up to twenty dollars a month for the first fifteen months for help in establishing paternity."[13] Establishing the principle that unwed fathers are as responsible for children as unwed mothers is designed to enforce the establishment of permanent nuclear family households among today's poor, for these marginal people have been devising strategies of family living that impinge on the precepts as well as the pocketbooks of the taxpaying majority whose nuclear families are held up as the model of "right living."

The permanently unemployed, those underemployed, and immigrants and others who are marginally related to the economy—our society's reservoir of potentially employable personnel—pursue the dream of an independent nuclear family household often, but with only partial success.[14] What the recent poor do about family arrangements is varied. Carol Stack[15] lays bare how poor black people living in an urban industrial setting manage to feed themselves and their children. The nuclear family group is, at best, an ephemeral arrangement for many of them. Men can barely sustain themselves in the job market. Women do not do any better at earning a living but may work a bit more regularly, or get Aid to Dependent Children. Whether or not they bother to register their liaisons as marriages, men frequently find themselves unable to contribute to the woman whose children they call their own. Households change personnel. Women "go home to mother." Men, too, go home to mother. At home are parents and/or siblings who are able to contribute to one another financially and emotionally. In a household breakup the woman usually keeps the children, for she can count on some minimal support from the government. Her man cannot. The man may give her gifts for them when he can. If a woman maintains a household of her own, she can and may take a new man and/or shelter those of her kin or quasi-kin who need sheltering. She receives help from them in return. Friends are as reliable as relatives in this mutual support network. They too help, and even may take the kids for a few days. If a woman and her man find it impossible to live with each other for economic and emotional reasons, alternative arrangements are readily made. One does what one has to—to survive. But these alternatives are a last resort. Most (about 60 percent) poor families, black as well as white, are nuclear in form, in that a husband and wife live together under one roof with their children and work hard to remain together.

Poor white immigrants from Europe to America also have

resorted to "alternatives" to the independent nuclear family. An acquaintance of mine, the daughter of Hungarian-born parents, comes from a mill town in Pennsylvania. Her mother, widowed young, brought her up with the aid of aunts and uncles who lived in their neighborhood and worked in the factories. Whoever worked in this scattered extended kin group helped those not working. My acquaintance now sends presents to her uncles and aunts regularly and is helping her nephews and nieces, who are scattered all over the United States seeking schooling and upward mobility.

In my own background are Russian Jewish immigrant parents who had few relatives in this country. Our neighbors, in a building with fifty apartments, were similarly situated. Each apartment housed a nuclear group, but the support system, economic and emotional, was not nuclear. My father, a baker, brought home large quantities of bread and cake, more than we could eat. Our neighbors ate what we did not. The old lady who lived down the hall sewed clothes for me, and one of her daughters, who worked for a publisher, lent me books. Their phone was closer than the one downstairs in the lobby of the building and could be used in "an emergency." The man across the hall was an auctioneer for a wholesale fruit concern. He brought fruit in season. His wife looked in on my brother or me when my parents went out. From other neighbors to whom we gave bread and cake we got many things—whatever goods they could bring home from their jobs, or TV-viewing privileges, or shelter when our apartment was being painted or a family argument erupted, and "no interest" loans, which we made to them, too. The domestic economy of the apartment building was like that of an extended kin group.

There is a more kin-based variation of this sort of apartment building "household" economy in the north end of Boston.[16] Several generations of kinspeople, Italian by origin, may live together in two- or three-decker apartment houses, the building owned by an elderly couple, and the apartments rented to a married son or daughter, sister or brother, or a more distant relative. The men often work together—in small businesses or in the construction trades and municipal jobs where "knowing someone inside" is helpful for getting a job. The women keep their own apartments, usually immaculately, but visit one another, shop for one another, leave their children in each other's charge, and carry their cookery from one apartment to another.

In all of these economically insecure or uncertain situations, many kin and nonkinspeople are continuously involved in the domestic economy of a family unit. In none is the nuclear family group economically isolated or independent. As we shall see shortly, collector–hunters with and without nuclear-family arrangements are inevitably drawn into and enmeshed in mutual aid systems similar to these. Nuclear family households tend to be isolated and independent only under special circumstances in both collecting–hunting and industrial societies.

The People in the Middle—Steady Work and Nuclear Family Groups

In our society the well-to-do can afford to expand on the nuclear family group, and those whose incomes are marginal or erratic cannot afford not to. Those whose circumstances fall somewhere between these extremes make up the bulk of the population. It is among them, people with some reasonably steady way of supporting themselves, that the nuclear family form—a man and a woman sharing a common residence with their children and cooperating economically (independent of but keeping in touch with relatives)—is most prevalent. They are the laboring people, white-collar workers, and professionals with adequate and fairly steady wages and salaries who make up the vast work force that keeps the wheels of our industrial society turning.

The development of the nuclear family arrangement in this segment of the population does not go very far back in time, since this segment of the population itself is not very old. The ability to earn a living wage by selling one's labor was achieved only after factory forms of production were so widespread and stabilized that apprentices and employees began to form mutual support associations and agitate for higher pay. Subsequently, women and children were deemed capable of and eligible for wage work. Nostalgic and romanticized images of our past often see our nuclear family form as a modification or destruction of the extended-family households of other, less numerous segments of the population—rural farmers and small shopkeepers and professionals, the petty landowners, burghers and professionals—who kept their children with them as partners and heirs, and their wives at home as domestics.[17] The least pernicious version of such a romanticized image argues that by making women's work purely domestic, what happened in these sectors of past populations was crucial in shaping the nuclear family form. In this analysis, the traditional role of the housebound wife allowed men to be free to sell their working time and be used as full-time employees by emerging industry. Yet wage-earning women are not as new a phenomenon as this formulation suggests, and indeed income contributed by women and children was frequently all that permitted the independent nuclear household to endure among workers. An article in the April 1875 *Scientific American* contains the following highly illuminating paragraph.

> *An annual report of the Massachusetts Bureau of Statistics contains some interesting facts touching on the wages and manner of living of working people in that state. The*

statistics were gathered by personal visits with 397 families. Of the 142 families in which the father was the only worker, the average yearly income was $723.82; of the 255 families in which the wives or children assisted, the average income was $784.38. From the tabulated returns the bureau has concluded that in the majority of cases working men do not support their families by individual earnings alone but rely, or are forced to depend, upon their wives or children for from one-fourth to one-third of the family earnings. Children under 15 years of age supply, by their labor, from one-eighth to one-sixth of the total family earnings.[18]

It was not just a woman's housework but her wage work that allowed for the development of any sort of family unit in a segment of the population, wage workers, that had for a period lacked the chance to achieve an enduring family life. That people were and

A pantsmaker's workshop. The employees, members of one family, earned a grand total of $8.00 a week. The Bettmann Archive, Inc.

still are subject to the vagaries of a fluctuating job market, that incomes are uncertain (or low) for employed men in a society in which life-style as well as survival depend on the size of a paycheck, and that women worked and still work for wages are factors that played and continue to play a role in the development and persistence of the nuclear family form under industrialism.

For the working people who sought and found regular or steady employment in emerging industries and services—for the lone migrant women and men selling their labor on the open market— marriage and the mutual shared household it legitimated was desirable. It offered them legal sex, some emotional and economic strength and support, and children who might provide for their old age when the prospects for employment were dim and incarceration in a poor house rather than a stipend from the Social Security Administration loomed. Monogamy, the already established legal form of marriage in Europe, was well suited to the emerging economic order in Europe and again in America. While a working man benefited from a wife's domestic services and income, most working men could just about afford to have one wife, for the wages paid men were low. The wages paid women were even lower, so these wages were supplemental rather than sustaining. Additional wives might have been able to add a little in the way of money, but they also brought with them the possibility of more mouths to feed, hardly a situation to be sought after. While having more than one husband clearly could have been advantageous for a woman, the loss of jobs, the pursuit of more rewarding employment elsewhere could disperse multiple husbands and quickly rend asunder the household of a woman with several husbands. To cleave to one man and follow him, as law and religion required, and take in transient roomers, if she had to, offered more security than marrying many men. Monogamy survived as the legal and preferred marital arrangement, because the nuclear household it created was both mobile enough and self-sustaining enough to fit well into the urban industrial setting. Nevertheless, the relationships within the unit were subject to con- siderable stress and strain. Elites who themselves lived in extended family households, however, extolled the virtues and naturalness of an ideal nuclear family based on women's domesticity and men's bread- winning capacities, pointing out that women as wives and mothers were entitled to support and protection, and working men acquired a home and a castle when they married. That women's work stayed cheap and dirty was not noted. Idealizations aside, the nuclear unit as a residence group separated from that of other kinfolk and as a self-supporting economic entity permitted the men and women of the new mobile army of the employed to take care of each other and their children, to live better, enjoy sex legitimately, and solve some of the problems of dividing the tasks of day-to-day living—by assigning most of them to women.

In Western societies today those in the middle, like those who are poorest, face somewhat altered conditions than prevailed in the early days in industrialization. A mobile work force is still necessary, but working men and women earn livable incomes more easily and are both equally eligible for unemployment insurance. Hard-won pensions, subsidized medical care, and government stipends make old age less insecure. It is noteworthy that both marriage and divorce rates have climbed steadily in the wake of such changes. Despite the fact that people can live reasonably well without getting married and despite the fact that the unmarried state is propagandized as attractive, most people get married and set up nuclear family households. Many are subject to severe economic and emotional stresses and strains in these households and often seek sexual solace outside them. Yet most married couples do not resort to divorce. While the economic and social pressures that once forced people to remain together have eased considerably, the prospects of a reduced life-style and of emotional isolation do not encourage the dissolution of these households and families. The independent nuclear family survives as the main form of family under industrialism, for while economic forces shape and have shaped this form, emotional factors also play a part in solidifying it and making it endure.

The peculiarly isolating world inhabited by people who have to earn their livelihood in the impersonal organizations of industrialized societies makes the nuclear unit the only legitimate and genuinely rewarding sphere for emotional expression, sustenance, and enrichment. Our friends are often transient, our relatives distant. Most of us have address-book aunts and uncles, Christmas-card cousins, and siblings tied to our adult lives only by telephone wires. Our spouses and children are spatially and emotionally closer to us and fixed in our universes. A man may torment his wife and children with chronic agonizing, or furious deprecations of them, of his work life, of the world at large. A woman may bore or infuriate her husband and children with plaints about their failures, the political scene, or her domestic chores or job. There may be tantrums, arguments, prolonged silences in the severely pressured nuclear household. But the audience is a captive one. And it is a participant audience. No other institutionalized setting in industrialized society gives this richness and texture to an individual's life. There is nothing as satisfying as a "good" marriage (whatever that may be), and there are few social milieus that provide as much emotional saturation as a "bad" one. Despite the strains placed on the nuclear unit, it survives in our industrial world because most of us who depend on wages and salaries are incapable of accepting the diminished life-style and the emotional vacuum that are its alternatives. The options are very limited for us.

FAMILY ARRANGEMENTS AMONG
CONTEMPORARY COLLECTOR-HUNTERS

Contemporary populations of collector-hunters have as long a tradition of family behind them as we do. Their ancestors are also our ancestors. However, the family as an institution apparently emerged among collector-hunters long ago, among peoples with advanced foraging adaptations built on refined hunting tools and techniques. Industrial societies did not "invent" the family. By the time early capitalist industrializing societies appeared on the scene, the institution had been adapted to many settings and modified to accommodate to successive technological and social innovations wherever they appeared. The conditions that gave rise to capitalism and industrialization were not the same as those obtaining where collecting and hunting still provided the subsistence base. The forms of family in recent collecting-hunting societies—while sometimes strikingly similar to ours—are products of different sorts of circumstances and disparate pasts. Whether or not they take familiar forms, they are not living fossils that have survived unchanged for eons.

Although it is possible to trace the history of family forms in Western societies from documents, we cannot similarly review data on the history of family arrangements, nuclear or otherwise, among collecting-hunting peoples. No such data exist. Foraging peoples kept no retrievable records of their social lives, and all we have to work from are bits and pieces of their material culture. Those bits and pieces tell us some things about social organizational patterns, but not enough to reconstruct with any certainty what family arrangements were like. The reports of explorers and merchant adventurers and the work of assiduous anthropologists take us back only a short period. Far from adequate, they nevertheless indicate that things have changed radically in a few short centuries. Peoples who are collector-hunters today usually suffered the depradations of disease brought by colonizers. Some are peoples who lost lands they once cultivated. Most have been excluded from the richer foraging areas. Hunted as animals or treated as chattel, many fled to marginal regions unwanted by the technologically advanced and advancing foreigners. Their ways of living are, consequently, not "just like" those of ancient foragers.

Although things have changed, descriptions of the lives of contemporary remnant collecting-hunting groups are the best, in fact the only, sources on what family arrangements might have been like among ancient foragers. The tools, settlements, weapons, and shelters they use are similar and in some cases identical to those found in prehistoric archeological sites. While many of the game species both ancient and not so ancient hunters pursued are extinct, a few are not, and are taken with such traditional weapons. Since these so-called "primitive" contemporaries of ours live in a variety of ways, just as our common ancestors evidently did, presumably at least some of the social and family arrangements they have devised resemble those of the past.

With this reminder that the present is not identical to the past we will look at two situations—that of the Andamanese, where a nuclear family form predominates, and that of the Tiwi. The latter are unusual in several respects, not the least being their family arrangements. The descriptions of these peoples focus on matters relevant to what family is, how family arrangements vary, and the functions the family arrangements fulfill within the framework of how collecting and hunting are pursued.

The Andaman Islanders[19]

The people of the Andaman Islands, like the Semang of Borneo, the Ojibwa of Southern Canada, the Bushmen of the Kalahari, the Vedda of Ceylon, and yet other collector–hunters are generally regarded as having the nuclear-family form. Within the basic similarities of the economies of these peoples, there are differences as to adaptations to local circumstances and ecological accommodations. The Andamanese are unique in some aspects of their "nuclear" household arrangements and typical as regards others.

The islands that make up Great Andaman lie in the eastern part of the Bay of Bengal. They are small (total area is 2508 square miles), warm (temperatures range from 60 to 95 degrees Fahrenheit), moist (about 140 inches of rain falls in each year), and have a six-month-long rainy season (May to mid-November) and a severe dry season which affects food supplies adversely. Blessed by their isolation, strategic unimportance, lack of exploitable resources, and a reputation for cannibalism, the Andamanese were left pretty much to themselves until 1858, when the British claimed the islands for use as a penal colony and harbor facility. The hostility of the Andamanese was overcome by some jobs, houses, food, "protection," and medicine, the last a necessity since the British also introduced syphilis and measles, which quickly reduced the population to about one fourth of its original size. The Andamanese way of life discussed here was current in the late nineteenth and early twentieth centuries.

The son of the first British administrator of the islands, Edward Horace Man, published an account of his observations of Andamanese life in 1885, and A. R. Radcliffe-Brown began systematic field work among the islanders in 1906. Neither author refrained from describing what they had not seen, precontact practices with regard to sex and social patterns. Radcliffe-Brown and Man are not quite in agreement about them. Both note that before contact, traditional codes allowed for premarital sexual experimentation. Monogamy, they report, followed a period of sexual freedom. Man argues, however, that marital infidelity became common only after contact. Radcliffe-Brown, noting that the spread of syphilis was rapid even among groups with whom the British had no contact, questions his assumption. Yet Radcliffe-Brown also says that in precontact times, local groups separated by no more than 15 miles were unaware of each other. This statement reflects the now-passé belief that hunter–gatherers live in tight territorial groups. The statement does not reflect the likelihood of interlocality contact inherent in the pattern of seasonal migration and resettlement that both authors agree was imposed by environmental conditions long before the British appeared on the scene.

The natives of Great Andaman lived in small groups of between 30 and 50 individuals. Local groups or camps on the coast where resources were richest were larger and closer together than inland groups. Coastal groups moved around more than inland groups. Canoe travel was easy for them, easier than overland travel. Camp groups of less than 10 people were common. Occasionally, there occurred assemblages of as many as 300. Small groups were hunting parties. The very large temporary gatherings of people drawn from several localities testify to intergroup contacts.

During the rainy season when game was abundant and valued vegetable foods and honey were hard to get, groups of 30 to 50 people congregated in "permanent" camps. Most permanent encampments were either large doughnut-shaped communal huts (360 feet in diameter and 20 to 30 feet high) divided into separate sleeping sections for married couples with children (not necessarily their own) and bachelors and spinsters. There were also "permanent" camps made up of several huts clustered around a public dancing area. Large temporary encampments were always constructed in this way. In large camps the bachelors and widowers were responsible for the communal cook pot.

The main cooking hearth in a large camp was always located near the bachelor quarters. If food was sufficient or the weather prohibitive, no one went out to hunt. A large game animal such as a pig, if available, was partially cooked over the communal fire. It was then dismembered and distributed to the resident family groups and to the bachelors and spinsters. Whenever someone was hungry, the cooking was completed over a small fire. If hunting was possible, small groups, three to five men, left the campsite to hunt, and set themselves up in the smaller campsites that were scattered around the "permanent" settlement. All campsites were named and people identified themselves as belonging to one or another of the chief camping sites in the area of the local group with which they lived.

During the cool dry season, the "permanent" campsite stood empty. People dispersed. Married couples and the children in their charge moved together. Some family groups visited friends in other localities. Others went to the sites used by hunters during the rainy season. The dry season was heavily given over to gathering. People collected the abundant vegetable foods, insect larvae, and highly desired honey, which were easy to get when the rains abated. Men and women foraged together, performing the same tasks, although if a hive hung high in a tree, a woman was never asked to climb for it. The casually constructed huts of the dry-season camps, which were the base of operations for these activities, not only housed nuclear-family groups, but were also meeting places for spinsters and bachelors, for the dry season was the time for courtship and offered the opportunity of sexual exploration.

Prestige accrued to people who were very successful in subsistence activities. The man whose arrow first struck and wounded a large animal (a turtle, or dugong, or big fish or pig) was regarded as its "owner." Similarly, a woman was honored as the "owner" of the food, animal or vegetable, she brought in. The obligation to share food was strong, and ownership did not imply power over its distribution. Older men, respected for their former skillfulness as hunters and for their fairness, generosity, kindness, and good temper, divided and distributed all game. Influential men like these, and, women who played similar roles in the encampments, were local figures with no status beyond their local group.

A man or woman belonged to the group that inhabited the locality of his or her birth. Young people were free to choose a mate on their own, from their own generation and from whatever locality they wished to. Brothers and sisters were prohibited as mates. A marriage ceremony almost always formalized a sexual relationship that was already well advanced. The marriage rite consisted of a public presentation of the wife to the husband. The couple then moved into a hut of its own. The husband or the wife at this time might find it necessary to leave their locality of birth. Whoever left "home" took up residence and membership, with all its attendant rights and obligations, in the local group of the other spouse. Wherever the man and wife lived, the terms they both used to address the members of the local group they now belonged to were identical, for Andamanese kin terms are generational and do not distinguish between "own" family and "others" except through the personal pronoun. A child born to the couple would, for instance, call its father "my" father, and all other men of his generation "father." A marriage was not considered as consummated until a child was born. Adoptive children and parents specified adoption as their link. An adopted child became a member of its adopted parents' local group.

A mother was expected to assume the major responsibility for her children, but infants and children up to the age of four were suckled by other women in the local group. The children were cared for by and played with everybody in camp. By five years of age little girls and boys started learning the tasks associated with their sex. Children between the ages of six and ten were often adopted by foster parents or exchanged by families. Often the transaction involved moving the child or children to another locality. This afforded the natural and adoptive parents an excuse for intervisiting. A request for permission to adopt and the granting of the right to adopt were regarded as acts of friendship and esteem, and adopted children were always treated with warmth and affection.

The Andamanese have been classified by Coult and Habenstein[20] as having "independent families i.e. familial groupings which do not normally, or other than temporarily include more than one nuclear or polygamous family." Polygamy of any kind was rarely practiced. Andamanese household units were usually based on the link between one man and one woman—and classified as nuclear. But while marriage was monogamous, extramarital liaisons were taken for granted. While married couples and "their" children shared a common roof, children in a household were often not those born to the couple. Unlike the nuclear units of the Ojibwa or Eskimo, which sustain themselves for long periods in isolation, the Andamanese family unit was isolated only occasionally. Most of the time it participated in a cooperative communal economy, in which child rearing was a group responsibility, and producing and preparing food involved so much sharing that we cannot talk of an independent domestic economy. While the people in the Andamanese nuclear unit recognized their special relationship to one another, there were not even special kinship terms for members of the nuclear group. In many respects, then, the Andamanese "nuclear family" is very different from ours. It is clearly embedded in a network of kin and local ties. Ours is not. It produces goods that are consumed by its members and the members of its network, while ours earns a money income to purchase consumption goods just for its members. Emotional and caretaking ties are generalized and open, but ours are closed. Clearly the Andamanese nuclear-family group performs different "functions" from the type of nuclear-family group that predominates in industrial settings. Yet the functions it performs are also those found in other collecting–hunting settings, where the family arrangements are not necessarily nuclear at all.

Tiwi Family Arrangements[21]

The socioeconomic base on which marriage and family arrangements in collecting–hunting societies are built is perhaps clearest in a situation in which the nuclear family is not favored—that of the

Tiwi. The Tiwi are unusual as collector-hunters go. They have survived untouched until recently in an area rich with animal and vegetable foods. Seasonal variation there is slight, and the area lacks any really large game or herd animals. In this rich and even environment, the Tiwi practice polygyny extensively. As it happens, polygyny as a dominant marriage form is rare among collector-hunters, although in most collecting-hunting populations, polygynous or polyandrous marriages occur occasionally.

It was long a tenet of anthropology that where men take multiple wives, this happens only if a man produces a lot of food, or controls other people by force, or is exceedingly sexy. Tiwi men who manage to acquire many wives do not often display these talents. In fact, among the Tiwi, as in most other collecting-hunting populations, women provide most of the food, women are very influential, and women lead as complicated sex lives as men. The unusual polygynous households of the Tiwi are so nakedly based on the same sorts of economic considerations that affect other collector-hunters that they are of special interest here.

The Tiwis live on two islands, Melville and Bathhurst. These are separated from the coast of northern Australia by about 25 miles of open sea. Apparently, the Tiwi had little contact with their aboriginal mainland neighbors, for they never acquired from them either the boomerang or the spear thrower. Powerful currents apparently discouraged sea travel, and the Tiwi came to regard the misty coastline on their horizon as the home of the dead, from which no one ever returned. Europeans were made aware of the two isolated islands by Dutch mariners in the seventeenth century. In the eighteenth century Portuguese slavers raided them sporadically. The French explored the islands in the early nineteenth century, and the British surveyed the coasts and established a settlement in 1824. Within five years, however, the British abandoned their settlement, leaving behind some water buffalo. The Tiwi were left to themselves, again, and the buffalo ran wild and multiplied. At the end of the nineteenth century the marketable buffalo attracted the attention of an Australian adventurer. To harvest them he established a trading post. By the time the buffalo were exterminated (1915) by a small army of hunters he had brought over from the mainland, the Tiwi had been visited by Australian government officials and by missionaries. The trader's efforts to replace the defunct buffalo business with a lumbering operation was cut short, for the Tiwi met their aspiring "employer" with repeated armed confrontations. He was soon banished by Australian authorities.

Between World Wars I and II, foreign trade items flowed into the islands from Australia. They were brought in with the express purpose of discouraging the Tiwi from trading with the Japanese. As a result, during World War II the Tiwi did, in fact, cooperate with Allied military personnel. At the end of the war the bases were converted into government and missionary settlements. Throughout all this the Tiwi continued to live in the bush, engaging in traditional subsistence activities in traditional ways. A number of ethnographers managed to do fieldwork among the Tiwi before the 1960s, when a revived lumbering industry all but destroyed the landscape and changed the Tiwi way of life. The data here covers the period prior to this upheaval.

Only 3000 square miles in area, the islands include swamp, waterless desert, mosquito-infested mangrove jungle, and about 800 square miles of more livable terrain. The islands are rich in small fauna and vegetable foods, so rich, in fact, that they have a greater density of aboriginal populations than is found in almost any other part of Australia. The only native animal that does not lend itself to casual collection is the wallaby. Every other sort of native land animal—lizard, rat, iguana, snake, opposum—is collected, along with wild food plants and shellfish, by the women. Men typically fish and hunt birds, aquatic reptiles and mammals, and wallaby, year round.

Traditionally, the Tiwi did very little as a unified people and lacked any occasions or officials for super local assemblies, although all Tiwi speak a common tongue and recognize a common relationship. There were a number of recognized regional groupings (authors disagree on precisely how many) on both Bathhurst and Melville islands. Boundaries between these regions were recognized but were not clear-cut and one moved gradually out of one district into another. "People, especially women, changed their residence frequently in the course of their lives. . . . Being born into a band did not at all require permanent residence in that band either for males or females."[22] In fact, "the nature of Tiwi marriage customs often dictates that men leave the residential group of their birth,"[23] and "though related males share rights in a common territory they do not reside there together. . . [while] closely related women often congeal into local clusters."[24] Each region was thus occupied by a flexible and constantly shifting collection of individuals who identified themselves as fellow district members and utilized their resources in common. Each range area averaged about 200 square miles, and had between 100 and 300 inhabitants, who rarely, if ever, came together. Small local camps were the rule, yet even they were in constant flux.

Local groups consisted of ephemeral associations and assemblages of households. Tiwi household or domestic units were independent, nomadic, and found scattered over the countryside. Their members hunted as a unit, pooled the results of their foraging, threw up shelters together, and ate and slept together. A household's subsistence was largely derived from collecting activities (46 to 55 percent); hunting was secondary, and fishing and shell fishing filled out the larder.[25] There were large households and small ones. Smaller ones tended to follow and settle near larger units whose productive levels were more evenly maintained.

A large Tiwi household included an older man and his wives, his wives' children (not necessarily his), some of his sons, and his sons-in-law who were married to the "daughters" of his wives. Some of these "daughters" were not even as yet conceived, as we shall soon see. The women left early in the morning, alone or in groups, with baskets and babies. They foraged for vegetable foods, small nocturnal animals which they tracked to their nests, and edible grubs and worms. The husband, if he was not too old, might go out later to spear fish or hunt wallaby and birds. Men cannot readily wed until they are around 30, and lose their hunting efficiency by 45, so the young men in camp, alone or in groups, gathered the same foods as women, and in addition brought in whatever wallaby, birds, or fish they could as dividends.

The Tiwi viewed a large household as economically advantageous. A missionary preaching against plural marriage was told by the head of a large household, "If I had only two wives I would starve, but with my present ten or twelve [sic] wives I can send them out in all directions in the morning and at least two or three of them are likely to bring something back with them at the end of the day, and then we can all eat."[26] Obviously, marriage was treated as an economic arrangement devoid of sentiment.

A marriage involved an exchange. For the privilege of marrying a woman a man gave or promised another in return, or agreed to work for his mother-in-law, or do both. The right to give a woman in marriage passed from a woman's mother's father to her father (strictly speaking the first husband of her mother), thence to her brothers, and then to her sons. There were always some men around with so many living male relatives who stood in the way of their having a woman to give that they had no women to exchange for wives. Such men remained bachelors without households to call their own, poor in privilege, prestige, and resources. But though a bachelor's life was not a happy one, neither was it celibate. In households where women foraged in the bush, frequently alone, and men hunted game in the bush, frequently alone, angry accusations of adultery were justifiably often voiced by aged males.

Bachelors were common, but no woman remained a spinster. Before a girl was even conceived, when her mother had first begun menstruation, she and her sisters had been given to a man who had women to exchange—sisters, daughters, or even a widowed mother— women he could offer for the privilege of marrying an unborn girl. The man who was considered a girl's first or primary husband was inevitably as old or older than her mother. A woman's last husband might be as young as her son, for two bachelors, poor in women, could "give" each other their mothers so that each might have a wife. A woman had no chance of becoming a spinster, but the likelihood of her becoming a widow, sometimes before she even reached adolescence, was very high indeed.

When a woman was widowed all sorts of opportunities opened up. The contract that bound her to her husband was null and void. She could be "given" in marriage again. If her daughters, born and unborn, were promised, her widowhood was an opportunity to dissolve these contracts and send away sons-in-law for real or trumped-up failures. If her mother's father was no longer alive to insist on his contract rights, her mother's husband could try to marry her and her daughters off to men of his choosing. If he was gone, there were her brothers seeking to exchange her, and if they were out of the picture, she had her sons. A young girl could look forward to widowhood and many husbands. Although women were exchanged, they were not powerless pawns forever.

"Sons or brothers wishing to use their mothers or their sisters in their political schemes . . . could only do so with the active collaboration of the women concerned. . . . Young girls thus had no bargaining power but young widows had a good deal. Old mothers with influential senior sons were extremely powerful . . . and some of the strongest influence networks were alliances of several senior brothers in which their old mother seemed to be the mastermind and the senior sons largely the enforcers of what the old mother and her middle aged daughters (their sisters) had decided among themselves."[27] Thus women *and* men played active roles in establishing, manipulating, and renegotiating the marital networks that criss-crossed the islands.

While the marriage merry-go-round was marked by power plays and political jockeying it effectively discouraged the development of powerful localized descent groups. How it helped maintain dispersed networks of relationships between local groups of people who reckon descent unilineally is easy to see. The system worked as follows. A woman's brothers and sons were members of her matrisib. Her mother's husband and her mother's father were not, and these two men were not necessarily members of the same group. All these male relatives had some claim on using the woman in an exchange marriage. Since each man's interest was best served by making alliances for her that strengthened his position in his own group, there was inevitable conflict. Women married several times since widowhood was assured and marriage contracts could be broken without widowhood. With the cooperation of conniving male relatives, even a young woman could exercise choice as to whom she took for her current spouse. Since only "strong" men inherited hunting rights through their fathers and stayed on in the father's locality, women could arrange to move or not, with the cooperation of male relatives. Most men moved about regularly to work off the debts incurred in the process of getting a wife.

The development of strong local or unilineal descent groups was inhibited by the machinations involved in negotiating marriages and the constant departures of spouses.

Child rearing in this fluid setting took on an ad hoc character. A little girl might be moved to her husband's residence, and a little boy follow his mother to her latest spouse, pursued by accusations that his mother was a "stolen wife." Whether reared in a household that included one or both parents, or in a household of in-laws, on reaching puberty children had already learned all the adult subsistence skills they needed to know. Girls then consummated their marriages and boys began the long, sometimes fruitless task of getting a wife by ingratiating themselves with men and households with females to give and by cementing their relations with kinspeople who might help them get a wife. Children, especially girl children, were used to make marriages. Marriages were not used to "make" children.

That family arrangements in this fluid setting are intimately bound up with maintaining social and economic networks is eminently clear from what happens during the lives of young adults. When a young man or woman moved from one locale to another for marriage, visiting back and forth was frequent. Visiting was always marked by gift giving, from guests to hosts, and vice versa. Goods, especially iron from wrecked ships, were distributed over the islands through these gift exchanges. Quarrels sometimes arose over such exchanges. If unfriendly relations between groups developed, the visits of spouses to their parents or in-laws served to bridge gaps and arbitrate disagreements. It is interesting to note that visits designed to make peace between groups and reestablish trade and social exchanges were accompanied by the same emotional expression that was traditional at a marriage—weeping.

SUMMARY—NUCLEAR-FAMILY GROUPINGS AS ADAPTATIONS

As noted, the majority of foraging peoples favor nuclear-family groupings of some sort and bilateral descent systems. If we reviewed in detail several or all their situations, differences between their nuclear arrangements would become evident. The Andamanese, for instance, live in large, stable settlements for six months and disperse into smaller ones, some consisting of single families, the rest of the year. The Shoshone of the Great Basin live as independent dispersed moving family groups most of the year, but when the pine nuts are ready for harvesting, get together for awhile. The Polar Eskimo gather no vegetable foods, live in igloos, and hunt as isolated nuclear-family groups, except when the sea is open and families can assemble in old rock sheltered housing sites, to work and hunt with others for the season. Differences in family economics are directly related to such varied environmental conditions. But not all the differences in family-related behaviors we would see are of this sort. The Andamanese evidently were shrewd enough to express some doubts about the propriety of extramarital sex to their Western inquisitors. Among the Eskimo, extramarital sex is not only expected—it is called for at times.[28] Among the foragers of Arnheimland, where sex is a widespread pastime enjoyed by all who can take part, "women find pleasure in comparing the relative degrees of satisfaction obtained during coitus (with various men)."[29] The Bushmen of the Kalahari prohibit extra-marital relations but exchange spouses without violating community norms.[30] These cultural differences do not negate the fact that in all these societies the family arrangement, whether or not nuclear, articulates with the local foraging adaptation, and, more significantly, is the main or only channel for economic and social exchanges. While it is interesting that the Andamanese seem to adopt children regularly and more often than other foragers to facilitate network ties, they are unusual only in how much adopting they do, not in the fact that they adopt.

Additional descriptions would clarify that collector–hunters have many attitudes in common with each other as regards sex and family arrangements. Nearly all do not contract marriages to "get sex." Premarital affairs are normal and expected and only a few foraging peoples—evidently much influenced by missionaries—follow patrilineal descent systems, and value virginity and premarital chastity.[31] Where encampments are large babies are commonly cared for by many people. Consequently, babies are generally accepted whether born with or without the benefit of the informal ceremonies that constitute marriage[32] since there is no pressing need to marry to ensure child support. Marriage is always a significant socioeconomic transaction, however. Although individuals appear rather free to choose their lovers and spouses, marriages inevitably lead to exchanges between groups and are recognized as embracing many more people than the marrying couple. Children of a marriage are furthermore recognized as being located in the exchange network as well as destined for participation in future exchanges. Finally, foragers favor monogamy and a nuclear type of family group only where semi- or full nomadism and/or seasonal dispersal is usually necessary or advantageous. Such attitudes indicate that family arrangements per se are viewed by collector–hunters as serving somewhat different functions than family in our society, and that the forces that encourage the adoption of the nuclear-family arrangement in societies on this technological level are not altogether the same as those at work in the industrial setting, although in both settings a nuclear grouping occurs in conjunction with a need for mobility.

The Tiwi did not go in for nuclear family households. In their unusual and rich environment, large households and multiple spouses were the norm and considered to be economically desirable. Among them marriages were explicitly deemed useful for establishing social and economic ties and network affiliations. Less explicit about the economic character of their marriage and family arrangements, the Andamanese favored monogamy and nuclear family groupings. As in industrial societies a small family unit which is movable had a significant adaptive value for them. In the industrial setting it is the exigencies of a fluctuating job market which favor this minimal family unit. Among the Andamanese the need for seasonal dispersal was pressing. But in our society, that small family unit is legally "freed" from network entanglements and responsibilities and the support a network could provide. In our society nuclear groups are economically self-sustaining most of the time and utilize kin or local networks only in emergencies or under extreme conditions. Not so for the Andamanese. Their nuclear family units are economically independent and self-sufficient only seasonally or occasionally. Most of the time they are not. Thus for the Andamanese, exchange and network relationships are as important as for the Tiwi. As in other collecting–hunting societies, marriage contracts effectively tie individuals and groups of people into extensive and extended relationships. For us, marriage ties two people together while relatives, friends, and neighborhood cohorts may never exchange so much as a smile.

The bases of Western industrial society's domestic arrangements and family forms can be traced back through time to link up with traditions of earlier family arrangements. The background of the nuclear or any other family arrangements among collector–hunters cannot. While the origin of the family as an institution is buried from our view, it is certain that the institution is old, old enough so that nowadays human populations wherever they are found have a tradition of family and some form of family. The accumulating evidence points to the emergence of family under the conditions collector–hunters faced, at least by the Upper Paleolithic, when tools and weapons still used by foragers, and evidence of some long-distance trade is found in the archeological record. While it is doubtful that as families began to be regularized features of the social landscape only a nuclear type occurred, it is important to remember that among collector-hunters family units are based on marital contracts that specify which individuals are linked in marriage to one another, that the nuclear unit is common, and that for the majority of collector–hunters the conditions they face frequently call for seasonal or periodic dispersal and thus favor small nuclear-type family units—minimal dispersal groups consisting of a male, a female, and young.

The nuclear unit is not a universal form of family. It is not even universal among collector–hunters. It is however, the simplest and most straightforward expression of the principal features underlying family everywhere. As such it helps illuminate how family originated.

NOTES

1. Allan D. Coult and Robert W. Habenstein, *Cross Tabulations of Murdock's World Ethnographic Sample* (Columbia, Mo.: University of Missouri Press, 1965), p. 357.

2. Coult and Habenstein, *Cross Tabulations of Murdock's World Ethnographic Sample*, p. 528.

3. Coult and Habenstein, *Cross Tabulations of Murdock's World Ethnographic Sample*, p. 528.

4. M. F. Nimkoff, "The Social System and the Family," in *Comparative Family Systems*, ed. M. F. Nimkoff (Boston: Houghton Mifflin, 1965), p. 41.

5. Claude Levi-Strauss, "The Family," in *Family in Transition*, eds. Arlene S. Skolnick and Jerome H. Skolnick (Boston: Little, Brown, 1971), pp. 50–72, especially p. 71.

6. Gerald D. Berreman, "Pahari Polyandry: A Comparison," *American Anthropologist*, *64*, no. 1, pt. 1, 1963, pp. 60–75.

7. Levi-Strauss, "The Family," p. 64. The nation is England.

8. The law is being modified with regard to voluntary extramarital affairs. The headline "Wife Entitled to Take Lover, Judge Rules" in the *Boston Globe*, March 19, 1975, p. 8, refers to a landmark decision by Judge Isaac S. Garb of Bucks County, Pennsylvania, in which a husband's suit for damages against his wife's lover was denied on the grounds that "The principle that one person has a cause for action for money damages against another arising out of his spouse's voluntary . . . sexual activity with another person is abhorrent and repugnant to modern standards. . . ."

9. Phillipe Aries, *Centuries of Childhood: A Social History of Family* (New York: Random House, 1962).

10. Maxine Cheshire, "Jane Fonda's Family in Domestic Setting,"

Boston Globe, June 25, 1975, p. 44.

11. Peter Laslett, *The World We Have Lost* (New York: Charles Scribner's Sons, 1971). This book is an exciting, scholarly work that undermines many myths about the family in preindustrial Europe.

12. Karen Sacks, "An Evolutionary View of Capitalism," unpublished manuscript, 42 pages.

13. John Stowell, "Welfare Paternity Rules Issued," *Boston Globe*, June 26, 1975, p. 6. Further developments in the development of the machinery to pursue errant fathers are described by Wolfgang Saxon, "Welfare Drive Seeks to Locate Absentee Fathers," *The New York Times*, August 8, 1976, p. 49.

14. Elliot Liebow, *Tally's Corner: A Study of Negro Streetcorner Men* (Boston: Little, Brown, 1966).

15. Carol B. Stack, *All Our Kin: Strategies for Survival in a Black Community* (New York: Harper & Row, 1974).

16. Herbert J. Gans, *The Urban Villagers: Group and Class in the Life of Italian Americans* (New York: Free Press, 1962). While describing a neighborhood that no longer exists, the book provides a picture of Boston north end Italian families as they still are.

17. William J. Goode, *World Revolution and Family Patterns* (New York: Free Press, 1963), pp. 6ff.

18. "50 and 100 Years Ago Today," *Scientific American*, *232*, no. 4, 1975, p. 113.

19. The data on the Andamanese presented here are drawn from A. R. Radcliffe-Brown, *The Andaman Islanders* (New York: Free Press, 1948) and from Edward Horace Man, *On the Aboriginal Inhabitants of the Andaman Islands* (London: Royal Anthropological Institute, 1932).

20. Coult and Habenstein, *Cross Tabulation of Murdock's World Ethnographic Sample*, p. 530.

21. Jane Goodall, *Tiwi Wives* (Seattle, Wash.: University of Washington Press, 1971); her article "Marriage Contracts Among the Tiwi," *Ethnology*, *1*, no. 9, 1962, pp. 452–466; and C. W. M. Hart and Arnold Pilling, *The Tiwi of North Australia* (New York: Holt, Rinehart and Winston, 1960) are the ethnographic studies of Tiwi culture from which most of the data presented are taken.

22. Hart and Pilling, *The Tiwi of North Australia*, p. 12.

23. M. Kay Martin and Barbara Voorhies, *The Female of the Species* (New York: Columbia University Press, 1975), p. 200.

24. Martin and Voorhies, *The Female of the Species*, p. 203.

25. George Peter Murdock, "Ethnographic Atlas: A Summary," *Ethnology*, 6, no. 2, 1967.

26. Hart and Pilling, *The Tiwi of North Australia*, p. 34.

27. Hart and Pilling, *The Tiwi of North Australia*, p. 53.

28. Ernestine Friedl, *Women and Men; An Anthropologist's View* (New York: Holt, Rinehart, Winston, 1975), pp. 41–42.

29. Ronald Berndt, "Sub-incision in a Non Sub-incision Area," *American Image*, 1951, pp. 165–171.

30. Richard B. Lee, personal communication.

31. According to Martin and Voorhies, *The Female of the Species* (p. 189), a few groups, influenced by missionaries and colonizers, value virginity at marriage and follow patrilineal descent rules.

32. Philip E. L. Smith, "Stone Age Man on the Nile," *Scientific American*, 235, no. 2, 1976, pp. 30–45.

6

The Origin of Families

Two general types of theories attempt to account for the origin and universality of the institution of family among humans: the biological and the sociological. We shall examine each in turn.

BIOLOGICAL THEORIES OF FAMILY ORIGINS

Explicitly biological theories offer several different models of both the past and the present. At first biological theorists held that a genetic predisposition toward a family-like social entity, either a pair group or a male-centered harem (theorists disagreed), was something we shared with the apes. Since some researchers soon realized that human family arrangements are very varied, a modified version of the model took a slightly different tack. In this version our genes no longer carry these predispositions, although those of early humans did.

Tracing our behavior back to a common ancestor of apes and humans ceased to make much sense when reliable descriptions of the social behavior of our closest living primate relatives became available. Only one of our ape "cousins," it turns out, actually goes in for anything even resembling a human family arrangement, the pair group, and that ape, the gibbon, is a very distant cousin. Newer biological theories of the origins and basis of family among humans have therefore taken a different approach. The approach consists of pointing out that the living primate species physically closest to the human line live in environments that the ancestors of humanity deserted. Leaving these environments behind was a major factor in humanization. Obviously, then, we cannot learn much about our past from the behavior of our ape relatives, who have become adapted to an environmental setting that we left long ago. What is really important, this approach holds, is to take our models of early human behavior from the adaptations of monkeys that live on the ground just as proto-humans and early humans did. The new biological theories are ecologically oriented.

Bioecological theories come in several models. One model sticks to the notion that family-like groupings are part of a precultural heritage. It selects as its starting point the one-male groupings of terrestrial hamadryas baboons and argues that proto-humans must have lived much as they do. The behaviors leading to such one-male groupings became genetically established, so by the time successive generations of proto-humans evolved into cultural beings, family subgroupings were firmly part of our social heritage. Another bioecological model also sees the behaviors leading to family subgroupings in our genetic heritage, but says that these behaviors became part of it after the cultural adaptation of hunting appeared. In this version our earliest ground-living ancestors lived as savannah baboons do, in large groups with mother–child dyads but without family-like subgroupings. In such large troops the dangers of terrestrial life led the males to become more aggressive, protective, and hierarchically ordered as the females became more dependent on them. These sex-associated traits, the model holds, are the behavioral precondition for the cultural division of labor by sex, making males naturally inclined toward hunting and females to nurturing. The family became entrenched as some males became bonded to the passive, nurturant, sexy females they preferred. The offspring of these mate-bonded protector–hunter–fathers had a better chance to survive than the children of males not inclined toward bonding. Generation by generation, bonders grew in numbers, passing on their behavioral preferences through their genes. Eventually, they outnumbered those less possessive toward mates. Thus was "the family" established. A third bioecological orientation lies buried in several sociological discussions of family and kinship which regard family itself as a culturally based institution. As we shall discover shortly, in some "sociological" models of human family arrangements and their origins, men and women are seen as fundamentally different, each sex being governed by behavioral predispositions that were evolved in adapting to early or proto-human habitats.

The theories that place the origin and perpetuation of human family arrangements into the biological realm run into difficulty on several counts.

1. The diversity of human family arrangements, even among collector–hunters, is so great that no common genetically programmed behaviors seem to determine their forms.

2. Those primates most closely related to humans exhibit no family-like social adaptations.

3. The apes and monkeys that have family-like groupings are far removed from the human line.

4.   Populations of monkeys that have family-like groupings interbreed wlth populations that do not. (Hamadryas baboons interbreed with savannah baboon populations. Baboons and macaques interbreed with each other.)

5.   In captivity and in the wild, many monkey and ape species show a remarkable capacity for adapting their behaviors and social relationships to fit new circumstances. To emphasize this last point, the behavioral flexibility of one very well studied species of monkeys is well worth noting.

Researchers induced a number of Japanese macaques to move out of the forest onto beaches by providing a lot of attractive foods on a regular basis.[1] Once on the beach, where they were easily observed and photographed, the animals on their own initiative learned, among other things, to swim. They were introduced to sweet potatoes. One animal discovered how to wash a potato by dipping it in the ocean. Others followed suit. A monkey discovered how to sort wheat grains from sand by putting handfuls of the mixed grains in water and picking off the wheat, which floats while the sand particles sink. The others learned the trick, and also discovered that the candy bars left for them were delicious when unwrapped. As to the plasticity of the social relationships displayed by the animals, on the beach, where flight into the trees was no longer easy, males became very protective. Without any human intervention other than introducing new foods in a new setting, it became evident that the troops studied differ as to social patterns. The males of troops at Takasakiyama and Takahashi take turns looking after infants while their mothers feed. Males in other troops never do so.

It is, of course, possible that Japanese macaques are exceptional among higher primates and should not be regarded as telling us much about the behavioral capacities of other primates. It is, however, unlikely that these macaques are more adaptable than the hamadryas baboon males who grew up in a compound and "forgot" how to herd females or the old tradition-minded hamadryas female who took over the herding task the males reared in the compound never learned to perform.[2] Japanese macaques are exceptional only in that they have been systematically observed while undergoing change. As we have seen, field and laboratory studies of the ongoing social behaviors of other primate species indicate much the same sort of thing, that social learning and social malleability are often part of the species' heritage.

All in all, an overall survey of the evidence indicates that theories that presume that humans have a genetically based behavioral predisposition to forming family-like groups are ignoring a great deal of data. An inclusive approach to the data shows that modern humans and nonhuman primates are behaviorally malleable and suggests that behavioral adaptability runs far back into the primate heritage. Given this broad range of evidence, it is hard to believe that proto and early humans were not behaviorally adaptive and adaptable, too, or that as early humans took to hunting, they became less capable of modifying their social patterns than human and nonhuman primates are today.

SOCIOLOGICAL THEORIES OF FAMILY ORIGINS

Sociological theories of the origin of family were first proposed at a time when it was thought that the human species is unique. Theorists in that era did not care what our primate relatives are like, because it was held that human social behavior is the product of experience and intellect, and thus differs radically from the "instinctual" behavior of all other animals. However, Linnaeus had placed humans in the animal kingdom and Darwin effectively discounted Divine Intervention in the formation of the species. Darwin thus made it clear that humans are totally embedded in the animal kingdom. He consequently raised doubts about how unique human behavior is, and did so quite explicitly. Since Darwin did not have much information to go on, he assumed that monkeys and apes were dominated by instincts, and in the course of recognizing our close ties with the higher primates took the position that humans also derive some of their social patterns from instinctual behaviors. In his writings he presented the argument that the institution of the family derives directly from prelinguistic primate social patterns, patterns which selection had locked securely into our primate nature.[3] Sociologically inclined theorists promptly rejected Darwin's arguments on the grounds that the human capacity for language is unique and makes humans somewhat special in the animal world, even though they generally believed that our linguistic abilities derived from the vocal but nonverbal forms of communication found among primates. Humans, they held, are completely dependent on learning. Monkeys and apes, they argued, can rely on their instincts—unlearned behaviors. However, as information on nonhuman primate behavior was collected, some of these theorists began to realize that many primates are more like us than they had ever dreamed possible. Nonhuman primates, too, learn and transmit information. They, too, adapt and modify their social behavior. Some use their hands to reshape material objects and make tools to accomplish tasks, just as we do. A few of them are even demonstrating a capacity for language, learning to communicate as deaf mutes do, with nonvocal hand languages and through machines.[4]

Humans are not quite as unique as theorists who saw the family as a social invention were once forced to maintain. In fact, it seems that the only substantive difference between the adaptive modes of nonhuman and human primates is that while apes and monkeys adapt their behavior to fit immediate circumstances, they do not, as humans do, use language to shape and reshape social relationships. Humans are able to manipulate their behavior not just to suit immediate conditions but to achieve long-term goals. Nowadays, theorists who seek the basis of human family arrangements in sociocultural processes no longer insist that our species is very unique or deny the relevance of our primate genetic heritage. They regard information on the behavior of other primates as confirming their views.

It would seem from the above that the few sociological models of family origins recent researchers have built hold that biologically prescribed behavioral traits play or played little or no role in the origin of the family. This is not so. One of the newest works on hand illustrates this clearly. The ostensibly "sociological" theory proposed by Evelyn Reed[5] runs as follows. Like Marx, whose sociological orientation she claims to adhere to, she disavows the idea that incest taboos which force people to seek mates among nonrelatives are an extension of an innately programmed psychodynamic. She proclaims that the standard Marxist position is correct and says that she does not believe that humans are programmed to develop either a sexual abhorrence of, or a sexual attraction to, those with whom they are intimate in their growing-up years, but at the same time goes on to say that she finds it inconceivable that brothers and sisters in dynastic Egypt actually got married and mated with each other. Departing from Marxian historical materialism, which regards the incest taboo in a political and economic light, however, Reed deals with the incest taboo in quite another framework.

The incest taboo is not really a sex taboo or a proscription on mating practices, according to Reed. It is an elaboration of a food taboo. It was created by nurturant and vegetarian women who were little inclined toward meat eating, she says. The original taboo was designed to control the carnivorous, cannibalistic impulses of men, who by nature were, and are, sexually aggressive and generally violent. These male qualities made men dangerous to the survival of the women and their children. Totemic rules, which often include restrictions on who can eat what foods, and when a particular food may be eaten, are fundamentally taboos against eating the flesh of one's own kind, Reed notes. Women by creating totemic rules and taboos forced men to eat, and also to mate, at campfires other than those they grew up around. The brother–mates, dangerous to sister–wives and children, were forced to become stranger–husbands. Foreign to the groups they entered, their behavior was more easily controlled by women, who were neither bloodthirsty nor physically powerful, but who were unified as sisters in their home site. Thus, Reed argues, the incest taboo, essential to the formation of family, was a response to the inborn character differences between men and women.

The behavioral determinism in this quasi-sociological model of the origins of incest taboos hardly deserves further comment. The theory is barely sociological at all. It is worth adding here that Reed also derives the communes of sisters she envisions in early human society from the collections of related females found at the core of many, but by no means all, nonhuman primate groupings. Like other recent authors,[6] Reed regards the stability of such female groupings as the forerunner and foundation of the sexual division of labor. In Reed's formulation as a consequence of the power and self-sufficiency of women in groups, the family in its most primitive manifestation involved at best an ephemeral relationship, a man being tolerated temporarily as a mate by a woman and her group. The family as an institution, she holds, was firmed up only when men gained control over productive resources. How and why this shift in power was accomplished is not made clear, since Reed herself acknowledges that to this day, among collector–hunters, women generally still supply most of the food.

A far more prestigious—in fact, the most academically acceptable sociological model of the origin of incest taboos is that of Claude Levi-Strauss. Levi-Strauss, another theoretician acknowledging a debt to Marx, assumes in his early formulations of the problem[7] that the prehuman primate group or the early human one was "naturally" a closed group, although Engels, Marx's collaborator, visualized a loosely articulated herd-like aggregate as the primordial form.[8] According to Levi-Strauss' reading, the sexual division of labor developed in a variant of a closed troop as hunting replaced foraging as the mainstay of group subsistence. Women, the nursers and caretakers of infants who generation by generation grew progressively more dependent, were consigned to the unimportant collecting jobs while men undertook the most important subsistence task, the pursuit of game. Cooperative hunting activities cemented the male core of the closed group into a self-conscious brother unit. Pursuing game far afield brought the men into contact with other men. Although initially suspicious and hostile to these strangers, the economic advantages of exchanging goods with them overrode these feelings. Political-like kin relational ties were established as the hunters arranged to exchange "their" women to secure continuing trade relationships. The incest taboo forbidding men and women from taking mates from within their own group became institutionalized because of its economic advantages. Women, hampered in their mobility by their child care responsibilities, came to control the "domestic sphere" of activities and the hunter males secured dominance in the "political sphere."

Levi-Strauss' original model, as was pointed out in the Introduction, does not actually deal with the family directly. Although it does not embrace the sort of gross biological determinism inherent in Reed's model, despite its sociological orientation it is predicated on the notion that a tendency toward closed groups is or was inborn, and further suggests that although sex-role behaviors are not innately programmed, as a consequence of the biological necessities of pregnancy and nursing, women's roles are universally elaborated in one "sphere" and men's along different lines. These biological premises, at first unnoticed, have been subject to more and more criticism.

In a paper published in English in 1956,[9] Levi-Strauss considers more closely some of the issues raised by the model he presents in his early *Elementary Structures of Kinship*, and surveys the endless variety of ways in which societies divide labor between the sexes. In some societies, he correctly notes, men carry heavy burdens; in others, women do. In some societies women do agricultural work; in others, men do it. Women go to market in some while the men stay in their fields, and in other societies the reverse is true. There are even examples of women warriors and hunters, he points out. Yet every known human society has some sort of sex division of tasks. (The recently discovered Tasaday may be an exception.) He concludes from his thorough survey that the division of labor by sex is in no way a biological specialization, and that it must have some other purpose. "It is the mere fact of its existence which is mysteriously [sic] required."[10] In an interesting departure from the materialist and historical perspective that pervades his earlier work he adds, however: "The form under which it comes to exist (is) utterly irrelevant, at least from the point of view of natural necessity," and comes to the conclusion that: "The sexual division of labor is nothing else than a device to institute a reciprocal state of dependency between the sexes."[11] This device serves the purpose of ensuring that the smallest viable economic unit contains at least one man and one woman. In the final paragraph of the article, he also makes it clear that he believes "the small, relatively stable, monogamic family (is a) natural requirement without which there could be no society and indeed no mankind."[12]

In this later discussion of the sexual division of labor and its basis, this author indirectly addresses the problem of the family and its origins, tacitly recognizing that family is both a subunit of a larger social entity and that it involves links established between individuals as spouses. He suggests that the development of the sexual division of labor and the development of the nuclear family form are intimately related but refers only to vaguely stated "natural requirements" for the formation of family. At the same time, he stresses that his analytic

Diverse household family and kinship arrangements characterize human societies: (a) Two brothers and their wives—Italian immigrants—sit for a family portrait (b) In the Kalahari, a wife, her husband and children outside their hut in one of the campsites they share with relatives and friends (c) A wedding in Andros attended by relatives of both spouses (d) A Sherpa nuclear family in the kin-based village of Melenchi, Nepal (e) Alex Joseph, an excommunicated Mormon, with seven of his thirteen wives.

194

(c)

The Andros Islanders: A Study of Family Organization in the Bahamas,
Keith F. Otterbein, The University of Kansas Press, Lawrence, Kansas, 1966.

(d)

John Bishop

(e)

United Press International

195

approach discounts considerations of "natural necessity." By discounting the relevance of "natural necessity," he tempers the implication that biologically proscribed behavioral traits are responsible for the division of labor by sex and also for the origins of family. However, he also eliminates from analytic consideration other sorts of natural necessities—such as the material conditions humans faced. The analysis is therefore an abstract one, averring to grandly generalized universalistic "functions," as if these helped to explain how the family came to be. The analysis does not deal with the on-the-ground, everyday social processes of the collecting–hunting adaptation, nor does it provide a model of the kinds of circumstances that might have given rise to either the sexual division of labor or the small family grouping it is evidently linked to, which are analyzed as *faits accomplis*.

The descriptions of family arrangements in our own and other cultures presented earlier are designed to illustrate more than that human family arrangements take many forms, that sexual mores and codes of behavior differ widely in different cultural settings, and that what men and women do, even with respect to caring for children, is so varied that no single universal inborn species-wide patterning of behavior is discernible. These descriptions emphasize the ecological and economic factors that play a part in shaping local adaptations and point out where possible the historical forces that contributed to shaping them. The "sociological" theories of family origins offered by Reed and Levi-Strauss are based on similar data viewed from a similar perspective. Although there are other theorists with this perspective who also note that the cross-cultural data indicate that incest rules fundamentally serve as regulators of marriage and socioeconomic relationships (Leslie White, for instance), few of them have developed as extensive models of how the sex division of labor, incest taboos, and families originated as have Reed and Levi-Strauss. The work of these two theorists exemplifies the state of "sociological" theories of origins. Their models are either more biologically or less substantially sociological than one might expect from their theoretical orientation. Both authors reconstruct the material conditions of ancient economies with little recourse to solid or recent data. Although direct evidence of ancient ways of life will never be available to us, indirect evidence relevant to understanding early human adaptations and prehistory has been accumulating and allows us to make inferences of a more sociological character than those incorporated into their models.

UPDATING THE DATA

Like all scientific theories and models, those about the origin of incest taboos and family are tentative and the products of the times in which they are written. Theory building is, of necessity, a hazardous occupation, since it is designed to explain what has not been or cannot be observed directly. New observations change the analytic perspective rapidly. As knowledge or information accumulates, theories and models are overturned, modified, or expanded. One of the chronic occupations of scientists is trying to build better theories or more complete models than those which have been previously put forth. This involves (1) looking at information that was not available to past researchers; (2) looking at information that was available but distorted, misinterpreted, or poorly interpreted; and (3) looking at information that was little noted or overlooked. Let us briefly go through these three steps, reviewing points that have already been made (some several times) and adding a few that are relevant and suggestive of how some of the kinks in these current sociological models of family origins can be ironed out.

Most of the new information pertinent to the problem of family origins comes from the rapidly growing body of field and laboratory studies of primate behavior, some of which we examined earlier. From these studies we have learned that being able to manipulate objects, and to accommodate to and learn from one's social and physical environment, are biologically based aptitudes widespread in the primate order. This heritage of adaptability affects the behavior of both sexes. Despite sometimes dramatic sexual dimorphism in species, the sexes do not often play the standardized social roles we expect, and in many species the way males and females act toward each other, toward infants, and in groups is a product of local circumstances. We have learned that large groups of socially interacting primates are common in well-stocked arboreal semi- and fully terrestrial environments. Sometimes these large groups are no more than ephemeral assemblages. At other times large groupings are more or less permanent but fission into smaller ones when the situation warrants. Contrary to the long-held notion that males are central to the cohesiveness of such large groups, field data have revealed that adolescent and adult males frequently leave the groups and locales of their birth. Females, who have infants as soon as they reach adulthood, are much less mobile. While females with their young usually constitute the stable, core membership of larger groupings, they, too, sometimes move about. Terrestrial monkeys living where food is sparse and predators rare, the new data show, are the primates that most often forage in dispersed small groups containing at least one adult female and her young and a male. Similar small stable groupings are, however, found in richer arboreal settings, too.[13]

A lot of the information that was distorted or misinterpreted in the past has to do with collecting–hunting societies. The fact that the majority of collector–hunters reckon kinship bilaterally and live in loosely articulated groups with vague borders, and most allow a married couple to join either spouse's relatives or live where they wish[14] was obscured by notions of the "ecological necessity" of patrilineal patrilocal band organization.[15] That collecting rather than hunting provides the major part of group subsistence for most populations at the simpler levels of technological adaptation was little noted until Richard Lee[16] drew attention to it. Little acknowledgment was given to the important economic contributions women make as collectors[17] and even less to the role women play in the organized hunt or in bringing in animal protein in the form of small game, although many ethnographers testify to women's hunting activities.[18] Theories of the origins of incest and family suffered from these distortions and misinterpretations.

Although much about the variability of family arrangements in human society as a whole was well documented for a long time, as is evident from the ethnographies we reviewed earlier, analysts did not or could not come up with a comprehensive conceptualization of what "family" is, or a definition of family universalistic enough to encompass all its cross-cultural variants.[19] As a result, it was rarely explicitly recognized that the family is always a subunit (not necessarily a group) of a larger social entity. This led to confusions and miscon-strued analyses, so that when a theorist proposed that the "family level of socio-cultural integration"[20] was the simplest form of human social arrangement, he was promptly taken to task for implying what he had not intended, that the family group is the oldest form of human society and possibly of precultural origins. A further consequence of inadequate analysis was that little attention was paid to the fact that everywhere the marital contracts that generate family subunits specify individuals as spouses (irrespective of their sex or kin-group member-ship). This failure to explicitly articulate the individualized character of marital contracts allowed economic theories of the origin of incest taboos to stop at a halfway point, explaining why groups exchange people through marriage (although some groups do not) without examining why—or even if—groups subdivide into family units. Also, the failure to recognize that family subunits are "regularized" (e.g., persist in all environments) permits theorists, even now, to equate ecologically adaptive family-like groupings (such as those of the hamadryas baboons) with "family."

Little noted or overlooked in nearly all models of the origin of family are some aspects of sexuality, reproduction, and sex-role relationships, data that clearly have some bearing on how and why family as an institution got started. That cultural forces play a part in how humans view sex and sexuality as we have seen is well substantiated. Many readers are probably aware that heterosexual intercourse is regarded by some peoples as abhorrent, by others as a pleasure, and by still others as pleasurable for one sex and not for the other—with very little agreement as to which sex is the hungry aggressor and which the victim. Homosexuality is variously idealized, viewed as an illness, or as something one indulges in at specified stages of growth. Cultural norms about sexual appetites range from the belief that such appetites are nonexistent to the belief that they are insatiable. The prevailing sophisticated way of looking at this widely recognized variability of sex norms credits those who regard sex as negative or inconsequential with repressing, suppressing, or modifying powerful innately governed sexual impulses.

But field studies have made us conscious of the fact that most of our primate relatives are neither very sexually active nor very competitive about sex. Field and laboratory studies together show that the nurturing and parenting behaviors of higher primates are varied, variable, and influenced by social experience. The primate data consequently cast doubt on the notion that humans particularly are propelled by suppressed or repressed innately programmed sexual and mothering instincts. Recognizing these facts of life among nonhuman primates draws attention to a side of human sexuality which is little noted in discussions of how the family originated. Unlike other primates, humans can, and often do, exercise a high degree of direct control over their reproductive and nurturing activities.

The fact that humans are capable of exercising control over both their reproductive activities and how they care for infants has far-reaching implications for theory building. Because a sexual division of labor is "universal" in human societies, there has remained a subtle suspicion, even among sociologically oriented theorists, that this division of labor is based on biological imperatives. Yet the cross-cultural evidence, which is far more extensive than just the few situations described earlier, demonstrates that men's and women's tasks and roles vary within and between societies, and that the way tasks and roles are allocated is molded by ecological, economic, and historical factors. When the fact that humans control their reproductive and nurturing activities is taken into account, it becomes simple to acknowledge the significance of this cultural variability, to rethink the cultural foundations of the division of labor along sex lines, and to set aside this long-standing suspicion.

Rethinking Reproduction in Relation to the Division of Labor

In nearly all human societies females do not customarily have babies as soon as they are physically mature enough to do so. The females of primate species that show little interest in the intricacies of sex and sexual intercourse have infants almost immediately after becoming fertile, but women do not. This peculiarly human trait, the postponement of female reproductivity, demands analysis because how humans exercise control over reproduction and nurturance and what the exercise of these controls accomplishes have a direct bearing on building an adequate model of how family originated.

The postponement of reproduction is achieved in some human societies by discouraging newly mature adults from having intercourse. If we are like other primates and our urges toward sex are low—unless culturally stimulated—this tried and true method of pregnancy prevention may have been an early one, either casually or intentionally instituted. But among the majority of living collector-hunters, premarital sexual experimentation is expected and practiced. Since it is unlikely that meat-eating collector–hunters today suffer from some sort of adolescent sterility which does not afflict other primates, it rather looks like we cannot discount the sparse evidence that suggests that even though their technologies are simple, they do indeed know how to control reproduction. Pregnancy and birth are prevented by means as various as refraining from intercourse, interrupting intercourse before the male ejaculates, "dumping" the semen ejected into the vaginal tract, intercepting sperm en route to the uterus either with mechanical or medicinal preparations, aborting fetuses mechanically or medicinally, and, if all else fails, by infanticide.

Significantly, postponing a woman's first pregnancy guarantees that the woman, unlike the females of other primate species, is fully as mobile as an adult male during at least a period of her adulthood before she has a baby. Also significantly there is evidence that the mobility afforded her is not necessarily diminished by pregnancy or the birth of a child. Postreproductive nurturing can, and frequently is, manipulated. Many societies are articulated in ways that prevent women with babies and young children from moving about freely, but even nonhuman primates occasionally arrange for babysitters. In collecting–hunting societies, women not only postpone the birth of their first child, they do not usually permit themselves more than two or three carefully spaced children, and they avoid being tied down to them in a number of ways.

Before bottle feeding was invented and freed Western mothers who found themselves trapped alone in their nuclear-family households by dependent infants and children, Western European tradition allowed women who could afford to to pay for the services of wet nurses. Getting paid for breast feeding someone else's child reduces the whole matter of nursing to the performance of a demeaning job that requires no special skills. This no-longer-acceptable custom probably contributed to the conviction among many Western women that nursing is an unpleasant task, best dispensed with, and that nursing another woman's child is either a violation of natural law or a terrible intrusion on the privacy of a mother's relationship with her own infant.

(This is, of course, in addition to the fact that in Western tradition breasts are regarded erotically, and the preservation of an adolescent upstanding profile becomes an obsession, keeping men interested rather than babies fed being the goal.) Yet allowing infants access to many women's breasts sometimes has distinct advantages for everybody involved. Passing babies from hand to hand and breast to breast is commonly done in non-Western societies and occasionally, although very quietly, done in our own society. (I know of several such arrangements.)

Another woman's breast milk and bottled animal or soybean milk are far from being the only foods not administered by a mother that will satisfy a hungry baby and quiet its insistent cries. As mothers who read the label on baby food jars and listen closely to their pediatricians know, "solids" can be introduced to very young infants. (My firstborn took to bits of steak when she was three weeks old and her sister was given solids even earlier.) Meats, vegetables, fruits, and grains can be reduced to a consistency babies can manage by being pulverized, prechewed, or boiled into a thin gruel. The food can be placed in or near a baby's mouth with a finger, a stick, a spoon, or with a substitute teat (something like the squeeze bags used to decorate cakes) made of cloth or skins. Anyone with a modicum of dexterity can feed an infant. In at least some collecting–hunting societies many women find it necessary or just plain pleasant to leave their infants or youngsters in the care of others for a while.

Among the !Kung of the Kalahari desert of South Africa, the requisites of collecting–hunting are such that a similar degree of mobility is demanded of both sexes. There is a lack of rigidity in sex typing many adult activities. Domestic chores, child care and socialization, and food collecting are everybody's business. Women do not chase big game animals but do go as far away from camp as men do in their food searches (unaccompanied by men to "protect" them, by the way) and return with information about the traces of animals they have seen. "A common sight in the late afternoon is clusters of children standing on the edge of camp, scanning the bush with shaded eyes to see if the returning women are visible. When the slow-moving file of women is finally discerned in the distance, the children leap and exclaim. As the women draw closer, the children speculate as to which figure is whose mother and what the women are carrying in their karosses (carrying bags)."[21] "A similarity in the gathering work of women and the hunting work of men is that both activities take adults out of the camp, sometimes all day for several days each week."[22] Where the circumstances of collector–hunters call for women to be as mobile as men, matters are arranged so that they are as mobile as men.

One model of early human social arrangements has it that women are and always have been restricted by their nurturing activities and therefore were the core of the early groupings in which incest taboos and family arose. Another model has it that because males are inevitably more mobile than females, they took over the hunt, became providers, protectors and politicians, and the core of such groups. Yet men and women can both move about with equal facility, if necessary, and members of either or both sexes can be the core of whatever sort of groupings is found adaptive. However, it is not always the case that females with young and males can move about equally freely. (We will return shortly to examining the circumstances under which constraints on behavior are imposed on both sexes.)

Among baboons living on the savannah, groups of related females do, in fact, constitute the core of troops and do not wander as widely as males. Chimpanzees, however, live in open, ever-changing aggregates. Related females with young do not stay together in tight clusters, but appear to be as actively mobile as males. These nonhuman primates do not postpone female reproductivity, nor do the females of these two species, to my knowledge, nurse or feed each other's young. The females of other primate species may. Presumably our proto-human primate ancestors who moved into a totally terrestrial setting were at least as capable as chimpanzees of moving about flexibly, and as likely as savannah baboons to adopt a stable troop pattern when necessary. Undoubtedly the females of the proto-human type were like those of other primate species, early bearers and somewhat bound by nursing.

Someplace along the line to humanity things changed, and it can be argued from indirect evidence that postponing reproduction, controlling the number of births, and distributing child care responsibilities, all of which result in females having as much mobility as males, occurred before humans faced any "natural necessity" for a sexual division of labor. The way labor is actually divided between the sexes so diversely today in human societies has no correlation with any of the biological or physical attributes of the sexes. This by itself suggests that control over reproduction, and the mobility it conferred, may have been attained before a sexual division of labor became institutionalized. But there are other more direct kinds of evidence that suggest more strongly that arranging things so that women are as mobile as men preceded the division of labor along sex lines.

1.   Living collector–hunters range far more widely in their daily activities than other primate foragers. Increasing the range of foraging activities appears to come about with the help of some simple tools. Digging sticks, hand axes, edge-finished pebbles, and carrying bags make foragers more efficient, allowing them to seek out new and different foods, and to look for them farther and farther afield. Ancient butchering sites to which carcasses were carried and then cut up

indicate that game, at least, was not always consumed on the spot where it was taken.[23]

2.   Simple tools made of imperishable materials which can be used for cutting, chopping, and digging are, in fact, the only tools that occur in conjunction with early upright plains living hominid fossils, and these tools were around for a long, long time. Whoever used them undoubtedly foraged widely, more widely than other primates, and foraging widely puts a premium on the mobility of both males and females. Those with the foresight to make such tools were probably quite capable of taking steps to ensure that women were mobile enough to forage widely alongside men.

3.   The users of these tools either took small animals sporadically like chimpanzees and baboons do or organized into work groups and surrounded or stampeded medium-sized herd animals such as antelopes and pigs into natural traps, or when the opportunity presented itself, slaughtered and butchered occasional bigger animals that had become mired in mud or were already wounded and weakened by age, infirmity, or carnivores. The archeological evidence is inconclusive with regard to how much and by what means our early ancestors acquired the meat they occasionally ate except in one respect. There are no projectile points in their tool kits. Whatever hunting they did was apparently the kind of group or individual hunting in which women are customarily involved.

4.   The projectile points and tools associated with one kind of hunting in which a fairly rigid sex division of labor is maintained do not appear until the Middle Pleistocene, long after our upright ancestors were able to range widely in their daily quest for subsistence. An established pattern of delaying reproduction would have made it relatively easy for people to disperse into the small, wide-ranging groups which the new projectile weapons made profitable. From such groups it is but a short step to the yet-more-dispersed minimal family-like grouping in which a division of labor along sex lines is a practical solution to real-life problems and not just an instrument serving generalized societal functions.

One other point deserves comment with respect to whether controlling reproduction preceded the establishment of the sexual division of labor. If, as I argue in Chapter 2,[24] sexual dimorphism (i.e., well-marked physical differences between the sexes) evolved in primate populations in which active, growing, well-traveled males had the greatest breeding successes, then a long period of high female mobility and equal opportunity on the plains helps explain why men and women are more similar in size than the males and females of other terrestrial primate species.

Arriving at a Division of Labor by Sex: A Sociocultural Model

The model of family origins presented in the Introduction argues that the equipment which made possible the active pursuit of medium-sized and large animals encouraged our foraging ancestors to disperse into smaller groups more frequently. It also holds that such minimal groups made a division of labor by sex a necesssity. Small groups undoubtedly always have been common in settings where resources are scarce. But where the environment is generous and plains are fruitful, animals of many species and sizes congregate, big carnivores flourish, and human foragers can live well on vegetables and small animals only in large groups that can intimidate potential predators. However, on foot, with weapons no more elegant than clubs or sharpened sticks, large groups cannot get much meat very often.

Massed groups of predatory people scare off herds of skittish herbivores more easily than small groups. A surround or drive is best accomplished by masses of individuals who—at a crucial point in the proceedings—noisily show themselves to their prey. With only clubs and sticks in hand, they come face to face with their victims and slaughter as many as they can. Animals that escape are forever after alerted to the dangers of getting too close to these two-legged assailants and avoid them. If no animals escape, that settles the matter. There is no game left to hunt. But sneaking up on game and suddenly launching projectiles at it is another matter entirely. This can be done by a few skilled stalkers and hunters, who, working from a distance, are not readily perceived by their victims as the source of death-dealing destruction. The hunters may only maim or kill one or two animals, all that a small group can make immediate use of. If necessary, the hunter or hunters may follow an animal that has been wounded and left behind by its companions at a discreet distance until it is so weak or exhausted that it can be approached and dispatched. With projectile hunting tools instead of clubs, even big beasts, which, unless already incapacitated, are dangerous when cornered or in their death throes, become fair game. The appearance of projectile points in the archeological record accompanies a startling increase in the amount of debris from butchered animals, large and small. Evidently, projectiles made meat a more regular part of the human diet. With these tools human hunting is most efficient when it involves small groups of hunters. The invention of projectile equipment favors dispersal into small groups even where resources are rich.

Half a dozen to a dozen adults of various ages with half again as many children at different stages of development constitute a smallish group. A group in this size range can spare some of its members from the steady and secure procurement of food derived from collecting activities for the uncertain task of tracking and pursuing game. Although the chances are poor that a group of this size will include two or more women breastfeeding simultaneously, the possibilities of a mother leaving her infant or child under someone else's care are not entirely absent. A day or two away for the mother of an infant can easily be arranged, since some adults or older children are always around the campsite to care for the infant. A nursing mother need suffer no discomfort from engorged breasts if she periodically expresses some of her milk while she is away from her infant. A division of labor that excludes women from participating in the chase or from foraging far afield—as Bushmen women do—is not absolutely necessary. It is when game is scarce, meat a regular part of the diet, and dispersal into yet smaller groups is called for that a woman with a child or two finds herself truly encumbered and unable to go far from camp.

A very small collecting-hunting group consists of no more than two or three adults. While two or three women sometimes get together and take turns hunting and caring for children,[25] and two or three men often join forces, every woman with a child needs some sort of companion, either to hunt for her or to leave with her child. Although our primate background indicates that human sex drives are not particularly overpowering, women who have experienced intercourse usually find the joys of sex worthwhile, especially if reproduction can be controlled. Experienced men usually agree and pass on the information. When our projectile-equipped ancestors were, on occasion, forced to disperse in minimal groups, their aroused sexual interests probably led most of them to go off in pairs, one adult male with one adult female. Since men can feed babies but cannot bear or nurse them, since hunting alone with a spear, a sling, or bolas is dangerous and hunters can get themselves killed, the expendable partner in a minimal pair group equipped with such weapons is the one who is not capable of bearing or of nursing babies. In such a minimal group whose members want to eat meat regularly, the woman's mobility is diminished and the man must take on the job of hunting. A division of labor is practical. Since skill in hunting is acquired through training, some differential training of the sexes in hunting tasks is appropriate and firmly establishes a division of labor along sex lines. Once a division of labor along sex lines becomes established, men and women are forced into mutual dependency. The minimum viable economic unit capable of sustaining itself becomes one that includes one male and one female. This minimal group looks very much like a nuclear family.

As the model presented in the Introduction points out, the

self-sufficient minimal dispersal group is not a family unless it is in some way dependent on other people (a subunit of a larger social entity) and unless it is durable and maintained in all environments, even where dispersal is not necessary (regularized). While the imminent possibility of having to disperse or move about freely would encourage people equipped with projectile weapons to choose sexually and economically compatible individuals for a period of dispersal, the economic advantages of trading with people outside a local group or area are strong enough to help explain why, at some point, choosing one's partner from another group and making the partnership a durable one was institutionalized.

Exchanging goods with other peoples obviously makes available to the traders things they might otherwise not have access to. It also provides back-up resources if supplies fail locally but remain abundant elsewhere. Requiring people to seek mates from a group other than their own is a way of stabilizing trade relationships. People who move to other groups provide services if goods are scarce. Those who move can represent "pledges" or "hostages" against debts on goods. They also can be channels through which goods are passed over the years. Whether or not mates are "exchanged" tit for tat, sending a male or a female into another group—marrying them out—is an economic transaction involving an exchange of services and gifts. The institutionalization of incest taboos and contractual marriages serves as a means of generating political as well as economic alliances, creating ties between peoples who shared or came to share common sets of concerns.

THE ORIGIN OF FAMILY RECONSIDERED

The habit of requiring that marital contracts link specific individuals for long periods of time and the conditions favoring monogamy and the nuclear-family groups that are so common in collecting–hunting societies must have involved something besides ecological necessity, since dispersal into minimal groups is not called for or imminent everywhere that collector–hunters roam or roamed. The factors leading to normalizing marital contracts that link specific individuals as spouses seem to have been several. First there is the fact that human populations usually have about the same number of young adult men and women, and pairing them off meets practically everybody's needs, sexual and social. Second, the generally loose structure of the population characteristic of most collector–hunter adaptations (and of many nonhuman primate adaptations as well) is a structure that allows individuals to move as individuals. Finally, there are the advantages afforded subgroups in the population when member individuals establish distinct and separate marital ties, creating for them group links with many people from many places. Trade networks resulting from such diffused marital alliances are far more advantageous for such subgroups than simple trade partnerships with but one or two or three other groups, for networks provide a diversity of goods and the stability of alternative sources for goods which a limited number of exchange partnerships cannot. Establishing and maintaining wide-flung networks requires sending individuals in many directions for a long time or for the rest of their lives. Making sure that specific individuals are parties in marital contracts also helps perpetuate a network of relationships from generation to generation, for assigning children through each contract to their parents' kin groups makes clear with whom the children belong and who they can or cannot marry. If descent is recognized as going though the individuals who are "parents," and children are required to marry away from their close kin, a highly adaptive tapestry of interdependent families loosely spread over wide areas is effectively standardized. What results is a pattern of social and economic relationships which, it turns out, is characteristic among collector–hunters up to the present day.

A summary of the kinds of material conditions and social processes that current data indicate may have brought about the emergence of the family, or better said, families, runs as follows. Minimal family-like groups are called for when resources are sparse and dispersal into tiny groups a necessity. However, the need to disperse into minimal groups does not explain why humans took to establishing regularized, durable family subgroupings in all environments. A number of cultural developments ultimately led to making family subgroups worthwhile all the time. The invention of projectile weapons increased hunting efficiency. Relatively small foraging groups became advantageous as meat became a more regular and sought-after part of the human diet. Wherever and whenever a minimal group of a man and woman with children occurred, the new tools and the increased reliance on meat forced the unencumbered man to take on the dangerous task of hunting. The habit of excluding women from tracking and/or hunting big game spread to or was continued in large groups as it became apparent that if a woman who had a child and child-care responsibilities was killed or incapacitated, the loss caused more problems than when a man was temporarily or permanently removed from productive and reproductive activities. The preferential training of boys for hunting became common. The resulting institutionalized division of labor by sex set the stage for the mutual dependency between the sexes that is one of the cornerstones of family. Once a pattern of dividing labor by sex was established, large groups and small ones which found that greater economic security and richer repertoires of resources are gained when goods are exchanged with other peoples also found that they could cement and stabilize trade relationships by "offering" to groups other than their own, men and women who could perform specialized duties. The institutionalization of incest taboos helped guarantee that men and women would move to seek mates. Marriage contracts that made mates into spouses helped prolong trade ties, and perpetuated trade ties over generations by the simple expedient of specifying the exact place of children in the economic and social universe. Ultimately, the individualization of marital contracts, which is a key element in maintaining the family as a subunit of larger social entities, was favored by the security and well-being gained from the flexibility of the trade and political networks that were created by allowing or sending people, one by one, to be contracted as spouses in many different directions to many groups.

The model encapsulated above integrates all the current information bearing directly or indirectly on the problem of family origins that its author has been exposed to. While this book provides only a sampling of that information, hopefully it is enough of a sample to support the major premises on which this model is built, and to indicate why the details of this model's structure appear to the author to be valid. Nevertheless, the model will be subject to rapid modification whenever new data which indicate that the model needs changing come to hand.

PREDICTIONS, PAST AND FUTURE

The pieces of the jigsaw puzzle of social evolution are few and far between. Social scientists who play with those pieces are genuinely interested in understanding what people are like, how they got to be that way, and where human society is going. Most have private prejudices and preferences about what "human nature" is and what kind of world they expect or hope to see in the future. But as scientists they are committed to rising above their prejudices. As new bits and pieces of data become available, scientists are obliged to deal with them, whether or not these fit into their current or preferred models. One researcher or another is bound to try to account for unexplained or contradictory data, and since new pieces in the puzzle of human evolution keep turning up, no model of social evolutionary events is likely to remain unchanged for long.

No one knows exactly how the family originated—and without time machines to transport observers into the past, no one will ever know—for sure—what events led directly to its emergence. Was the family invented once or many times? In several places or one?

Gradually or quickly? We cannot be certain. Social relationships in prehistoric epochs are deduced from the archeological record; they are not written clearly in it. From the fragments of ancient humans, their artifacts, their garbage heaps, and their settlement sites, and from the behavior of contemporary humans and their closer primate relatives, we infer what these social relationships might have been. Our speculative reconstructions are speculative and reconstructions. Nevertheless, they are not empty exercises in imaginative logic, devoid of scientific method or significant social value. Like all scientific models or theories, they are built out of data. Such reconstructions are also used to make predictions. Like other science theories, they try to predict what evidence that is not yet available will be like and what it will reveal. If research turns up information that supports or fits the model or theory, the theory—for the time being—will stand confirmed. If not, the new materials will force a revamping and reconceptualizing of the problem, the building of a new theory, and a search for further evidence. As in all scientific theorizing, developing reconstructions of evolutionary events involves a process, repeated over and over, until at last a model that adequately and concisely accounts for all the data, new, old, and continuing to emerge, is developed. Until a reconstruction is tested in this way it is not possible to hold that as an evolutionary theory or model it is well substantiated.

A well-substantiated scientific theory should not be confused with that elusive thing called "truth," however. Scientists may aspire to truth but the best they can offer are ways of looking at reality that explain phenomena elegantly and predictably. When we look closely at science, it is not so much a method as the whole business of asking, searching, explaining, testing by further searching, and then if necessary reexplaining, researching, and reformulating hypotheses until predictability is achieved. Some scientists attempt to predict what we will find about the past and the present, and others restrict themselves to predicting the outcome of carefully controlled laboratory events. The problems these two kinds of scientists try to solve are different. The methods they use are different. But the questions and their basic orientations to problem solving are the same. Although those who work with social evolutionary problems can never be as certain about their constructs as are scientists who work with hypotheses that are testable under controlled laboratory conditions, they are nonetheless scientists as long as they respect and use their data.

In the light of all this, it looks as if the origin of family is a legitimate scientific concern, but not necessarily one that everybody will find relevant, worthwhile, or productive. After all, what happened in prehistory is done and gone. What happens in the future is what scientists are supposed to be able to predict, and—if possible—help prevent or make happen more easily. Scientists interested in social evolution seem to be concerned only with the past. Yet theories about the origin of family by their nature imply things about the present and future. Since family is a peculiarly human institution which raises serious questions about what can or should happen in human societies and what we can or should do about controlling events, it is extremely important to recognize that models of the past often contain hidden prescriptions for social action and predictions about the effects of particular social actions. Thus social evolutionary models that seem to deal only with the past are, in fact, predicting things about society that most people find very relevant to their own lives. Presumably "better" models allow us to make "better" predictions. A good evolutionary model may not be one that allows us to make very precise predictions, however. What the model of family origins presented here indicates as to what we can anticipate in the future of the family tells us more about social processes than it does about the exact forms that families will take.

Family as it manifests itself in all human societies today is extremely variable. Its form and arrangements are so diverse that they indicate not only that humans can survive, reproduce, and live out their lives (not necessarily happily) in a great many ways, but that family as an institution has been found adaptive in all sorts of societies. The institution seems to have originated out of socioeconomic considerations that lent adaptive advantages to collecting–hunting populations which adopted rules that created family subunits. Since that early innovation, one that appears to have taken place sometime during the mid-Pleistocene, family arrangements have been reorganized time and again. The simple rules generating family subunits have proved to be capable of producing different sorts of locally adaptive familial patterns of relationships, most of the time nuclear ones. So adaptive is the family in its many manifestations for human societies that the same sort of arrangement can serve very different ends. For instance, while the nuclear group among collector–hunters cements trade bonds, the parents of spouses in a nuclear unit may not even know each other in an industrial setting. In the industrial setting the nuclear form of family is adaptive not because it cements trade networks, but because it provides the society at large with a movable work force of men and women who when they jointly contribute as spouses to it, as has been the case among working people for at least a century, achieve an improved standard of living. Since the industrial setting is what it is—impersonal—the nuclear group also is often the only place an individual can blow off emotional steam and react to pressures in ways that must be kept in check elsewhere. So the nuclear family persists in part despite its disadvantages because it serves ends that could be served in quite other ways with different arrangements.

Other forms of family continue to coexist alongside the nuclear form and to also serve these ends. Clearly, the adaptability of family and its dependence on broader economic consideration tells us only a little about what we can expect from the future.

We are in the midst of a major social revolution. It began when human labor became a saleable commodity. The revolution accompanied and made possible rapid technological changes and allowed humans to manipulate nature more effectively. The revolution is still in progress. While people can produce more goods with less effort than ever before, and can survive in greater numbers than ever before, more and more people have seen themselves chronically jeopardized, not by natural cataclysms but by the vagaries and daily violence of an economic system that puts profits before people. The parts of the world in which this system no longer has absolute sway are ever increasing, and the effects of this continuing revolution on family forms are illuminating. In the industrialized and industrializing new socialist nations, children are reared by nonparents earlier and more often than is the case in Western capitalist states. In them, sex and sexuality are viewed as consequences, not causes, of the organization of social life. Yet family units continue to exist in these new nations and, interestingly, a small, monogamously based nuclear unit prevails. In capitalist industrial nations, much concern over higher and higher divorce rates is being expressed, and people who are afraid of major social changes say that these changing rates are signaling the destruction of the family and augur the destruction of human society in general. However, the data demonstrate that our form of family is but a transient one on the social evolutionary scene, and families of some sort have survived both past and present revolutions. A world in which humans with sophisticated and complex ways of producing and distributing goods and services will eliminate all forms of family is, it seems, unlikely.

Aldous Huxley's imaginative projections of the future notwithstanding, babies born in test tubes and raised by icy technicians are prohibitively expensive. A technology for mass-producing babies by such means is not worth speculating on simply because older, tried-and-true methods make more efficient and economic use of readily available resources. Despite Huxley's dim view of what goes on in biological laboratories, the scientific experimentation on reproduction which he so disparaged has helped to control human reproductive activities and not to dispense with them.

Sex for sex's sake is safer than ever. Although it is less inhibiting to explore the joys of sex, à la Alex Comfort, without fear of pregnancy, without children to tire one out or to cramp one's athletic creativeness, it seems that at least some people will continue to find having babies, interacting with children, and participating in the development of people fun, fascinating, and worth the trouble and discomfort. Humans, I am convinced, do not live by sex alone, nor are families built on just the joys of sex and their sidelights.

My hunch, an informed hunch but nevertheless just a hunch, is that the family will persist, predominantly in a nuclear form but, as has always been the case, with variations. Once economic security and child-care services are assured, some people will undoubtedly prefer to raise children without spouses, with sexual partners of the same sex, with several sexual partners ready at hand, or in groups with mutual sexual access to everybody in them, but, since it is easiest, generally, in our flux-filled lives to establish but one intimate heterosexual bond at a time, and that as durable a one as possible, my hunch is that the majority of people will continue to establish basically nuclear types of family groups when they want children.

Knowing that family has taken many forms in many societies should ease the hearts and minds of those who see doom in the signs of change around them. Knowing that a nuclear type of family persists in socialized industrial nations should give pause to those who see changing the family as the key to revolutionizing human relationships. The model of the origins of the family presented here and the many forms of family arrangements found in living human societies indicates that the family is an instrument of larger economic forces, and not vice versa. I must admit to feeling uncomfortable with predictions of what sort of family will prevail in the future, predictions that are customary nowadays at the end of every book about family, because I do not think the problem of what family will be like is *the* crucial issue. Far more important is the question of how we are going to solve the general economic crisis of inequitable distributions of wealth and power. What form or forms of family emerge in the future will depend on how that problem is solved.

NOTES

1. Marvin Harris, *Culture, People and Nature* (New York: Crowell, 1975), pp. 58-62. The data on Japanese macaques is taken from a section entitled "Infra-Human Culture."

2. Thelma Rowell, *The Social Behavior of Monkeys* (Harmondsworth, England: Penguin, 1972), pp. 81-84.

3. Lila Leibowitz, "Dilemma for Social Evolution: The Impact of Darwin," *Journal of Theoretical Biology*, 25, 1969, pp. 255-275.

4. Joyce Dudney Fleming, "Field Report: The State of the Apes" *Psychology Today*, January 1974, pp. 31-50. This is a popular and readable report on the rapidly expanding experimental work on the language acquisition capacities of nonhuman primates.

5. Evelyn Reed, *Woman's Evolution: From Matriarchal Clan to Patriarchal Family* (New York: Pathfinder's Press, 1975).

6. Sally Slocum, "Woman the Gatherer; Male Bias in Anthropology," pp. 36-50, and Kathleen Gough, "The Origin of the Family," pp. 51-76, in *Toward an Anthropology of Women*, ed. Rayne R. Reiter (New York: Monthly Review Press, 1975). See also M. Kay Martin and Barbara Voorhies, *Female of the Species* (New York: Columbia University Press, 1975), pp. 108-144.

7. Claude Levi-Strauss, *The Elementary Structures of Kinship* (Boston: Beacon Press, 1969), Published first in France in 1949 under the title *Les Structures élémentaires de la parenté*.

8. Frederick Engles, *The Origin of the Family, Private Property and the State* (New York: International Publishers, 1971).

9. Claude Levi-Strauss, "The Family," in *Family in Transition*, eds. Arlene S. Skolnick and Jerome H. Skolnick (Boston: Little, Brown, 1971), pp. 50-71.

10. Levi-Strauss, "The Family," p. 63.

11. Levi-Strauss, "The Family," p. 63.

12. Levi-Strauss, "The Family," pp. 71-72.

13. See Chapter 2 for details and references.

14. M. F. Nimkoff, "The Social System and the Family," in *Comparative Family Systems*, ed. M. F. Nimkoff (Boston: Houghton Mifflin, 1965), pp. 37-60.

15. See, for example, Julian Steward, *Theory of Culture Change: The Methodology of Multilinear Evolution* (Urbana, Ill.: University of Illinois Press, 1955); Elman R. Service, *Primitive Social Organization* (New York: Random House, 1962); and Marshall D. Sahlins and Elman R. Service, *Evolution and Culture* (Ann Arbor, Mich.: University of Michigan Press, 1960).

16. Richard B. Lee, "What Hunters Do For a Living; or How to Make Out on Scarce Resources, in *Man the Hunter*, eds. Richard B. Lee and Irven DeVore (Chicago: Aldine, 1968), pp. 30-43.

17. Slocum, "Woman the Gatherer: Male Bias in Anthropology," p. 36ff.

18. A few of the older ethnographies describing women's hunting activities are Martin Gusinde, *The Yahgin: The Life and Thought of the Water Nomads of Cape Horn* (Molding bei wiem, Anthropos Bibliothek, 1937; H.R.A.F. translation New Haven, Conn., 1962); Daisy Bates, *The Passing of the Aborigines* (London, John Murray, 1938); Ruth Landes, *The Ojibwa Woman: Male and Female Life Cycles Among the Ojibwa Indians of Western Ontario* [first published 1938 and reprinted (New York: W. W. Norton, 1971)]; and Phyllis M. Kaberry, *Aboriginal Woman: Sacred and Profane* (London: Routledge and Kegan Paul, 1939).

19. This problem is discussed in detail in the Introduction.

20. Steward, *Theory of Culture Change*.

21. Patricia Draper, "!Kung Women: Contrast in Sexual Egalitarianism in Foraging and Sedentary Contexts," in *Toward an Anthropology of Women*, ed. Rayne R. Reiter (New York: Monthly Review Press, 1975), p. 82.

22. Draper, "!Kung Women," p. 87.

23. For an overview of the archaelogy of the Paleolithic, see Chester S. Chard, *Man in Prehistory* (New York: McGraw-Hill, 1975).

24. Lila Leibowitz, "Perspectives on the Evolution of Sex Differences," in *Toward an Anthropology of Women*, ed. Rayne R. Reiter (New York: Monthly Review Press, 1975), pp. 20–35.

25. Landes, *The Ojibwa Woman*.

Selected Bibliography

SEX AND SOCIAL BEHAVIOR: ANIMALS OTHER THAN PRIMATES

Abdel-Hameed, F., and R. N. Shaffner, "Intersexes and Sex Determination in Chickens," *Science, 172,* May 28, 1971, pp. 962-964.

Barley, Theodore N., "The Elusive Bobcat," *Natural History, 81,* no. 8, 1972, pp. 42-49.

Calhoun, John B., "Population Density and Social Pathology," *Scientific American, 206,* no. 2, 1962, pp. 139-148.

Cimino, Michael S., "Meiosis in Triploid All-Female Fish (*Poeciliopsis poecilidae*)," *Science, 175,* March 31, 1972, pp. 1484-1485.

Clough, Garrett C., "A Most Peaceable Rodent," *Natural History, 82,* no. 6, 1973, pp. 67-74.

Creighton, William S., "Living Doors," *Natural History, 86,* no. 10, 1969, pp. 71-73.

Estes, Richard D., "Predators and Scavengers," *Natural History, 76,* no. 3, 1961, pp. 38-47.

Estes, Richard D., "Showdown in Ngorongoro Crater," *Natural History, 82,* no. 8, 1973, pp. 71-79.

Forbush, Edward Howe, *A Natural History of American Birds of Eastern and Central North America.* New York: Bramhall House, 1955.

Gould, Stephen Jay, "The Misnamed, Mistreated and Misunderstood Irish Elk," *Natural History, 82,* no. 3, 1973, pp. 10-19.

Hailman, Jack P., "How an Instinct Is Learned," *Scientific American, 221,* no. 6, 1969, pp. 98-106.

Hohn, Otto, "The Phalarope," *Scientific American, 220,* no. 6, 1969, pp. 105-111.

Klopfer, Peter H., "Aggression and Its Evolution," *Psychiatry and Social Science Review*, *3*, no. 3, 1969, pp. 2–7.

Koffan, Karoly, "The Ways of a Parasitic Bird," *Natural History*, *82*, no. 6, 1963, pp. 48–53.

McMillan, Vick, "Maturing of the Fathead," *Natural History*, *81*, no. 5, 1972, pp. 72–78.

Robertson, D. S., "Social Control of Sex Reversal in a Coral Reef Fish," *Science*, *177*, September 15, 1972, pp. 10007–10009.

Schaller, George B., "Predators of the Serengeti, Part I," *Natural History*, *81*, no. 2, 1972, pp. 38–49.

Smith, C. Lavett, "Hermaphroditism in Bahama Groupers," *Natural History*, *72*, no. 6, 1964.

Thorpe, W. H., "Duet Singing Birds," *Scientific American*, *229*, no. 2, 1971, pp. 70–79.

Vaurie, Charles, "So Fair and Foul a Bird," *Natural History*, *82*, no. 6, 1973, pp. 60–65.

Watts, C. Robert, and Allen W. Stokes, "The Social Order of Turkeys," *Scientific American*, *224*, no. 6, 1971, pp. 112–118.

Weber, William J., "A New World for the Cattle Egret," *Natural History*, *81*, no. 2, 1972, pp. 26–33.

Wilson, Edward O., *The Insect Societies*. Cambridge, Mass.: Harvard University Press, 1971.

THE SOCIAL BEHAVIOR
OF THE NONHUMAN PRIMATES

Alexander, B. K., "Parental Behavior of Adult Male Japanese Monkeys," *Behaviour*, *36*, 1970, pp. 270–285.

Burton, Frances D., "The Integration of Biology and Behavior in the Socialization of *Macaca sylvana* of Gibralter," in *Primate Socialization*, ed. Frank E. Poirer. New York: Random House, 1972, pp. 29–62.

Carpenter, Clarence R., "Life in the Trees, The Behavior and Social Relations of Man's Closest Kin," in *A Reader in General Anthropology*, ed. Carleton S. Coon. New York: Henry Holt, 1948.

Carpenter, Clarence R., "A Field Study in Siam of the Behavior and Social Relations of the Gibbon," in *Naturalistic Behavior of the Nonhuman Primates*, ed. Clarence R. Carpenter. University Park, Pa.: Pennsylvania State University Press, 1964.

Chamove, A., H. F. Harlow, and G. D. Mitchell, "Sex Differences in the Infant-Directed Behavior of Preadolescent Rhesus Monkeys," *Child Development, 38*, 1967, pp. 329–335.

Crook, John H., "The Socio-Ecology of Primates," in *Social Behavior in Birds and Mammals*, ed. John H. Crook. New York: Academic Press, 1970.

DeVore, Irven, ed., *Primate Behavior*. New York: Holt, Rinehart and Winston, 1965.

DeVore, Irven, and Sherwood L. Nashburn, "Baboon Ecology and Human Evolution," in *Readings in Anthropology*, eds. J. D. Jennings and E. Adamson Hoebel. New York: McGraw-Hill, 1966.

Frisch, John S. J., "Japan's Contribution to Modern Anthropology," in *Readings in Anthropology*, eds. J. D. Jennings and E. Adamson Hoebel. New York: McGraw-Hill, 1966.

Galdikas-Brindamor, Birute, "Orangutans: Indonesia's People of the Forest," *National Geographic, 148*, no. 4, 1975, pp. 444–472.

Goodall, Jane Van Lawick, "Chimpanzees of the Gombe Stream Reserve," in *Primate Behavior*, ed. Irven DeVore. New York: Holt, Rinehart and Winston, 1965.

Goodall, Jane Van Lawick, *In the Shadow of Man*. New York: Dell, 1971.

Goy, Robert W., "Hormones and Psychosexual Development," in *The Neurosciences*, ed. F. O. Schmidt. New York: Rockefeller University Press, 1970, pp. 203–219.

Harlow, Harry F., "Love in Infant Monkeys," in *Psychobiology—The Biological Bases of Behavior*, readings from *Scientific American*. San Francisco: W. H. Freeman, 1966, pp. 100–106.

Harlow, Harry F., and Margaret Kuenne Harlow, "Social Deprivation in Monkeys," in *The Nature and Nurture of Behavior: Developmental Psychology*, readings from *Scientific American*. San Francisco: W. H. Freeman, 1973, pp. 109–116.

Kummer, Hans, and F. Kurt, "Social Units of a Free-Living Population of Hamadryas Baboons," *Folia Primat, 1,* 1963, pp. 4-19.

Lahiri, R. K., and C. H. Southwick, "Prenatal Care in Macaca Sylvana," *Folia Primat, 4,* 1966, pp. 257-264.

MacRoberts, M. H., "The Social Organization of Barbary Apes (*Macaca sylvana*) on Gibralter," *American Journal of Physical Anthropology, 33,* 1970, pp. 83-100.

Mitchell, Gary, and E. M. Brandt, "Behavioral Differences Related to Experience of Mother and Sex of Infant in the Rhesus Monkey," *Developmental Psychology, 3,* July 1970, p. 149.

Mitchell, Gary, William K. Redican, and Jody Gomber, "Lesson from a Primate: Males Can Raise Babies," *Psychology Today, 7,* May 1974, pp. 63-68.

Reynolds, Vernon, and Frances Reynolds, "Chimpanzees of the Budongo Forest," in *Primate Behavior,* ed. Irven DeVore. New York: Holt, Rinehart and Winston, 1965, pp. 698-707.

Rowell, Thelma, "Female Reproductive Cycles and the Behavior of Baboons and Rhesus Macaques," in *Social Communication Among Primates,* ed. Stuart A. Altman. Chicago: University of Chicago Press, 1967.

Rowell, Thelma, *Social Behavior of Monkeys.* Harmondsworth, England: Penguin, 1972.

Schaller, George B., "Mountain Gorilla Displays," *Natural History, 70,* no. 7, 1963, pp. 10-17.

Schaller, George B., *The Year of the Gorilla.* Chicago: University of Chicago Press, 1964.

Singh, Sheo Dan, "Urban Monkeys," *Scientific American, 221,* no. 1, 1969, pp. 108-115.

Southwick, Charles H., Mirza Ashar Beg, and M. Rafiq Siddiqi, "Rhesus Monkeys in North India," in *Primate Behavior,* ed. Irven DeVore. New York: Holt, Rinehart and Winston, 1965.

Teleki, Geza, "The Omnivorous Chimpanzee," *Scientific American, 228,* no. 1, 1973, pp. 32-42.

Zuckerman, Solly, *The Social Life of Monkeys and Apes.* London: Routledge and Kegan Paul, 1932.

HUMANS IN CULTURES

Aries, Phillipe, *Centuries of Childhood: A Social History of Family*. New York: Random House, 1962.

Berreman, Gerald D., "Pahari Polyandry: A Comparison," *American Anthropologist*, *64*, no. 1, 1962, pp. 60–75.

Bohannon, Paul, *Social Anthropology*. New York: Holt, Rinehart and Winston, 1963.

Brown, Judith K., "Economic Organization and the Position of Women Among the Iroquois," *Ethnohistory*, 1970, pp. 151–167.

Callahan, Daniel, *Abortion, Law, Choice and Morality*. New York: Macmillan, 1970.

Devereaux, George, *A Study of Abortion in Primitive Societies*. New York: Julian Press, 1955.

Fortes, Meyer, "An Ashanti Case Study," in *Social Structure*, ed. Meyer Fortes. New York: Russell and Russell, 1963.

Fox, Rubin, *Kinship and Marriage*. Harmondsworth, England: Penguin, 1967.

Gans, Herbert J., *The Urban Villagers: Group and Class in the Life of Italian Americans*. New York: Free Press, 1962.

Goodall, Jane, *Tiwi Wives*. Seattle, Wash.: University of Washington Press, 1971.

Gough, Kathleen, "The Nayars and the Definition of Marriage," in *Cultural and Social Anthropology*, ed. P. B. Hammond. New York: Macmillan, 1964, pp. 167–180.

Gusinde, Martin, *The Yahgan: The Life and Thought of the Water Nomads of Cape Horn*. H. R. A. F. Yale translation, 1962.

Hart, C. W. M., and Arnold Pilling, *The Tiwi of North Australia*. New York: Holt, Rinehart and Winston, 1960.

Heider, Karl, *The Dugum Dani: A Papuan Culture in the Highlands of West Guinea*. New York: Wenner-Gren Foundation for Anthropological Research, 1970.

Kay, Herma Hill, "The Family and Kinship System of Illegitimate Children in California Law," in *The Ethnography of Law*, ed. Laura Nader, *American Anthropological Association Publication*, *67*, 1965, pp. 57–81.

Kenkel, William F., *The Family in Perspective*. Englewood Cliffs, N.J.: Prentice-Hall, 1973.

Kolata, Gina, "!Kung Hunter-Gatherers: Feminism, Diet and Birth Control," *Science, 185*, 1974, pp. 932–934.

Landes, Ruth, *The Ojibwa Woman: Male and Female Life Cycles Among the Ojibwa Indians of Western Ontario*. New York: W. W. Norton, 1971.

Laslett, Peter, *The World We Have Lost*. New York: Charles Scribner's Sons, 1971.

Leach, Edmund R., "Aspects of Bridewealth and Marriage Stability Among the Kachin and Lakhar," in *Rethinking Anthropology: Collected Essays*. London: Athlone Press, 1963.

Lee, Richard B., "What Hunters Do for a Living: or How to Make Out on Scarce Resources," in *Man the Hunter*, eds. Richard B. Lee and Irven DeVore. Chicago: Aldine, 1968, pp. 30–43.

Liebow, Elliot, *Tally's Corner: A Study of Negro Streetcorner Men*. Boston: Little, Brown, 1966.

Linton, Ralph, "The Marquesas," in *The Individual and His Society*, ed. Abram Kardiner. New York: Columbia University Press, 1939.

Man, Edward Horace, *On the Aboriginal Inhabitants of the Andaman Islands*. London: Royal Anthropological Institute, 1932.

Mead, Margaret, *Sex and Temperament in Three Primitive Societies*. New York: William Morrow (Mentor edition), 1953.

Mencher, Joan P., "The Nayars of South Malabar," in *Comparative Family Systems*, ed. M. F. Nimkoff. Boston: Houghton Mifflin, 1965, pp. 163–191.

Middleton, Russel, "A Deviant Case: Brother–Sister and Father–Daughter Marriage in Ancient Egypt," in *The Family: Its Structure and Function*, ed. Rose L. Coser. New York: St. Martin's Press, 1964, pp. 74–92.

Money, John, and Anke E. Ehrhardt, *Man and Woman, Boy and Girl*. New York: New American Library, 1972.

Murdock, George Peter, *Social Structure*. New York: Macmillan, 1949.

Nimkoff, M. F., ed., *Comparative Family Systems*. Boston: Houghton Mifflin, 1965.

Parsons, Talcott, "The Incest Taboo in Relation to Social Structure," in *The Family: Its Structure and Functions*, ed. Rose L. Coser. New York: St. Martin's Press, 1964, pp. 48–69.

Radcliffe-Brown, A. R., *The Andaman Islanders*. New York: Free Press, 1948.

Ransil, Bernard, *Abortion*. Paramus, N.J.: Paulist Press, 1969.

Reiter, Rayne, ed., *Toward an Anthropology of Women*. New York: Monthly Review Press, 1975.

Sangree, Walter, "Going Home to Mother: Traditional Marriage Among the Irigwe of Benue-Plateau State, Nigeria," *American Anthropologist, 71*, no. 6, 1969, pp. 1046–1056.

Sangree, Walter, "Secondary Marriage and Tribal Solidarity in Irigwe, Nigeria," *American Anthropologist, 74*, no. 5, 1977, pp. 1234–1243.

Spitz, René A., "Hospitalism," in *The Family: Its Structure and Functions*, ed. Rose L. Coser. New York: St. Martin's Press, 1964.

Stack, Carol B., *All Our Kin: Strategies for Survival in a Black Community*. New York: Harper & Row, 1974.

Stephens, William N., *The Family in Cross-Cultural Perspective*. New York: Holt, Rinehart and Winston, 1963.

Talmon-Garber, Yonina, "The Case of Israel," in *The Family: Its Structure and Functions*, ed. Rose L. Coser. New York: St. Martin's Press, 1964.

Turnball, Colin, *The Forest People*. New York: Simon and Schuster, 1962.

EVOLUTION:
PHYSICAL AND CULTURAL

Buettner-Janusch, John, *Physical Anthropology: A Perspective*. New York: John Wiley, 1973.

Campbell, Bernard, *Human Evolution*. Chicago: Aldine, 1966.

Engles, Frederick, *The Origins of the Family, Private Property and the State*. New York: International Publishers, 1971.

Friedl, Ernestine, *Women and Men: An Anthropologist's View*. New York: Holt, Rinehart and Winston, 1975.

Galle, Omer R., Walter R. Gove, and J. Miller McPherson, "Population Density and Pathology: What Are the Relations for Man?" *Science, 176*, April 7, 1972, pp. 29–30.

Goode, William J., *World Revolution and Family Patterns*. New York: Free Press, 1963.

Harris, Marvin, *Culture, Man and Nature*. New York: Thomas Y. Crowell, 1971.

Harris, Marvin, *Culture, People and Nature*. New York: Thomas Y. Crowell, 1975.

Kurten, Bjorn, *Not from the Apes*. New York: Random House, 1972.

Leibowitz, Lila, "Dilemma for Social Evolution: The Impact of Darwin," *Journal of Theoretical Biology*, 25, 1969, pp. 255–275.

Levi-Strauss, Claude, *The Elementary Structures of Kinship*. Boston: Beacon Press, 1969.

Levi-Strauss, Claude, "The Family," in *Family in Transition*, eds. Arlene S. Skolnick, and Jerome H. Skolnick. Boston: Little, Brown, 1971, pp. 50–71.

Margulis, Lynn, "Symbiosis and Evolution," *Scientific American, 225*, no. 2, 1971, pp. 49–57.

Martin, M. K., and Barbara Voorhies, *Female of the Species*. New York: Columbia University Press, 1975.

Parsons, Talcott, *Societies: Evolutionary and Comparative Perspectives*. Englewood Cliffs, N.J.: Prentice-Hall, 1966.

Pfeiffer, John E., *The Emergence of Man*. New York: Harper & Row, 1969.

Reed, Evelyn, *Women's Evolution: From Matriarchal Clan to Patriarchal Family*. New York: Pathfinder's Press, 1975.

Service, Elman R., *Primitive Social Organization*. New York: Random House, 1971.

Sohlius, Marshall D., and Elman R. Service, *Evolution and Culture*. Ann Arbor, Mich.: University of Michigan Press, 1960.

Steward, Julian, *Theory of Culture Change: The Methodology of Multi-Linear Evolution*. Urbana, Ill.: University of Illinois Press, 1955.

Williams, Sharlotte Neely, "The Argument Against the Physiological Determination of Female Roles," *American Anthropologist*, 75, no. 5, 1973, pp. 1725–1728.

Index